Placemaking

Placemaking: People, Properties, Planning

EDITED BY

DAVID HIGGINS
Higgins Research, UK

AND

PETER J. LARKHAM
Birmingham City University, UK

United Kingdom – North America – Japan – India – Malaysia – China

Emerald Publishing Limited
Emerald Publishing, Floor 5, Northspring, 21-23 Wellington Street, Leeds LS1 4DL

First edition 2025

Editorial matter and selection © 2025 David Higgins and Peter J. Larkham.
Individual chapters © 2025 The authors.
Published under exclusive licence by Emerald Publishing Limited.

Reprints and permissions service
Contact: www.copyright.com

No part of this book may be reproduced, stored in a retrieval system, transmitted in any form or by any means electronic, mechanical, photocopying, recording or otherwise without either the prior written permission of the publisher or a licence permitting restricted copying issued in the UK by The Copyright Licensing Agency and in the USA by The Copyright Clearance Center. Any opinions expressed in the chapters are those of the authors. Whilst Emerald makes every effort to ensure the quality and accuracy of its content, Emerald makes no representation implied or otherwise, as to the chapters' suitability and application and disclaims any warranties, express or implied, to their use.

British Library Cataloguing in Publication Data
A catalogue record for this book is available from the British Library

ISBN: 978-1-83753-131-8 (Print)
ISBN: 978-1-83753-130-1 (Online)
ISBN: 978-1-83753-132-5 (Epub)

Printed and bound by CPI Group (UK) Ltd, Croydon, CR0 4YY

INVESTOR IN PEOPLE

Contents

List of Figures and Tables	*vii*
About the Editors	*xi*
About the Contributors	*xiii*
Preface	*xvii*

Chapter 1 Introduction — *1*
Peter J. Larkham and David Higgins

Chapter 2 The Reality: The Legal Framework and Placemaking — *13*
Amanda Mundell and Hazel Nash

Chapter 3 Placemaking: Creating Value With Smart Spaces — *31*
David Higgins, Peter Wood and Chris Berry

Chapter 4 Placemaking, Nature, and the Promise of Digital Transformation — *47*
Mike Grace

Chapter 5 The City as a System of Places: Smart Placemaking for Future Living — *75*
Vahid Javidroozi

Chapter 6 Placemaking and Sustainability: Moving from Rhetoric to Transformative Sustainability Policies, Mindsets, and Actions — *91*
Claudia E. Carter

Chapter 7 Placemaking, Conservation, and Heritage — *125*
Peter J. Larkham, Emma Love and Miguel Hincapié Triviño

Chapter 8 Handmade Spaces: Creative Placemaking in a Local Neighborhood *145*
Silvia Gullino and Heidi Seetzen

Chapter 9 The Political Dimension of Making a Place: Framing the Right to the City in Placemaking *163*
Débora Picorelli Zukeran, Claudia E. Carter and Miguel Hincapié Triviño

Chapter 10 Placemaking on a Wider Scale: Seeing the Bigger Picture *179*
Kathryn Moore, Alex Albans and Peter J. Larkham

Chapter 11 Conclusion: The Future of Placemaking *197*
Peter J. Larkham and David Higgins

List of Figures and Tables

Figures

Chapter 3
Fig. 3.1.	Emerging Drivers of Real Estate Performance.	34
Fig. 3.2.	Examples of Major Black Swan Events.	35
Fig. 3.3.	Property Owners' Income: Smart Flexible Office Space.	39
Fig. 3.4.	Property Owners' Income: Co-living Space.	41

Chapter 5
Fig. 5.1.	Key Elements of Systems Integration.	80
Fig. 5.2.	A Framework for the City as a System of Smart Places.	86

Chapter 6
Fig. 6.1.	Commonly Used Generic Representations of Various Weak and Strong Sustainability.	96
Fig. 6.2.	Principles and Goals for (Strong) Sustainable Development Which Seek to Create and Maintain Healthy Economies and Societies Both of Which Are Intricately Linked With and Reliant on the Environment With Its Ecosystems.	103
Fig. 6.3.	Hadley's Bar, Hamburg Which Hosts the Zwischenraum Regular Debates and Events.	110

Chapter 7
Fig. 7.1.	(A) Johnstone Castle, Scotland: Remains of Fortified House Surrounded by Modern Housing. (B) Recent Housing With Traditional Thatched Roofs, Tolpuddle, Dorset.	126

Fig. 7.2. (A) Old Doorway Incorporated Into New Office Block, Hamburg; (B) Medieval Church in Exeter Incorporated Into Guildhall Shopping Precinct. 128

Fig. 7.3. (A) Moseley Road Baths and Library. (B) Example of Campaigning and Events in the Derelict Baths: "100 Swimmers." 130

Fig. 7.4. Before, During, and After Intervention of a Heritage Building in Bogota Historic Centre – La Candelaria. 132

Fig. 7.5. Before and after Intervention of a Heritage Building in Bogota Historic Centre – Santafe Neighborhood. 132

Fig. 7.6. Neighbor in Las Herrerias Street, Supporting the *Minga*. 133

Fig. 7.7. Before and After the Herrerías Maintenance Campaign. 134

Fig. 7.8. Graffiti on Abandoned Housing, Preston Road, Hull. 135

Fig. 7.9. Graffiti in Doel. 137

Fig. 7.10. Graffiti in the Leake Street Tunnel. 138

Chapter 8

Fig. 8.1. Bonnington Square, London, in the 1970s. 151

Fig. 8.2. Example of a Mosaic Located in Harleyford Road Community Garden. 152

Fig. 8.3. The Pleasure Garden and, in the Background, an Old Mill Wheel Rescued From a Nearby Marble Factory. 154

Fig. 8.4. A Written Note Left on the Community Board, Found During Our Fieldwork. 155

Chapter 9

Fig. 9.1. Digbeth Community Garden. 171

Fig. 9.2. Garrido Boxe gym in São Paulo. 172

Chapter 10

Fig. 10.1. A Refinement of the Proposal for the Tame Valley Landscape Vision: An "Unthreatening Drawing." 188

Fig. 10.2.	A Contour-Based Analytical Map of the Tame Valley.	189
Fig. 10.3.	A Contour and Waterway Analytical Map of the Blythe and Tame River Catchment.	190

Tables

Chapter 6

Table 6.1.	The 10 Melbourne Principles for Sustainable Cities.	93
Table 6.2.	Characterizing Different Forms (or Stages) of Sustainable Development.	97
Table 6.3.	Characterizing Typical Urban Sustainability Elements and Goals From a Weak and Strong Sustainability Perspective.	106
Table 6.4.	Seven Key Principles of QoL Planning.	115

About the Editors

Peter J. Larkham is a Professor of Planning at Birmingham City University. He is an urban geographer by background, with degrees from the Universities of Manchester and Birmingham. He has published extensively on how towns and cities change over time, focusing particularly on the changes after the destruction of the Second World War and on aspects of urban conservation.

David Higgins was Professor of Real Estate at Birmingham City University, and he is now a Real Estate Consultant, has founded Higgins Research, and is a Visiting Academic at several universities. He is a Fellow of the Royal Institution of Chartered Surveyors, and his research interests include property marketing, the role of space and place in the future of the office, property forecasting, and extreme risk events and their impact on real estate markets.

About the Contributors

Alex Albans is a Research Fellow at Birmingham City University's West Midlands National Park Lab. He has a background in historical geography, landscape architecture, and conflict mediation. Alex's research interests include site interpretation and analysis in design process pedagogy, and an emerging enquiry into reconciliation as an approach to addressing global landscape challenges.

Chris Berry is a Lecturer in Real Estate, teaching on the undergraduate and postgraduate courses at the Birmingham City University. He has a background in public sector real estate consultancy, and his research interests focus on local authority investment and operational property portfolios and bringing about regeneration through public funding initiatives.

Claudia E Carter is a Professor in Environmental Governance and Planning at Birmingham City University and a Chartered Town Planner. Her research concerns the links between climate, ecological, and social-technological changes and what sustainable development actually means. Claudia's main research interests are the opportunities and barriers to low-impact living and the emergence of transition initiatives and economic–political transformation propositions to facilitate a low-carbon, sufficiency-oriented economy and society that enables ecological recovery.

Mike Grace is a Senior Research Fellow at Birmingham City University and a Chartered Town Planner. He has extensive experience in land use planning and placemaking from working in UK local authorities and national government agencies. He was formerly the Head of Planning Services at Carlisle City Council and the Head of Profession for Sustainable Land Use at Natural England. Mike's research interests include smart sustainable and green cities including the development of national standards for urban green infrastructure for England.

Silvia Gullino is a Professor in City Making at Birmingham City University. Her research relates to policies and practices of city and community development, with a focus on networks and self-organized groups, through digital technologies to make cities more inclusive and sustainable.

Miguel Hincapié Triviño is a Lecturer in Urban Planning and Sustainability at Birmingham City University. He has a PhD in Urban Planning from University College London. His research interests include community and social actors' participation in city planning, the conservation of cultural landscapes, and the role of public institutions in urban design quality.

Vahid Javidroozi is an Associate Professor in Smart City Systems at Birmingham City University, working on various research projects in the field of information systems engineering, smart city development, digital transformation, artificial intelligence (AI), process modeling, ERP, and supply chain management.

Emma Love is a Senior Lecturer at Birmingham City University and teaches on the Building Surveying courses. Her research explores the sociocultural aspects of graffiti, exploring its role as a dynamic and often controversial component of urban environments. Emma's academic journey is marked by a passion for understanding how graffiti both reflects and influences the identity of urban spaces, exploring the intersection of this subculture and public discourse.

Kathryn Moore is a Professor of Landscape Architecture at Birmingham City University and a Past President of the International Federation of Landscape Architects. She has published extensively on design quality, theory, education, and practice. Her ideas for a West Midlands National Park are receiving widespread support in the region and nationally. She was the Chair of the pilot HS2 rail link landscape specification guidelines and served as a member of the UK Government HS2 Design Review Panel from 2015 to 2024.

Amanda Mundell is a Senior Lecturer teaching Planning and Property Law at Birmingham City University. Having spent her early career in a commercial property law department, her research interest relates to the application of planning law and policy in land use decision-making, with a particular focus on community and individual interaction with the planning system. Most recently, she has developed an interest in the use of nose-work dogs in the identification of endangered species on proposed development sites.

Hazel Nash is a Consultant in planning law, formerly a Senior Lecturer in Planning and Property Law at Birmingham City University. With a background in professional practice, her research interests sit within the application of law and policy in land use planning and real estate management. In particular, Hazel's interests lie in permitted development rights and use classes, farm diversification, and the role of environmental certification in the assessment and conditioning of nonresidential development proposals.

Débora Picorelli Zukeran is an Urban Planner who has practiced in Brazil, Germany, and South Africa. She is currently a Doctoral Researcher at Birmingham City University, researching community-led public spaces. Her research interests include participatory planning, public spaces, placemaking, and informal urbanism.

Heidi Seetzen is an Artist and a Lecturer in Sociology at Kingston University. Her artistic practice is predominantly sculptural – using everyday materials (such as fencing wire) to explore human experience and emotion. Her academic research focuses on urban change, creative practices and placemaking, as well as barriers to social inclusion and forms of community participation.

Peter Wood was a Senior Lecturer in Real Estate at Birmingham City University, and he is now part of the real estate team at Oxford Brookes University. Peter remains embedded in industry with his research focus on hybrid real estate portfolios and delivering alpha + returns in a risk-adjusted manner, bringing this knowledge both into the classroom and back to industry.

Preface

In recent years, anyone with a professional interest in the built environment will have become aware of the idea of "placemaking" – particularly in town planning, urban design, or property development. It has become prominent in planning education and academic research, where it has also spread into other disciplines. So, when the "property, planning and policies" academic team at Birmingham City University was considering how to reposition our work to engage interest – with colleagues at BCU and other universities, with practitioners, and with current and prospective students – placemaking became a useful focus on which most of us could agree most of the time. We initially collected our thoughts, drawing on our interests and knowledge, and produced a short illustrated booklet aimed at a professional readership. This has been the nucleus of the current book: much extended and updated, with an interdisciplinary focus, seeking to extend placemaking ideas – but still the product of the BCU team.

David Higgins
Peter J. Larkham
Stratford on Avon, 2024

Chapter 1

Introduction

Peter J. Larkham[a] and David Higgins[b]

[a]Birmingham City University, UK
[b]Higgins Research, UK

Abstract

This introductory chapter discusses the concept of "placemaking" and how it has developed and expanded since its relatively recent origins. This book extends the remit of placemaking further to consider issues such as finance, law, and digital technologies, in addition to some more familiar applications. The structure of the book and the contents of the following chapters are introduced.

Keywords: Urban design; community neighborhoods; real estate renewal and repurposing; multidisciplinary perspectives; built environment sustainability

Introduction

The power of "placemaking" is in transforming spaces – creating a sense of place, shaping an identity. It offers stakeholders – residents, businesses, local governments, and organizations – meaningful places, whether by deliberate or accidental process. The character and identity of places are linked with the people who created and shaped the space, their values and aspirations for the places in which they live and work, and the society within which they operate. Stern (2014) relates this concept with the creation of significance or meaning.

This significance, the importance of a space, therefore needs to be identified, and the physical product – the place – needs to respect and reflect that meaning (Hes et al., 2020). Of course, many places will have multiple layers of meaning, of different significances to a variety of entities. As shaping places is usually an expensive process, placemaking is mediated through consideration of finance and other resources, and thus, the implications of related objectives such as sustainability, gentrification, and economic development must be recognized. But we should also recognize that placemaking can operate at a wide range of scales, from the very small scale and local to areas and districts within cities (probably the most commonly considered scale) but also to entire settlements or even wider regions (perhaps least-considered). The term "placemaking" has come to be applied principally to the shaping of new developments, although it can logically and appropriately also be applied to the reshaping of existing neighborhoods, towns, and cities. Placemaking as generally conceptualized, as a formal activity, tends to offer specific and broad solutions, this fuzziness of scale and application could also lead to fuzziness of concept (Cilliers et al., 2015; Stern, 2014).

In many uses, "placemaking" has become almost synonymous with "town planning" and "urban design." The United Kingdom's Royal Town Planning Institute, for example, supports its members "to deliver outstanding placemaking that creates inclusive, healthy, prosperous, sustainable and happy communities" (RTPI, 2024a). There is also an uneasy relationship with "urbanism" – is "guerrilla urbanism" not just a bottom-up expression of placemaking (Foth, 2017; Hou, 2020)? However, this usage may be little more than current professional and political fashion, and a deeper exploration of the ideas and applications is timely.

This book explores a multidisciplinary perspective on placemaking, examining both some familiar applications and making links with some less-familiar themes including legal, financial, and digital. In looking outside the more familiar boundaries of the concept, we can explore the wider relevance of placemaking: its connections with the ways in which society and cities work and with how the world is rapidly changing. We argue that placemaking is central to the urban future, but that future will be very different from even the recent past.

Developing the Idea

Placemaking (as we represent the term simply for convenience, although "place-making" or even "place making" are often used – see Lew, 2017) is an interdisciplinary concept that has become increasingly prominent in academic research and teaching and professional practice, since the mid-1970s (Jeleński, 2018). It emerged principally from the closely related disciplines of town planning, urbanism, and urban design, albeit that urban design was itself a new concept and urbanism a more Europe-centric one. Indeed placemaking is often seen as an approach to, or facet of, urban design (Madden, 2011; Thomas, 2016) or the link is strongly expressed but in other ways (for example, for historical districts: Li et al., 2020). It developed particularly in response to criticisms of modernist urbanism, after rapid urban redevelopments and expansion – particularly that following the Second World War and, in the countries affected, the extensive wartime damage. The speed, scale, and nature of these changes were increasingly identified and generating concern, even from the late 1960s as causing a lack of place in cities: they were losing individuality (Aldous, 1975) and becoming placeless (Relph, 1976). There were widespread – and continuing – discussions about the need to return to human-centered urbanism (Aravot, 2002; Kent, 2019; Strydom et al., 2018) and the approaches and techniques that could foster this

(Choi et al., 2016; Hyden, 2020 are examples). A pro-conservation movement emerged as one popular public and professional response (Cherry, 1974).

More recently, the growth in placemaking-related interest and activity has led the concept to have noticeable visibility in global environment-related discussions, to the extent that it has become embedded in major international agendas and declarations, such as the Sustainable Development Goals (UN, 2015) and UN Habitat's New Urban Agenda (UN, 2017). The placemaking connection to sustainability aspirations and goals often involves incorporating innovative design features such as green infrastructure, public accessibility, and renewable energy sources (for example, Dreiseitl, 2015; Donaldson & João, 2020; Schaeffer & Smits, 2015). These positive initiatives contribute to environmentally sensitive approaches which can mitigate the increasing threat of the changing climate and extreme weather events, particularly as the world's population, and particularly its urban population, continue to grow and consume finite resources.

Overall, placemaking has emerged as a social process focusing principally on the creation and management of public places that are characterful, vibrant, and safe: they function well for those who use them. This is particularly the view of the Project for Public Spaces, a prominent North American placemaking organization (PPS, 2011), although some might extend the approach to semi-public, if not also private, spaces. There is a focus on generating economic growth through this activity, much of it from tourism, especially cultural tourism. Placemaking is thus inescapably intertwined with property ownership and financial returns (Canelas, 2019, gives a London example). A legitimate question emerges from this: to what extent is placemaking distinct from other planning-related activities including master planning and urban design? According to Cilliers et al. (2015, p. 351), placemaking "differs from traditional masterplanning in the sense that its principal goal is to create a public place that attracts a wide variety of people and offers an experience that makes people return to the space." This is a narrower focus and, perhaps, a narrow interpretation of placemaking.

Although placemaking has become a widely recognized concept, familiar to many built environment professionals and at least recognizable to a wider public, it remains problematic in terms of its meaning, objectives, applications, and scale. The term's widespread use across a variety of academic disciplines, professions, and applications is likely to be largely responsible for this (Hes & Hernandez-Santin, 2020). As in the early days of "urban design," the term sounds comprehensible and familiar, but it lacks a commonly accepted definition and has multiple interpretations. Is it a theoretical framework for urban policy and design, a methodology or set of tools for practitioners? Recently, experts and academics have categorized it as both an "art" and a "science" (Fincher et al., 2016) – aligned to the United Kingdom's Royal Town Planning Institute and its focus on the "art and science of town and country planning" (RTPI, 2024b). As a result, the concept has been criticized – for example, in Punter's terms as an "increasingly vacuous mantra" (Punter, 1991, p. 352). It is right that we should be cautious of overuse and under-thinking as some terms become more familiar and more widely used. Is placemaking as we use it in this book related to "place(making)" as applied to conservation activism in Indianapolis by Lockwood and Heiderscheit (2023) or to its use applied to crocodiles and their interactions with humans on a farm in Australia (Baynes-Rock, 2019)? Both papers challenge us to consider nonhuman agency and different applications of placemaking. However, since Punter's words were written, uses of placemaking in built environment professional contexts have arguably become more nuanced and sophisticated.

As with urban design (Rowley, 1994), placemaking can be considered as both process and product. One approach, derived principally from cultural geography, defined placemaking as "how a culture group imprints its values, perceptions, memories, and traditions on a landscape and gives meaning to geographic space" (Lew, 2017, p. 449). This definition focuses more on people and culture rather than physical or procedural aspects. In contrast, according to the Project for Public Spaces, placemaking is not just a final outcome but a means to an end (PPS, 2020). The process of placemaking allows a community to identify and prioritize its own needs. The academic literature for this approach commonly uses terms such as "sense of place," "place identity," and "place attachment," although each has its own separate and sometimes lengthy history of development and research (see Jivén & Larkham, 2003, on sense of place, for example).

A separate, but related, process-based literature focuses on participatory placemaking. Again, this has a very long history in town planning, focusing on the nature and extent of participation in a wide range of planning and environment-related issues and, particularly recently, on the use of technology including social media to extend participation including facilitating access for some traditionally difficult-to-reach groups in society (at the risk of creating more such groups among the less digitally literate) (Foth, 2017; Frith & Richter, 2021; Gonsalves et al., 2021; Morrison, 2022; Shtebuanev et al., 2023). We do need to identify and recognize the diversity of interests and potential actors in placemaking activities, and it is indeed possible that nonhuman agency and interests are under-considered.

Placemaking can be seen as both top-down and bottom-up (Platt & Medway, 2022). It is increasingly being recognized that placemaking is not (or should not be) solely the act of official actors such as planners, designers, and politicians but also needs to involve the active participation of local residents, users, and communities (Friedmann, 2010).

As vibrant places attract people and business, they will appeal to the commercial real estate industry. Remade places can attract and energize communities, leading local economies to prosper and attract local businesses. Placemaking at the scale usually practiced – street blocks to urban quarters – leads to communal areas (though not necessarily in public ownership) that promote social interaction, cultural diversity, local entrepreneurship, and economic growth. These factors directly affect the success, and hence the value, of real estate (principally commercial property, as placemaking initiatives rarely take place in locations affecting privately owned residential property). Through placemaking, it is recognized that (commercial) real estate investors and developers can enhance the overall appeal, functionality, and value of their properties and surrounding areas (Hines, 2023). The impact of small-scale and local placemaking, often carried out without official sanction, on the social, psychological, and financial value of property tends to be less well considered.

There is an extensive product-based literature, but this tends to focus more on identifying examples of best practice, guides to "good places," and criteria such as "habitability" and "walkability" by which a good place – and, by implication, a good placemaking process – can be identified. The early-21st century focus on "tools and toolboxes" is certainly present (*Urban Design*, 2024).

Overall, therefore, placemaking is a relatively recent concept. It has relatively rapidly gained widespread visibility and use but in a wide range of applications and generating multiple definitions, approaches, and tools. It is a field sufficiently mature to have generated a substantial Routledge *Handbook* (Courage et al., 2021). It is useful to take stock of the position so far, but perhaps less useful to be too concerned about definitions, variations, and what is included or excluded. We argue that it is more constructive to explore range and variety, how placemaking can help us reposition urban places for an increasingly uncertain future, and therefore how placemaking needs also to be considered alongside issues such as law, finance, and digital thinking and technology.

The Shape of This Book

Chapter 2 examines placemaking and the United Kingdom's legal framework. Places are the product of a myriad of influences and a complexity. However, underpinning placemaking activity in each country is the legal and regulatory framework which provides a set of governing principles concerning the use of land that includes planning and development considerations. In the United Kingdom, the laws governing the planning system have changed over time and dispersed into separate and increasingly disparate jurisdictional laws and policies. Nevertheless, successive recent governments have been clear in criticisms of the planning system, describing it as "outdated and ineffective," recognizing the need for simplicity, clarity, and faster results. This chapter discusses the role and scope of law and policy in placemaking. It particularly explores the use of flexibility in responding to the impacts associated with the recent global coronavirus pandemic and the UK government's "build, build, build" economic agenda in a local context. In addition, this chapter considers the future of the planning system: exploring, among other things, the emerging priority of beauty in placemaking.

Chapter 3 discusses a real estate perspective on placemaking: creating value with smart spaces. As placemaking is rapidly changing the urban landscape, the ways in which we view real estate assets and their value need to adapt to meet evolving community demands, where people create places where they want to actually live, play, and work. Increasingly, space in the city is linked to younger generations and the emerging knowledge (gig) economy. This interconnection is shaping current and future urban skylines, with buildings that offer new – and often combined – working and living environments. Foremost are co-living/coworking spaces, where owners and developers are looking beyond the offering associated with traditional office and apartment complexes. Owners and investors need to understand the new avenues to create real estate value and seek opportunities to reap commercial rewards far beyond the historical property investment arrangements.

Chapter 4 examines placemaking and connectivity, in the new era of big data and smart cities. The governance of our towns and cities requires an approach that connects people with nature and places. Previous and current approaches have rarely done this effectively. Digital technology can be the glue that does this, provided that it serves the needs of the various stakeholders including urban communities. Identifying the potential connections across people, digital, and place themes, there is a need to identify and examine successful approaches, exploring some of the current practice (or lack of it) in spatial planning and smart cities. This can be considered by the use of a range of Internet of Things (IoT) technologies and methodologies which combine the use of socioeconomic data. This might include data collected from "wearables" or personal devices of users of the urban environment. This ambient domain sensing can provide the ecological data to show how digital connectivity is addressing the placemaking challenges alongside providing implications for urban governance and communities.

Chapter 5 recognizes that placemaking plays a crucial role in enhancing the quality of life in cities, necessitating a holistic approach and the incorporation of smart strategies. This chapter addresses the gap in existing research by exploring the integration of systems thinking and systems integration in smart placemaking within cities to make the placemaking more resilient, connected, and smart. The city is viewed as a system of interconnected and integrated smart places, where attractions, communication hubs, public spaces, and infrastructures seamlessly connect. The outcomes of smart placemaking include economic prosperity, environmental sustainability, health and well-being, safety and security, cultural preservation, innovation, and resilience. This chapter develops a framework that highlights the interconnectedness and interdependencies between systems thinking, systems integration, and smart placemaking. The framework provides guidance for city planners, urban designers, and policymakers in implementing effective strategies for creating vibrant, inclusive, and sustainable public spaces within the broader context of a smart and interconnected city.

Chapter 6 situates placemaking in the rhetoric and reality of sustainability and the need for transformative policies and actions. Sustainability features in the national and local policies of many countries but often lacks clarity in what it means in practice. Interpretations of sustainable development (or sustainable cities and places) vary widely between different countries and social, economic, political, and environmental actors and interest groups influenced by underlying values and specific contexts. Considering the already-evident impacts of rapid climate change and ecological breakdown, continuing with business as usual will add more pollution, resource depletion, and lead to economic and societal turmoil and collapse. A significant factor in past and current policy failures is that "weak" rather than "strong" sustainability models have been adopted laced with a voter-enticing rhetoric yet delaying painful, but essential, changes in production and consumption and a shift in focus away from profit toward human and ecological well-being. Making this shift requires a clear and ambitious regulatory framework yet also flexible approaches and "agency" of citizens, employees, employers, and politicians for transformation across different geographical and institutional levels, moving away from competition and strive and making room for experimentation and creativity and new forms of collaboration and sharing. Relevant concepts, examples, and critiques can be gleaned from the ecological economic and social–ecological transformation literature, offering direction for the kinds of shifts in placemaking to achieve social and environmental justice.

Chapter 7 examines the linkages between placemaking, conservation, and heritage: a key aspect of this relates to place identity. Particularly in response to rapidly changing circumstances and environments, conservation (also widely known as "historic preservation") involves identifying and retaining an element of heritage, stability, and familiarity in both existing areas and informing the design of new areas. Yet this is a complex and contested process. It involves processes of valuation and selection: so whose heritage is being selected, prioritized, promoted, and retained, and whose is marginalized, redeveloped, and vanished? And individuals and communities do change over time, so the views and values of those communities are also likely to change. Incomers don't necessarily share the same values as long-term residents. On a wider scale, what is generally accepted as worthy of conservation also changes with, for example, postwar modernism, brutalism, and postmodernism becoming accepted; but difficulties with problematic heritage of war, destruction, slavery, and exploitation, for example, being contentious and potentially splitting communities. What one generation values, particularly if it is (relatively) new, can be seen by others as disfiguring, and this is very evident in the heritage and conservation of urban art and graffiti. A range of less-common examples from the United Kingdom, Europe, and elsewhere are used to identify and critique the processes and products – the landscapes of heritage manipulation, the decision-making processes, the power of individuals and communities. All these are critical factors in the complex interrelationship between placemaking and conservation, new and old.

Chapter 8 discusses the findings of a research project rooted in the unique context of a late-Victorian square in south London, which had become largely occupied by squatters in the 1980s and 1990s. Over three decades, squatters (some of whom later became "legalized" as homeowners and tenants) mended derelict houses, created two community gardens and green streets, and set up a vegetarian café. The square, an oasis in the middle of London, is now a fashionable neighborhood to live and visit because of its enduring artistic flair and alternative cultural "feel." Through ethnographic methods, this chapter's authors focused on how residents transformed derelict buildings and neglected spaces, and on the evolving dynamics of this neighborhood as it underwent progressive gentrification, reflecting similar trends in many other neighborhoods in London. This chapter analyses these informal practices and interprets them as examples of creative placemaking. Framed by the intricate interplay between the community's initiatives and the challenges posed by contemporary processes of regeneration and gentrification, they explore how such practices shaped both the material fabric of the place as well as its immaterial character: its sense of community and identity and the feelings and memories associated with its built environment.

Informed by Lefebvre's theories on the social production of space and the "right to the city," this analysis emphasizes the importance of informality, everyday practice, spontaneity, and self-management in shaping and sustaining a vibrant urban culture. By exploring how these elements intersect with forces of regeneration and gentrification, this chapter aims to contribute to a nuanced understanding of creative placemaking, the complex dynamics at play in the ongoing transformation of urban spaces, and the resilience of bottom-up, community-driven placemaking initiatives in the face of external pressures.

Chapter 9 focuses on the political dimension of placemaking. While placemaking has the potential to foment political change, recent discussion about placemaking seems to revolve more around its methods and outcomes. Departing from the perspective of placemaking as outcome, this chapter positions placemaking as a dynamic process, shifting attention to the actors involved and their motivations. This political dimension is explored, like Chapter 8, by adopting the framework of the "right to the city," enabling a critical examination of existing power structures and circumstances in the transformation of the urban landscape. Two cases of small-scale, informal, and "unauthorized" placemaking illustrate the questions about who has the right to make places, emphasizing the need for structural change in the transformation of urban spaces for public use. As the current approach for placemaking is criticized for fueling social inequalities, asymmetrical political processes and spatial issues, such as gentrification and displacement, a new framework is required to reorientate placemaking toward a people-led approach. The right to the city interprets placemaking beyond its physical outcomes but as a unique set of conditions and circumstances that facilitates or hinders people's ability to make a place. Moreover, the right to the city provides a lens to examine the processes involved in the transformation of the urban landscape and acknowledges the potential of placemaking to challenge these processes.

Chapter 10 outlines a selection of significant ideas emerging from research investigating the implications of the redefinition of theories of perception presented in the book *Overlooking the visual* (Moore, 2010). This is based on a sequence of case studies beyond the academic world, establishing a strategic landscape-led approach to placemaking at a regional scale that culminates in the West Midlands National Park, a radical new interpretation of the national park concept launched in 2018 at Birmingham City University. This chapter argues that this is the perfect time to take stock, see the bigger picture, and take a new look at regional planning – not as it has been traditionally conceived but from a landscape perspective. This is "landscape regional design." This is essential if we want to create better, more resilient places.

In the final chapter, we reinforce the overall premise of the book: placemaking is here to stay, has become an integral part of decision-making for the built environment, and has much of value to offer. Nevertheless, even dominant paradigms need critical attention, and this chapter reinforces the contributions of the individual chapters and the overall message that placemaking needs to be more holistic, to demonstrate more "joined-up thinking," in a fast-changing world in which our growing urban areas need to prepare for climate change and other uncertainties. Perspectives and actors that have been under-represented in placemaking thinking and actions need to receive greater consideration and to become integral parts of the process.

References

Aldous, T. (1975). *Goodbye, Britain?* Sidgwick & Jackson.
Aravot, I. (2002). Back to phenomenological placemaking. *Journal of Urban Design, 7*(2), 201–212.
Baynes-Rock, M. (2019). Our precious reptiles: Social engagement and placemaking with saltwater crocodiles. *Area, 51*(3), 578–585.
Canelas, P. (2019). Place-making and the London estates: Land ownership and the built environment. *Journal of Urban Design, 24*(2), 232–248.
Cherry, G. E. (1974). The conservation movement. *The Planner, 61*(1), 3–5.
Choi, J., Kim, S., Min, D., Lee, D., & Kim, S. (2016). Human-centered designs, characteristics of urban streets, and pedestrian perceptions. *Journal of Advanced Transportation, 50*(1), 120–137.
Cilliers, E. J., Timmermans, W., Van den Goorbergh, F., & Slijkhuis, J. (2015). Green place-making in practice: From temporary spaces to permanent places. *Journal of Urban Design, 20*(3), 349–366.
Courage, C., Borrup, T., Rosario Jackson, M., Legge, K., Mckeown, A., Platt, L., & Schupbach, J. (Eds.). (2021) *The Routledge handbook of placemaking*. Routledge.
Donaldson, G. H., & João, E. M. (2020). Using green infrastructure to add value and assist place-making in public realm developments. *Impact Assessment and Project Appraisal, 38*(6), 464–478.
Dreiseitl, H. (2015). Blue–green social place-making: Infrastructures for sustainable cities. *Journal of Urban Regeneration and Renewal, 8*(2), 161–170.
Fincher, R., Pardy, M., & Shaw, K. (2016). Place-making or place-masking? The everyday political economy of "making place". *Planning Theory & Practice, 17*(4), 516–536.
Foth, M. (2017). Lessons from urban guerrilla placemaking for smart city commons. In M. Rohde, I. Mulder, D. Schuler, & M. Lewkowicz (Eds.), *Proceedings of the 8th International Conference on Communities and Technologies* (pp. 32–35). Association for Computing Machinery.
Friedmann, J. (2010). Place and place-making in cities: A global perspective. *Planning Theory & Practice, 11*(2), 149–165.
Frith, J., & Richter, J. (2021). Building participatory counternarratives: Pedagogical interventions through digital placemaking. *Convergence, 27*(3), 696–710.
Gonsalves, K., Foth, M., Caldwell, G., & Jenek, W. (2021). Radical placemaking: An immersive, experiential and activist approach for marginalised communities [conference presentation]. In *Connections: Exploring heritage, architecture, cities, art, media*. University of Kent. https://architecturemps.com/wp-content/uploads/2020/06/Kavita_Gonsalves_etal_Radical-Placemaking_Abstract_Canterbury_20.pdf
Hes, D., & Hernandez-Santin, C. (Eds.). (2020). *Placemaking fundamentals for the built environment*. Palgrave Macmillan.
Hes, D., Mateo-Babiano, I., & Lee, G. (2020). Fundamentals of placemaking for the built environment: An introduction. In D. Hes & C. Hernandez-Santin (Eds.),

Placemaking fundamentals for the built environment (pp. 1–13). Palgrave Macmillan.
Hines. (2023). How important is placemaking in commercial real estate? Hines. https://www.hines.com/the-point/development/how-important-is-placemaking-in-commercial-real-estate
Hou, J. (2020). Guerrilla urbanism: Urban design and the practices of resistance. *Urban Design International, 25*, 117–125. https://doi.org/10.1057/s41289-020-00118-6
Hyden, S. (2020). *Meaningful urbanism: A human-centered approach to placemaking using form-based zoning codes*. Unpublished doctoral dissertation. University of Texas at Austin.
Jeleński, T. (2018). Inclusive placemaking: Building future on local heritage. In G. Amoruso (Ed.), *Putting tradition into practice: Heritage, place and design. Proceedings of the 5th INTBAU International Annual Event* (pp. 783–793). Springer.
Jivén, G., & Larkham, P. J. (2003). Sense of place, authenticity and character: A commentary. *Journal of Urban Design, 8*(1), 67–81.
Kent, E. (2019). Leading urban change with people powered public spaces. The history, and new directions, of the placemaking movement. *The Journal of Public Space, 4*(1), 127–134.
Lew, A. A. (2017). Tourism planning and place making: Place-making or placemaking? *Tourism Geographies, 19*(3), 448–466.
Li, X., Jia, T., Lusk, A., & Larkham, P. J. (2020). Rethinking place-making: Aligning placeness factors with perceived urban design qualities (PUDQs) to improve the built environment in historical districts. *Urban Design International, 25*, 338–356.
Lockwood, B., & Heiderscheit, D. (2023). Place(making) for conservation activism: Materiality, non-human agency, ethics and interaction in Indianapolis. *Area, 55*(4), 558–564.
Madden, K. (2011). Placemaking in urban design. In T. Banerjee & A. Loukaitou-Sideris (Eds.), *Companion to urban design* (pp. 654–662). Routledge.
Moore, K. (2010). *Overlooking the visual: Demystifying the art of design*. Routledge.
Morrison, J. (2022). Heritage, digital placemaking and user experience: An industry perspective. In F. Nevola, D. Rosenthal, & N. Terpstra (Eds.), *Hidden cities* (pp. 39–58). Routledge.
Platt, L. C., & Medway, D. (2022). Sometimes… sometimes… sometimes… Witnessing urban placemaking from the immanence of "the middle". *Space and Culture, 25*(1), 105–120.
Project for Public Spaces (PPS). (2011). *Place-making for creating lively cities*. Training Manual. PPS. http://www.lively-cities.eu
Project for Public Spaces (PPS). (2020). *The lighter, quicker, cheaper transformation of public spaces*. PPS. https://www.pps.org/article/lighter-quicker-cheaper
Punter, J. V. (1991). Participation in the design of urban space. *Landscape Design, 200*(1), 24–27.
Relph, E. (1976). *Place and placelessness*. Pion.
Rowley, A. (1994). Definition of urban design: The nature and concerns of urban design. *Planning Practice and Research, 9*, 179–197.
Royal Town Planning Institute (RTPI). (2024a). *About us*. RTPI. https://www.rtpi.org.uk/about-the-rtpi/about-us/

Royal Town Planning Institute (RTPI). (2024b). *Policy and research.* RTPI. https://www.rtpi.org.uk/policy-and-research/

Schaeffer, C., & Smits, M. (2015). From matters of fact to places of concern? Energy, environmental movements and place-making in Chile and Thailand. *Geoforum, 65,* 146–157.

Shtebuanev, S., Gullino, S., & Larkham, P. J. (2023). Planning the smart city with young people: Addressing teenagers' perceptions, values and visions of smartness. *Urban Planning, 8*(2), 57–69.

Stern, M. J. (2014, May 30–31). Measuring the outcomes of creative placemaking. In *The role of artists & the arts in creative placemaking* (pp. 84–97). Goethe-Institut.

Strydom, W., Puren, K., & Drewes, E. (2018). Exploring theoretical trends in placemaking: Towards new perspectives in spatial planning. *Journal of Place Management and Development, 11*(2), 165–180.

Thomas, D. (2016). *Placemaking: An urban design methodology.* Routledge.

United Nations. (2015). *Transforming our world: The 2030 agenda for sustainable development.* United Nations. https://sustainabledevelopment.un.org/post2015/transformingourworld

United Nations. (2017). *New urban agenda.* United Nations. http://habitat3.org/the-new-urban-agenda

Urban Design. (2024). Theme issue on placemaking tools. *Urban Design, 169.*

Chapter 2

The Reality: The Legal Framework and Placemaking[1]

Amanda Mundell[a] *and Hazel Nash*[b]

[a]Birmingham City University, UK
[b]University College of Estate Management, UK

Abstract

Places are the product of a myriad of influences and complexity. However, underpinning all placemaking activity is the legal and regulatory framework which provides a set of governing principles concerning the use of land that includes planning and development considerations. In the United Kingdom, the laws governing the planning system have changed over time and dispersed into separate and increasingly disparate jurisdictional laws and policies. Although this is a system created by central government it, amongst others, has been clear in criticisms of the planning system, describing it as outdated and ineffective, recognizing the need for simplicity, clarity and faster results. This chapter discusses the role and scope of law and policy in placemaking. In addition, it examines the future of the planning system, exploring, among other things, the emerging priority of beauty in placemaking.

Keywords: Legal framework; statutory process; development plan; material considerations; planning law

Introduction

Any consideration of "placemaking" needs first to examine the judicial and planning systems of the location. These underpin all relevant planning and development activities, setting boundaries on what is and is not possible, and the procedures for considering and approving – or rejecting – proposals. Therefore, to

---

[1]In this chapter, legal cases are referenced in footnotes using the style common to English legal writing.

underpin this book, this chapter examines the United Kingdom, but specifically English, planning system and how placemaking can operate within it.

There are many theories about what makes a "place" rather than a "development space." Consideration needs to be given not only to the need for a development but also to the quality of the place being created and to the legacy future communities will inherit. Foremost is an appreciation of markets and frameworks within which these places are formed. This must include the supply of appropriate land and competing demands for that land, as well as the planning policy frameworks and processes that seek to deliver quality developments in places and of a type(s) where it is needed and at the appropriate time. Coupled with this should be a prerequisite to provide a benefit to the local economy, have a positive effect on the environment, to ensure that the "place" will be created within the overarching objective of the planning system which, in the United Kingdom, is to contribute to the achievement of sustainable development (Department for Leveling Up, Housing and Communities [DLUHC], 2023). The success or failure of placemaking needs to be measured not only through the social and environmental lens but also through its economic effects including measures of performance.

At the heart of this process, in every country, is the legal and policy framework within which development stakeholders operate. This framework underpins the various stages of any scheme, from land acquisition and the considerations at preconstruction phase through construction to disposal and the requisite ongoing estate management. Within this framework, planners – in collaboration with local communities, developers, and landowners – seek to plan the area by creating the places that people need and want by proactively deciding where they want to put these places.

However, the current UK planning system restricts the ability of stakeholders at the forward planning stage as they can only review those sites that are actively put forward for development by landowners or their development partners. This is not only an issue facing local planning authorities (LPAs), but developers and communities experience similar issues. Meeting the environmental, social, and economic challenges expected of the planning system, while also allocating land in the right places at the right time to deliver healthy and beautiful places to live and work, requires a system that is based on up-to-date data and the appropriate and accurate analysis of that data. The current system is struggling to meet these requirements. It is an outdated system that has been analogue from its inception and is still largely the same nearly 80 years later. The data gathered in relation to an area and proposed/existing development are one-use only, leading to missed opportunities in relation to a coordinated, integrated strategic approach.

Placemaking

In order to create the places in which we want to live and work, placemaking has been identified as a key theme in planning policy (DLUHC, 2023, para. 20). The concept has been prioritized through the following:

- appropriate evidence-based policies in the statutory development plan which fulfill the needs of their community;
- requiring sufficient details on planning applications to enable the proper planning of an area, e.g., submission of a masterplan for phased developments;
- providing additional guidance, e.g., on design;
- placing an emphasis on meaningful community engagement;
- ensuring that the vision for the development is not "watered-down" during the planning application process and that conditions attached to the planning consent are met;
- securing a contribution from the development to enable the provision of the infrastructure necessary to support it.

In a placemaking context, planning policy presents a number of difficulties, not least with regard to its perceived vagueness. Planning policy is, by its very nature, open to interpretation with professional planning officers having their own understanding of the intentions of policies "which might change depending on their mood, the timing or even the individual looking at a specific application" (Farrer & Co, 2023). Indeed, the discretionary nature of planning in terms of applying planning policy, both national and local, in decision-making is established in law (Planning and Compulsory Purchase Act [P&CPA] 2004, s. 38(6)). Such ambiguity inevitably leads to challenges being instigated either through the planning appeals process (Town and Country Planning Act [T&CPA] 1990, s. 78) or on a point of law through judicial review. While it is important for LPA decisions to be open to question and accountable, such disputes serve to add delay to delivering development.

The planning process can, however, be a positive tool ensuring that the "vision" for an area put forward by a developer and endorsed by the LPA by virtue of its granting of planning permission is an opportunity for collaboration between the parties. LPAs have powers to enforce the delivery of the development as approved and to rectify any breaches of planning control ensuring that the vision of place is maintained (T&CPA, 1990, Part VII). In reality, however, given the ongoing economic challenges, which has seen a decrease in local planning authorities' net spending per person dropping by 59% between 2009 and 2021, taking enforcement action is likely to be weighed against the expediency of pursuing the breach.

The National Planning Policy Framework (NPPF) sees this "carrot and stick" approach as important in "maintaining public confidence in the planning system" (DLUHC, 2023, para. 59). During and following completion of a development, LPAs, developers, landowners, and the community can also ensure that the quality of place is maintained through the use of legal tools such as section 106 agreements, community infrastructure levy, the imposition of conditions, restrictive covenants, and stewardship schemes to provide a degree of control after disposal and foster a sense of community ownership.

Legal Framework

The legal framework surrounding the planning system has developed since its inception in 1947 and has had subsequent additions, amendments, and consolidations through the imposition of various acts and regulations to create the plan-led planning system we have today. This has been an unusually long-lived and generally robust planning system (Cullingworth, 1999), and despite substantial changes in the early 2000s, it is still recognizable.

Development plans are central to the operation of the planning system with a statutory requirement that planning decisions must be plan-led. Plans establish the vision and provide a framework for the development of an area through a set of planning policies. In implementing these planning policies in a way that reflects the aims, ambitions, and needs of a local authority's area, LPAs need to balance the "needs and opportunities in relation to housing, the economy, community facilities, and infrastructure – as well as being a basis for conserving and enhancing the natural and historic environment, mitigating and adapting to climate change, and achieving well designed places" (DLUHC, 2021).

Planning policy within the United Kingdom is established through a hierarchical system of documents. The system of land-use planning is a devolved matter, and thus, Wales, Scotland, and Northern Ireland have and continue to develop their own increasingly different planning policies and underpinning legal frameworks. In England, the NPPF sets out the government's planning policies and how it expects these policies to be applied, through the local development framework produced by LPAs, down to plans produced by communities at a neighborhood level, referred to as Neighbourhood Development Plans (NDPs). While not law, the NPPF is a material consideration and must be taken into account in planning decisions. However, if decision-makers determine not to follow the NPPF in making any determination on a planning application, they must provide clear and convincing reasons.

Plans go through consultation and other processes, including being tested for "soundness," passing environment and viability assessments, undertaking and acting on the Statement of Community Involvement, having to meet the duty to cooperate between LPAs, and responding to challenges from third parties before completing the adoption processes and being accepted as the planning policy at national or local level. There is an emphasis on consultations with communities at this stage of the planning process so that they are able to have a say in how their area is to develop over the life of the local plan. However, most communities currently do not get involved at this stage in the process, but rather respond to notifications of specific planning applications. This process is complicated and can take on average 7 years to complete satisfactorily, resulting in an adopted plan (Pritchard, 2012). So although it is a statutory requirement for LPAs to have an up-to-date local plan, many fall short. As plans progress through these procedures, their policies may be accorded weight in the decision-making process where policies are relevant and in certain defined circumstances (DLUHC, 2023, para. 48). The amount of weight that a decision-maker can give to such emerging policies is dependent upon a number of factors:

- What point within the adoption process the emerging plan has reached.
- Whether there are objections to the relevant emerging policy which have not been resolved.
- The degree to which the identified emerging policy conforms to the National Planning Policy Framework.

(DLUHC, 2023, para. 48).

While each level of policy documents is required to be in conformity with those above it and should have a consistency of message within its own policies, one of the main issues in relation to planning policy continues to be the tensions created between the policies contained within these numerous documents. As a result, it is not uncommon for planning policies which are relevant to a particular development to be in conflict with one another.

Making Plans

For a plan-led system to function effectively, it is paramount that the framework of documents contains clear and up-to-date policies to "provide a positive vision for the future of each area; a framework for meeting housing needs and addressing other economic, social and environmental priorities; and a platform for local people to shape their surroundings" (DLUHC, 2023, para. 15). The development plan must, therefore, contain strategic and nonstrategic policies which are in conformity with government guidance contained in the NPPF but which are tailored to the priorities and needs of that particular area, meeting the test for soundness. Strategic policies should look ahead to the desired pattern, scale, design, and quality of places for an area over the life of the plan. The provision of infrastructure and community facilities must also be sufficient to support the proposed developments while enhancing and conserving the environment. Nonstrategic policies are used to provide more detail relating to specific types of development or specific areas within the remit of the LPA.

Neighbourhood Development Plans (NDPs) provide a further layer of policy. These plans are created by communities which are able to form a vision for their area provided that it is in conformity with the strategic development plan policies. NDPs are part of the statutory development plan and are to be considered in the decision-making process. An NDP which has been accepted after a referendum has the status of an adopted development plan in the decision-making process. By virtue of the T&CPA 1990 (section 70(2), as amended), regard must be given to a postexamination draft plan as far as its policies are material to the development proposal. Prior to formal examination, an emerging NDP may also be considered as a material consideration. The weight which may be given to neighborhood plan policies which are pertinent to the proposed development is set out in paragraph 30 of the NPPF and is determined with regard to the same criteria as local plan policies. Indeed, the Neighbourhood Planning Act 2017 s. 1 inserts into the T&CPA 1990 at s. 70(2) that LPAs have a duty to have regard to a postexamination draft NDP. While the NDP is not part of the development plan until it has been considered and approved by the community in a referendum, in determining a planning application, the LPA should evaluate any evidence of local support for an emerging plan and should apply weight to it as appropriate.

Plans set out policy considerations at various levels providing a clear vision for development. However, some policy considerations are supported by further guidance documents. As an example, while the NPPF identifies high-quality design – which creates better places – as being central to the development process, LPAs are expected to elaborate on this consideration within their local plan by providing clear policies which reflect their area's defining characteristics and goals and provides certainty for developers as to what will be required to achieve an approval. To this end, national design principles are supported by the National Design Guide (Ministry of Housing, Communities and Local Government [MHCLG], 2021a) and National Model Design Code (MHCLG, 2021b). To provide further clarity with regard to design at a local level, it is expected that LPAs will prepare design guides and codes which are in conformity with national principles to create beautiful places but which reflect local area distinctiveness (DLUHC, 2023, para. 130).

In theory, at a fundamental level, there should be no conflict between national policy and those in local planning and neighborhood documents or within each of the documents themselves. Sustainable development is at the core of NPPF policy, and section 39(2) of the P&CPA 2004 requires LPAs to prepare their local plans with the objective of contributing to sustainable development. Each level of policy documents is required to be in conformity with those above it and should have a consistency of message within its own policies. The complexity in meeting the test for soundness and navigating the procedure for the adoption of a local plan also provides opportunities for challenge and effectively slows the process to adoption leading to complexity in giving weight to draft, emerging, and adopted policies in decision-making.

Other Material Considerations

What Is a Material Consideration?

There has been very little guidance from Government policy and Ministerial advice with regard to what matters can or cannot constitute a "material consideration" in planning decision-making. Paragraph 11 of the supplementary planning document to Planning Policy Statement 1 (Office of the Deputy Prime Minister [ODPM], 2005) quoted from *Stringer v Minister of Housing and Local Government* stated that "In principle...any consideration which relates to the use and development of land is capable of being a planning consideration. Whether a particular consideration falling within that broad class is material in any given case will depend on the circumstances".[2]

The supplementary planning document also refers to the determination made in *R v Westminster City Council, ex parte Monahan*, which concluded that, in

---

[2]*Stringer v Minister of Housing and Local Government* (1970) 1 WLR 1281.

order to be considered as a material consideration, the matter must be regarded as being a genuine planning consideration, i.e., it must be related to the development and use of land in the public interest, and must also fairly and reasonably relate to the development proposal in the application concerned.[3] Although it is the courts which are the final arbiters of whether a matter constitutes a material consideration (ODPM, 2005, para 12), it has been established that all of the fundamental factors involved in land-use planning such as the number, size, layout, siting, design and external appearance of buildings and the proposed means of access, together with landscaping, impact on the neighborhood and the availability of infrastructure, are considered to be material considerations (Development Control Practice, n.d.).

Which particular factors should be considered to be material considerations in relation to land-use planning matters has also been the subject of litigation. The judge in *Stringer v Minister of Housing and Local Government* considered that "material considerations ... must be considerations of a planning nature ... any consideration which relates to the use and development of land is capable of being a planning consideration."[4] However, it was also established in this case that the materiality of any particular issue may depend upon the particular circumstances in each particular case. Although this decision provides some guidance on what issues could be a material consideration in planning terms, it also leaves the term open to wide interpretation.

The courts have, in general, therefore taken a liberal approach, in considering the question of whether a matter can constitute a material consideration. However, cases have been brought which have established that certain matters may be considered to be a material consideration. Therefore, material consideration includes the following.

Resource and Economic Issues

The overarching aim of sustainability and sustainable development policies permeates through all levels of planning policy and seeks to ensure that new development has the minimal impact possible on resources.[5]

Social and Cultural Issues

The effects of a potential new development on the existing environment and uses should be assessed and whether they are socially or morally desirable or harmful. Matters which may be considered relate to the social structure of communities,

---

[3]*R v Westminster City Council, ex parte Monahan* (1989) JPL 107.
[4]*Stringer v Minister of Housing and Local Government* (1970) 1 WLR 1281, reaffirmed in the more recent case of *Northumberland County Council v Secretary of State for the Environment and British Coal Corporation* (1989) 2 WLUK 292.
[5]*Niarchos (London) Limited v Secretary of State for the Environment* (1977) 35 P&CR 259; *R v Westminster City Council, ex parte Monahan* (1989) JPL 107.

questions of human rights, morals, religion, culture, and race. Within development proposals, these issues are usually raised during the consideration of proposals for new housing development, e.g., the percentage of affordable/social housing required to be included within a development scheme and the distribution of this percentage in terms of the total development site.[6]

Layout, Design, and Amenity Issues

The materiality of the effect that the design and layout of a new development may have on the existing development and uses in an area and on the future occupants of the new development should also be considered (Moore, 2010). Indeed, the NPPF identifies that central to the planning process should be "the creation of high quality, beautiful and sustainable buildings and places" (DLUHC, 2023, para. 131). A report by the Building Better, Building Beautiful Commission supported the inclusion of the term within the NPPF with the report suggesting that the planning system should "ask for beauty" (Building Better, Building Beautiful Commission, 2020, p. 9), with the term becoming a clear focus in the NPPF between 2019 and 2021 as the number of uses of the term doubled. However, beauty is not seen as interchangeable with design and amenity, in fact all these elements are seen as independent.

For decision-makers, the difficulty is in defining and assessing beauty in the context of a planning application before them. The weight to be given to the beauty of a project may also be difficult for the decision-maker to evaluate: however, as it is a distinct material consideration, it is essential that beauty is considered in the decision-making process in order to comply with the statutory requirements of s. 70 of the T&CPA (1990) and s. 38(6) of the P&CPA (2004). Normally, in matters of interpretation, the courts would use legal rules to determine the meaning of the word in dispute, but this may be rather difficult with a term such as beauty which is fluid and so much within "the eye of the beholder."

The key to achieving sustainable development is, therefore, beautiful high-quality design which creates places that are better to live and work in and that help communities accept new developments within their area. Good design has been identified as having a number of characteristics, namely identity; context; life space; resources, homes, and buildings; uses; public spaces; nature; movement and built form (MHCLG, 2021a).

Existing Site Uses and Features

In some cases, it may be desirable to retain the existing site uses or features. In order to be able to consider this as a material consideration, it is necessary for the

---

[6]*R v London Borough of Tower Hamlets, ex parte Barrett Homes Limited* (2000) JPL 1050.

LPA to undertake an assessment to ascertain whether it is reasonable to conclude that, should the proposed development be refused, the existing uses or features will be retained.[7] The opposite view to the retention of uses, but within the same category in terms of material consideration, is where the LPA can see planning gains which may be achieved by the removal or consolidation of undesirable site uses.[8]

Requirements of Other Authorities or Service Providers

With any new development proposal, other Government, local government departments and agencies either internal or external to the LPA, statutory bodies, or privatized service providers will have duties, policies, and requirements which will apply to the proposal.[9]

Precedent Creation

The LPA may be aware that, in granting a particular development proposal, it may set a precedent for further similar development proposals to be approved. The cumulative effects of such development may alter the character of an area and erode the objective of planning policies and principles. The LPA is, therefore, able to consider the materiality of the effect of setting such a precedent. However, in order to rely on precedent creation as the reason for refusal of a development proposal, there must be more than "mere fear or generalised concern. There must be evidence ... For the reliance on precedent".[10]

Government Policy

At the inception of the modern planning system, s. 1 of the T&CPA 1947 stated that the minister with responsibility for the planning function within the United Kingdom was required to provide national policy relating to the use and development of land in order to provide a consistent approach to decision-making.[11] Section 1 was repealed in 1970; however, in 2011, the judge in the case of *Cala Homes (South) Ltd v Secretary of State for Communities and Local Government* held that this was still a valid description of the Secretary of State's responsibility in relation to planning policy.[12] Care must be taken, however, to distinguish between statements that are formal policy statements which are material to a

---

[7] *London Residuary Body v Lambeth London Borough Council* (1990) 1 WLR 744; *South Buckinghamshire District Council v Secretary of State for the Environment and Berkley Homes Limited* (1999) JPL 1340.
[8] *WG Tolley & Son Limited v Secretary of State for the Environment* (1998) 75 P& CR 533.
[9] *Roger Lethem v Secretary of State and Worcester City Council* (2003) JPL 332.
[10] *Collis Radio Limited v Secretary of State for the Environment* (1975) JPL 221.
[11] *Stringer v Minister of Housing and Local Government* (1970) 1 WLR 1280.
[12] *Cala Homes (South) Limited v Secretary of State for Communities and Local Government* (2011) EWHC 97 (Admin).

determination of an application and other, more informal, strategy documents, or draft policies which have no statutory, or pseudo-statutory, status.[13] LPAs are, therefore, under no obligation to consider government policy guidance which does not form part of the development plan in making their determination on any proposal for development. While there is no obligation, it is widely accepted that as far as it is relevant to the development proposal, informal policy should be recognized as a material consideration and should be regarded as "obviously material" within the remit of the Findlay tests.[14–16]

Public Opinion and Personal Pleas

These considerations are probably the most relevant in relation to the rise of public involvement being recognized as important within the planning system. This area considers the materiality of the views expressed by applicants and local residents to a proposed development. The LPA also has to consider the weight which may be accorded to these personal rather than planning factors in their decision-making. The assertion that a development will reduce the market value of a person's property is not a material consideration in planning. Neither is a request by the applicant's wife not to approve the proposal on the basis that her husband intends to do all the work himself, and she is concerned about the impacts of this on his physical health. These are just two examples experienced by the authors in practice.

Material considerations have traditionally, therefore, been focused on assessing matters relative to the application that can be considered as being capable of being objectively assessed. While the courts are willing to assess whether a decision-maker has identified and considered the correct material considerations in relation to a particular development proposal, the role of the decision-maker in identifying and attributing weight to material considerations is adding another level of complexity and discretion to the decision-making process in relation to planning applications. The courts have largely refused to become involved in assessing the weight to be attributed to material considerations, meaning that the decision-maker has wide-ranging discretion. Accordingly, the role of the courts is to determine the lawfulness of the decision and whether all material considerations have been taken into account, but the role does not include attributing weight to these considerations. This remains a matter of planning judgment.

---

[13] *Cala Homes (South) Limited v Secretary of State for Communities and Local Government* (2011) EWHC 97 (Admin).
[14] *Gransden v Secretary of State, ex parte Richmond L.B.C.* (1996) 1 WLR 1460, 1472.
[15] *Cala Homes (South) Limited v Secretary of State for Communities and Local Government* (2011) EWHC 97 (Admin).
[16] Re Findlay (1985) A.C. 318 (Approved as a "correct statement of principle" the observations made by Judge Cooke J in *Creed N.Z. Inc. v Governor-General* (1981) 1 NZLR 172 (at p.183)).

Making a Decision

There is a general presumption in favor of sustainable development, and LPAs should consider proposals for development which meets the sustainability economic, social, and environmental objectives for an area in a positive way seeking to approve those applications wherever possible (DLUHC, 2023, Section 2). Current Government guidance encourages preapplication discussions prior to the submission of a planning application between the LPAs, developers, communities, and other relevant consultees, both statutory and nonstatutory, with the aim of improving the efficiency of the planning system and improved outcomes for all parties involved (DLUHC, 2023, paras 39–46). This part of the process is designed to consider the fundamental issues relating to the principle of development in a particular circumstance, but for it to contribute positively to the planning process relies on the timely provision of responses from all those involved. An important aspect of this procedure is the identification of information that will be required by the LPA upon the submission of a planning application in order for it to make a determination on the development proposal.

It has already been identified that current Government guidance refers to the UK planning system as being a "plan-led" system. The "plan-led system, and the certainty and predictability it aims to provide, is central to planning and plays the key role in integrating sustainable development objectives" (ODPM, 2004).

The move toward a plan-led system was first introduced by the Planning and Compensation Act (1991), s. 26 of which inserted a new section (s. 54) into the T&CPA (1990). This new section required that "in making any determination under the Planning Acts, regard is to be had to the development plan, determination shall be made in accordance with the plan unless material considerations indicate otherwise." The section was re-enacted at s. 38(6) of the P&CPA (2004). However, this is virtually identical to the wording contained within s. 54: "If regard is to be had to the development plan for the purpose of any determination to be made under the Planning Acts the determination must be made in accordance with the plan unless material considerations indicate otherwise." Given that the two tests are so similar, many of the principles established through litigation in relation to s. 54 are also considered pertinent with regard to the application of the test under s. 36(8). Section 38(6) of the P&CPA (2004) must also be read in conjunction with section 70(2) of the T&CPA (1990), which requires an LPA in determining applications for planning permission to "have regard to the development plan, so far as it is relevant, and other considerations that are 'material' to the determination."

There are four features of the plan-led system that were identified by the House of Lords prior to their replacement by the Supreme Court under the Constitutional Reform Act 2005:[17]

---

[17] *City of Edinburgh Council v Secretary of State for Scotland* (1997) 1 WLR 1447.

(1) "The decision maker must take in to account the development plan and other material considerations."[18]
(2) "The development plan will have priority in the decision making process."[19]
(3) "That this priority is not a 'mere mechanical preference'. There is an 'element of flexibility' within the process; and if there are other considerations which would indicate that the development plan should not be followed a decision based on other considerations can be made."[20]
(4) "It is for the decision-maker to assess the facts and weigh the material considerations."[21]

It was observed by Lord Hope that elements of development plan policies may become "out-dated as national policies change, or circumstances may have occurred which show that they are no longer relevant".[22] When this occurs, it is for the decision-maker to determine how a balance is to be struck between the outdated development plan policies and any other relevant material, i.e., what weight should be accorded to policy and material considerations. Given the cumbersome and lengthy process for developing and adopting a new Local Development Plan, as discussed above, situations occur frequently where policies in development plans become outdated. Of course, where there is an emerging new local development plan at an advanced stage, weight can be accorded to the relevant draft policy. It is worth noting that certainty and clarity of planning decision-making from a public perspective can be harmed by this type of situation and so, too, can the general reputation of the planning system.

In making a decision on a development proposal where there are both development plan policies and "other material considerations," the weight to be given to each of the material considerations in coming to a decision on an application is in the hands of, and at the discretion of, the decision-maker – provided that they have had regard to the presumption in favor of the development plan contained within s. 54A of the TCPA (1990) and s. 38(6) of the P&CPA (2004). An LPA is, therefore, entitled to deduce, having applied the relevant test, that notwithstanding the policies contained in their development plan, which may clearly support the development proposal, should there be material considerations which indicate otherwise a decision contrary to the development plan can be made.[23]

A distinction has, however, to be made – a fact acknowledged in the courts – between the factors that should be acknowledged as material considerations in

---

[18]Ibid Lord Clyde p. 1457 F-H, citing Lord Guest in *Simpson v Edinburgh Corporation* (1960) SC 313, at pp. 318–319.
[19]Ibid Lord Clyde at p. 1458B.
[20]Ibid Lord Clyde at p.1458F.
[21]*City of Edinburgh Council v Secretary of State for Scotland* (1997) 1 WLR 1447; Lord Clyde p. 1458G-H, p. 1459D-H, Lord Hope p.1450D.
[22]Ibid p.1458D.
[23]*Council of London Borough of Bexley v Secretary of State for Communities and Local Government and Arslanboga* (2009) EWHC 2325 (Admin), *North Wiltshire District Council v Secretary of State for Communities and Local Government* (2007) EWCH 886.

relation to a development proposal and the weight which should be accorded to that material consideration in the making of a determination on that particular development proposal. As stated by Lord Hoffmann, materiality is a question of law, whereas the weight to be accorded to any material consideration is a matter for the decision-maker.[24]

It is, therefore, the responsibility of the decision-maker to identify policies and material considerations that are relevant to the development proposal and to allocate weight to each of these, possibly conflicting elements, in making their determination on a planning application. As an added pressure, government guidance requires that decisions on applications are to be made as speedily as possible and within timescales laid down in statute unless the applicant has agreed with the LPA to a longer deadline, referred to as an extension of time (UK Parliament, 2015, s. 34). Once a decision has been made by an LPA (or if they fail to make a decision by the deadline), it is open to challenge by applicants through appeal to the Planning Inspectorate (in England) or the Planning Environment Decisions Wales (in Wales), Planning and Environmental Appeals Divisions (Scotland), and Planning Appeals Commission (Northern Ireland). In approximately one-third of appeals, the LPA decision is overturned. For appeals decided in November 2023, the timescale for householder appeal decisions in England was 17 weeks. For written representations, the median timescale was 33 weeks, for hearings 27 weeks and for inquires 30 weeks (Planning Inspectorate, 2023). As a result of these long appeal decision times, there is more of an incentive to compromise with the LPA in order to gain approval, and there is equally less motivation to pursue a nondetermination application.

All the Cs: Challenges, Criticisms, and Change

The planning system has evolved from its inception in 1947 through a series of additions, amendments, and consolidations. These changes have brought not only advances and finessing of the system but also a level of intricacy and ambiguity which has led to uncertainties and delays. Planning decisions are currently based on the application of the test set out in s. 38(6) of the P&CPA (2004) and the interpretation and application of the policies contained within the various layers of the policy framework on a case-by-case basis by individual planning officers. This again provides uncertainty within the system, potentially discouraging investment in development projects, overburdening the appeals process, and prolonging the time taken to obtain an approval.

In making decisions on applications, planning officers must first consider the local plan. The time taken to produce a local plan is also contributing to confusion within the system as many of the policies within the adopted plan are effectively out of date or being contradicted by emerging plan policies. The lack of digitization of these plans and the data upon which the policies are based also

---

[24]*Tesco Stores Limited v Secretary of State for the Environment* (1995) 1 WLR 759 (at p.661B-C).

leads to a lack of joined-up working in relation to development and infrastructure projects. At a local level, there is also an increasing emphasis on design and the creation of beautiful places which aim to enhance the environment, health, and character of the area. The policies surrounding these requirements are written policies open to interpretation and negotiation by individual officers rather than visual design codes which provide transparency and certainty.

Planning for Change

The existing planning system has numerous problems which hamper the delivery of the vision set out by national and local government, needed by the environment and desired by communities. Further amendments to the current system are unlikely to be able to reform the system so that it can better deliver on these goals and are more likely to produce greater complexity and confusion. This realization has led to calls for a major overhaul of the system of planning in England with many backing the vision of wholesale reform over piecemeal changes to provide a simpler framework which supports developers and provides more resilient places (Mullane, 2023). The government has therefore proposed a review and has put forward a number of reforms to the current system for consultation. The 2020 White Paper *Planning for the Future* (MHCLG, 2020) was hardly welcomed; Howes Percival (2022) refers to the sheer number of consultations over the past 3 years seeking views on planning reforms to be a "merry-go round."

The numerous layers of policy containing sometimes contradictory and vague written policies reformed at all levels, with national policy focusing on general planning policy areas and with local planning authorities concentrating on site- and area-specific issues. The policy area of design, with an emphasis on beauty, is to be given more weight in decision-making with the aim of enhancing rather than doing no harm to the built and natural environment of an area. Policies dealing with the issue of design are to move from design guidance to a clearer locally produced design code. The process that plans have to navigate is also proposed to be simplified, with the removal of the test for soundness and the duty to co-operate and its replacement with the need for the plan to comply with a single statutory sustainable development test which clearly links to planning having sustainability at its core. The proposed changes set out in the 2020 White Paper also aim to abolish many of the obligations and challenges which cause delay under the current system and seek to impose a maximum statutory timetable for the adoption of a local plan of 30 months – greatly reducing the time currently taken by some LPAs to reach this end goal. This aims to ensure that all local authorities have an up-to-date local plan in place to guide development of their area.

While there have been a number of initiatives to engage communities at the plan-making stage of the process, taking up of these opportunities remains low, and consultations are often seen as tokenistic (Department for the Environment, 1995; Healey, 1993, 1996; Norton et al., 2018). The proposed reforms aim to re-emphasize the importance in community engagement in the formulation of planning policy for their area in order to front-load the process, thus allowing a streamlining of the community opportunities at the planning application stage. This is an effort to speed up the process once an application is submitted and to assist LPAs in meeting their determination targets.

In making decisions on applications, there is a renewed focus in the NPPF on sustainability and design which emphasizes the goal of planning to create beautiful places and shifts the requirement from "do no harm" to "create a net gain" in the creation of place. Accordingly, developments which meet the requirements for high-quality design while reflecting local character and preferences are encouraged to be automatically approved (DLUHC, 2023, para. 11): design/beauty is, by its very nature however, very much a matter of opinion, and not all members of a community will agree on what is good design and/or beautiful. The consideration of this emotive and highly subjective factor in the determination of planning applications has the potential to lead to greater uncertainty within the process.

Design requirements should move away from vague policy statements toward a system of tailored design codes and guidance which reflect local views and are central to decision-making – however, how do we decide whose good design/beauty should be codified? As the interpretation of the terms is subjective, these may lead to the view of beauty from those responsible for the creation of the design codes being perpetuated to the exclusion of other viewpoints.

The focus on sustainability, and all that this entails, leads to an expectation that planning will be playing a pivotal role in meeting the United Kingdom's commitment to net zero by 2050. The purpose of reforming the system is, therefore, to enable planning to meet some of the key environmental challenges facing the United Kingdom and world today while enhancing the built and natural environment in which we live and work and, at the same time, making the planning system simpler, faster, more efficient, and with more certain outcomes for prospective developers.

Conclusion

In considering the development process – and in the context of this book the placemaking process – it is, therefore, essential to give due consideration to the legal framework that will surround the project from its initial stages of land acquisition to disposal and beyond. It not only imposes restrictions on landowners, developers, and the community on what development can take place but also creates the structure within which stakeholders can ensure that the needs of a community are established, that appropriate high-quality developments are brought forward to meet those needs, and that development contributes to sustainability goals while creating the places that people and communities want. This is how placemaking functions within the planning system.

References

Building Better, Building Beautiful Commission. (2020). *Living with beauty: Promoting health, well-being and sustainable growth*. MHCLG. https://www.gov.uk/government/publications/living-with-beauty-report-of-the-building-better-building-beautiful-commission

Cullingworth, J. B. (Ed.). (1999). *British planning: 50 years of urban and regional policy*. Athlone Press.

Department for Levelling Up, Housing and Communities. (2021). *Guidance: Plan-making*. DLUHC. https://www.gov.uk/guidance/plan-making

Department for Levelling Up, Housing and Communities. (2023). *National planning policy framework*. DLUHC. https://assets.publishing.service.gov.uk/media/64f991c99ee0f2000fb7c001/NPPF_Sept_23.pdf

Department of the Environment. (1995). *Attitudes to town and country planning*. HMSO.

Development control practice. (n.d.). *Material considerations*. DCP. https://www-dcp-online-co-uk. Accessed on January 30, 2024.

Farrer and Co. (2023). *Place-making: A patient approach to creating communities*. Farrer & Co. https://www.farrer.co.uk/campaigns/placemaking-a-patient-approach-to-creating-communities/#:~:text=Despite%20the%20best%20of%20intentions,looking%20at%20a%20specific%20application

Healey, P. (1993). The communicative work of development plans. *Environment and Planning B: Planning and Design*, *20*(1), 83–104.

Healey, P. (1996). The communicative turn in spatial planning theory and its implications for spatial planning strategy formulation. *Environment and Planning B: Planning and Design*, *23*(2), 217–234.

Howes Percival. (2022, March 9). *The planning reform merry-go-round*. Howes Percival. https://www.howespercival.com/articles/the-planning-reform-merry-go-round/

Ministry of Housing, Communities and Local Government. (2020). *Planning for the future*. White Paper. MHCLG. https://assets.publishing.service.gov.uk/media/601bce418fa8f53fc149bc7d/MHCLG-Planning-Consultation.pdf

Ministry of Housing, Communities and Local Government. (2021a). *National design guide: Planning practice guidance for beautiful, enduring and successful places*. MHCLG. https://assets.publishing.service.gov.uk/media/602cef1d8fa8f5038595091b/National_design_guide.pdf

Ministry of Housing, Communities and Local Government. (2021b). *National model design code*. MHCLG. https://www.gov.uk/government/publications/national-model-design-code

Moore, V. (2010). *A practical approach to planning law* (11th ed.). Oxford University Press.

Mullane, J. (2023, August 3). *Call for planning system overhaul as applications drop to a record low*. Homebuilding & Renovating. https://www.homebuilding.co.uk/news/calls-for-planning-system-overhaul

Norton, P., Hughes, M., & Brooke-Smith, L. (2018). *Public consultation and community involvement in planning: A 21st century guide*. Taylor & Francis.

Office of the Deputy Prime Minister. (2004). *Planning policy statement 1: Delivering sustainable development*. HMSO.

Office of the Deputy Prime Minister. (2005). *The planning system: General principles.* HMSO.

Planning Inspectorate. (2023, December 21). *Guidance: Appeals: How long they take.* Planning Inspectorate. https://www.gov.uk/guidance/appeals-average-timescales-for-arranging-inquiries-and-hearings

Pritchard, R. (2012). *How long does it take to make a local plan?* Planning Advisory Service. https://planningadvisor.wordpress.com/2012/06/18/how-long-does-it-take-to-make-a-local-plan/

UK Parliament. (2015). *Town and Country Planning (Development Management Procedure) (England) Order 2015.* HMSO.

Chapter 3

Placemaking: Creating Value With Smart Spaces

David Higgins[a], Peter Wood[b] and Chris Berry[c]

[a]Higgins Research, UK
[b]Wood Advisory Limited, UK
[c]Birmingham City University, UK

Abstract

As placemaking is rapidly changing the urban landscape, the way in which we view real estate assets and their value needs to adapt to meet evolving community demands, where people create places where they want to actually live, play, and work. Increasingly, space in the city is linked to younger generations and the emerging knowledge (gig) economy. This interconnection is shaping current and future cities skylines, with buildings that offer new working and living environments. Foremost are co-living/coworking spaces which are looking beyond the offering associated with traditional office and apartment complexes. Owners and investors need to understand the new avenues to create real estate value and seek opportunities to reap commercial rewards far beyond the historical property investment arrangements.

Keywords: Property markets; investors; owners; co-living; coworking

Introduction

Megatrends primarily built around emerging digital technologies are dramatically changing the way we live, work, and socialize. This was intensified by the recent COVID-19 pandemic lockdown and has led to major structural demand changes occurring in real estate markets. These changes already affect the ways in which we think about, manage, and use places. As part of the process, at a local level, it is integrating real estate investments into transformative placemaking strategies.

Critically, the requirement and operation of space has changed in cities, where rapid adoption of digital technologies and novel pandemic-generated work routines have changed the demand for space both by duration (shorter lease terms) and location (remote working). Organizations are embracing new work practices in an environment of ongoing uncertainty. To respond to these challenges, owners increasingly need to follow sustainable practices with the global pressures of climate change policies to preserve and repurpose individual real estate assets. Global guidelines have been developed for businesses to better integrate environmental, social, and governance (ESG) activities. ESG, as it has come to be known, has provided additional measurements of performance that can impact on the reporting and value of the real estate asset alongside owner/investors' operations. In the past, investors have traditionally looked to real estate as a secure and passive investment. The value of the income streams generated by fixed-term leases has been used to inform investment decisions based on property yields. Longer leases of large units to blue chip organizations have become the de facto standard for low-risk and low-hassle returns.

Property markets are dynamic in nature and will naturally respond to demand-side changes: for example, increasing online retail spending is occurring at the expense of the traditional High Street. This has led to recent structural changes in investment patterns, with real estate investors starting to adapt their investment strategies accordingly. This is especially evident in relation to secondary-grade investment building stock, particularly in towns and cities. These trends have long-term repercussions for owners and investors, who have, in the past, traditionally looked at real estate as standalone individual assets, offering a relatively secure passive investment with minimum hands-on asset management requirements.

In the current fast-changing environment, driven by technological advances, sustainability requirements, and increased extreme risk events, many owners and investors of primarily secondary-grade real estate realize that there is a need to adapt to occupiers' lower space requirements and shorter income streams. New real estate investment models are being promoted for owners and investors to maintain and grow their real estate portfolios. Foremost, there is a realization there needs to be a fundamental change from the traditional landlord and tenant arrangement to a proactive customer and service provider offering, for example, advanced digital connectivity, access to experts, hospitality, and well-being facilities. This can improve occupier retention alongside exploring better diversification of income streams.

Furthermore, in looking at the individual real estate asset, the surrounding environment also needs to be considered. In transforming urban locations, placemaking offers a smart approach to create vibrant, inclusive, and sustainable communities. These interactions can provide spaces which are attractive to people and businesses. This can boost foot traffic, the local economy, and associated real estate values.

To understand how smart space can create real estate value, this chapter discusses (i) the changing property market drivers, (ii) evolving urban landscape, (iii) new city-orientated working and living environments, and (iv) the new currency of real estate investment. In summary, this research looks at the new paradigms driving modern urban real estate markets for building owners and those that invest in urban real estate markets.

Changing Property Market Drivers

Land and property have always been factors of production along with labor, capital, and enterprise. While industry dominated western economies, real estate was intrinsically linked to industrial output. As economies transitioned away from industry and into services, businesses became more flexible in location but still required a physical space for staff and operations. Real estate became a separate capital entity, an investment asset class in its own right. Theoretical real estate models were developed to explain the emerging market. The Archer and Ling model developed in the mid-1990s (see Goodchild & D'Arcy, 2019) describes a cyclical property market where performance is based on three factors:

(1) Space market: this is focused on occupier demand and is driven by local economic conditions. In reflecting occupier needs, the space market can change rapidly depending on the economic environment.
(2) Property market: both property condition and new supply form part of this section, where the property is compared to alterative locations, and new supply absorption rates affect the choice and size of the selected property market.
(3) Capital market: this looks at the investment and finance markets, as compares real estate performance (risk and return) to alternative asset classes, and the cost of money which reflects the borrowing opportunities, as more often to buy physical real estate it requires substantial debt financing, due to challenges of high real estate costs, illiquidity, and divisibility (Higgins, 2017).

In detailing these determinants, the adapted Archer and Ling model can manage new specific space, property, and capital market inputs; however, widespread structural changes and extreme risk events can seriously influence the performance of real estate markets, to an extent that the traditional space, property, and capital market drivers are of lesser importance (see Fig. 3.1).

Also, Fig. 3.1 shows the emergence of two new mega drivers on real estate performance: extreme risk events and structural changes. There is plenty of evidence that their relevance and importance are increasing to an extent that underlying fundamentals may be of lesser significance. This is discussed as follows.

Extreme Risk Events

In the past, extreme risk events, such as plagues and major catastrophes, were considered location-specific and deemed, to many, to be part of the normal

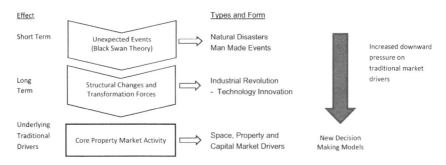

Fig. 3.1. Emerging Drivers of Real Estate Performance.

economic marketplace and so attracted relatedly little interest apart from the surrounding community. This has dramatically changed, with extreme risk events becoming more frequent and of a wider spatial scale, as is demonstrated by the recent Climate Central (2021) research on the frequency of billion-dollar weather disasters in the United States, being now about one event every 18 days. This compares to 82 days between such disasters in the 1980s.

Knowledge and the implications of extreme risk events have also significantly increased since the 2008 global financial crisis. The severe worldwide economic crisis provided the platform to support the popularity of the term "Black Swan Events" to describe these major incidents that can cause extensive destruction being a combination of low predictability, severe impact, and obvious in hindsight. This makes Black Swan events of considerable importance to society (Taleb, 2009).

In understanding the concept of Black Swan theory, catastrophic events can be grouped under defined headings relating to natural and man-made disasters. The impact of these events can vary depending on locality and category of risk. Fig. 3.2 details recognized major Black Swan events during the last 40 years.

Interestingly, on data recorded by Swiss Re (2023), the number and type of major disasters are changing, with man-made disasters in the past five years falling to an average of 109 events per year from a high of 220 events in the early 2000s. This compares to the steady increase in natural catastrophes from 140 events in the early 2000s to the current average of 189 events per year. In part, this represents increased extreme weather events, such as major floods, earthquakes, hurricanes, and so on. These extreme weather-related natural disasters now appear to dominate the insured catastrophes and are in excess of 60% of the annual value of overall recorded catastrophes (Swiss Re, 2023).

It is recognized by many that climate change is a key catalyst driving extreme weather-related natural disasters. There is considerable research on the topic, with general acknowledgment of the evolving risks that are shaping the global environment. These include rising temperatures and sea levels and extreme weather

Placemaking: Creating Value With Smart Spaces 35

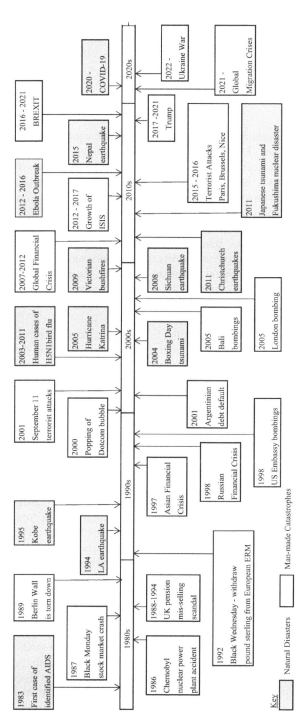

Fig. 3.2. Examples of Major Black Swan Events.

events, which can have potentially devastating effects on society. Leading global government-funded organizations have prepared extensive reports on climate change observations, causes (greenhouse emissions), projections, and impact (for example, see IPCC, 2022; WMO, 2023; World Bank, 2023).

Structural Changes

The permanent nature of real estate can create challenges when new products and processes enter the marketplace. Traditionally, these can be linked to major innovations which, in many instances in the past, have evolved with the phases of industrial revolutions. The most recent Fourth Industrial Revolution represents a fundamental change as it cuts across many sectors, with new digital technology offering increased interconnectivity and smart automation.

While technological development is occurring on several fronts, McAfee and Brynjolfsson (2017) identified five key parallel, independent, and overlapping areas. They developed the DANCE acronym, namely: data, algorithms, network, the cloud, and exponential growth in digital hardware. Together, the elements of DANCE are driving change with the explosion in artificial intelligence devices including robots, drones, autonomous cars, and many other machines that are deeply digital.

The speed of change is now intense and is leading to the emergence of new real estate opportunities. For example, computer data centers and large logistic warehouses are in demand globally; conversely, many prominent commercial buildings are becoming rapidly obsolescent, as is currently seen in city centers with strikingly high retail and office vacancy rates. This creates both opportunities and challenges, especially if we are trying to attract new inhabitants to work and live in the once vibrant city centers. This is at the essence of placemaking, as underutilized space can be transformed into meaningful places that can reflect the changing needs of the changing community.

In understanding the drivers of digital transformation, we have seen the recent emergence of the "gig economy", where knowledge workers, particularly younger generations – Generation Y and Z (19–42 years old) – are expressing an increasing demand for flexible and autonomous work, prompting many to engage in free-lancing work where they can work for a number of clients on a flexible basis. The emergence of digital talent platforms linking workers and employers is the driving force behind the increasing prominence of the gig economy (Forbes, 2021).

The Evolving Urban Landscape

Throughout history, rapid growth in urban populations has led to the rapid expansion of cities. In the past, cities have been a key catalyst for human progress, bringing together the movement of people, goods, and knowledge. Even with the recent digital trend of remote working, most people in cities are restricted in their ability to do their job remotely: for example, Schwebel et al. (2021) noted that about one in three workers can entertain remote working opportunities. To this backdrop, cities are an important part of society, as they now account for over half of the global population, with this share forecast to rise to two-thirds by 2050 (Goldin & Lee-Devlin, 2023).

In celebrating the success of cities, being the engine room for innovation, economic growth, and job creation, many locations have strikingly similar challenges: foremost of these is widespread demographic inequality. There is a gulf between professionals and knowledge workers, forming the cosmopolitan elite, and the low-skilled service workers, who support this prosperous society. In recognizing the issues, many cities are looking to better balance the social and cultural density of urban living, with reforms to education, housing, and public transport. The aim is to create communities offering opportunities to all those living within the city's perimeters and beyond. To many, this is the essence of placemaking.

Cities also have an important role in reducing the impact of climate change. Although urban areas represent just 1% of the earth's habitable landmass, approximately 57% of the world population live in cities and currently generate close to 70% of the world's carbon emissions (Ritche & Roser, 2019; World Bank, 2023). In acknowledging that this is a high figure, many cities have taken action to reduce carbon emissions by improving the built environment: requiring new buildings to be more energy efficient, encouraging old buildings to be retrofitted with insulation and sustainable technologies, promoting public transport, and encouraging electric cars, etc.

As the urban landscape changes, so do passive building owners and investors need to adapt to the new dynamic business environment driven by innovative technology and increased degrees of uncertainty. The attractiveness of cities can create placemaking opportunities to manage real estate obsolescence and dilapidations and offer smart solutions to meet the changing occupier space demands, whether it relates to their working or living requirements.

New Working and Living Environments

The following section explores the emerging coworking and co-living markets. For each market, the traditional operational approach is examined, followed by more recent changes, referred to as "generation one" and "generation two." These are the trade-off between risk and return as each successive model attempts to balance the higher risk of income stream with increased returns in order to maintain and enhance capital values. Both in coworking and co-living spaces, the level of services provided and short lease terms will affect the risk profile of the building owner and investors.

Coworking Space

As placemaking is rapidly changing the urban landscape, the way in which we view real estate value needs to adapt to meet evolving community demands, as people create places where they want to live and work. Increasingly, space in the city is linked to younger generations and the knowledge (gig) economy where shifting lifestyles and "open all hours" irregular work schedules will be the new normal. This interconnection is shaping current and future city office markets which look beyond the traditional space, financial, and lease demands to flexible operating platforms. Owners and investors need to understand the new avenues to create real estate value and seek opportunities to reap commercial rewards far beyond the historical office landlord and tenant arrangements.

While space, property, and capital markets have been the traditional real estate drivers, the knowledge economy provides an additional layer which is guiding occupier demand. The key elements cover digital connectivity, increased globalization, environmental concerns, and strategic resources alongside post-COVID-19 recognition of disaster preparedness. These megatrends are changing the working environment by improving an individual's work experience (productivity) and creating new workplace settings.

As technology redefines the workplace, younger generations are changing the traditional work contract, and the nomadic multitask workforce can move seamlessly between organizations, building a freelancing career on entrepreneurship and their interests. More often, being digital natives, they can take up remote and flexible working practices and are increasingly able to work anywhere, causing organizations to reconsider their real estate strategy and move toward more flexible options (Higgins & Wood, 2021).

To attract and retain the young knowledge workforce, the modern office setting is becoming more inviting and informal. New workplaces look to break down boundaries, in order to socialize and share knowledge with a focus on occupier experience and well-being. Ergonomic desks, meeting spaces, and social spaces offer a creative comfortable work environment where the smart office starts to become your sixth sense, as a personal assistant to support you in your daily activities (JLL, 2023; Raconteur, 2022).

In this environment, property owners still need to achieve attractive commercial returns. The convention of providing distance between themselves and tenants with long term "let and forget" full repairing and insuring (FRI) leases is being consigned to history, as more occupiers are increasingly seeking smart offices offering flexible terms, customer management, and service provisions. The imbalance has created opportunities for intermediates to offer operating models where a serviced office/co-working operator takes a long-term conventional lease in a building and then offers flexible smart office space – the traditional co-working model (Regus and WeWork, etc.). In the COVID-19 era, a generation 1 model emerged, whereby the flexible operators can no longer accept the risk transfer, with revenue-share models coming to the fore. Beyond this, landlords – or should we say customer service providers – are now realizing that they themselves can capture this margin and "white label" facilitators are rapidly evolving, a generation 2 model (Re-defined, Indego, etc.) (see Fig. 3.3).

In various forms, the intermediaries' (co-working operators') offer may provide attractive returns in buoyant markets, although less so in depressed markets, where flexible smart leases provide low security of income at the operational and ownership level with increased risk of vacancy. In short, with flexible smart leases,

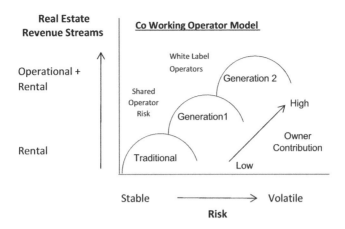

Fig. 3.3. Property Owners' Income: Smart Flexible Office Space. *Source:* (Higgins & Wood, 2020).

property owners will hold long-term assets with short-term liabilities; essentially, they need to become more than rent collectors, making a move to a strategic and human-focused property asset management strategy and so achieving maximum returns on the space they let. As has been used in the hotels market for some time, a cash flow approach with appropriate stress testing needs to be employed to allow a more holistic and representative valuation.

Beyond the physical bricks and mortar structure, property owners need to buy into the future business models and market dynamics of the knowledge workforce, by integrating the physical space with services and technology offering to create an enhanced customer experience. This creates a massive shift in the property owner's business model, where value is created by the offering rather than the location. To determine value, rather than reviewing the building's covenants and weighted average lease expiry (WALE) profile, future performance measures will consider on-demand facilities with key indicators covering footfall, short-term occupancy rates, service charges, and hospitality revenues.

In moving the income stream sources generated by real estate toward customer services, real estate values would need to reflect the changing risk profile. Initially, this suggests higher yields to embrace the increased uncertainty, with projections based on business valuation principles, which focus on an estimate of the economic value in the form of a going concern. This would place greater emphasis on asset utilization, efficiency, and occupier retention. In simple terms, using a cash flow approach, monetizing these diverse income streams would generate a higher margin, and a higher yield would be applied.

Co-living Space

As the future of work is changing, we now find ourselves at a stage where demand for quality, convenience, and flexibility in urban living is not being met by traditional inner-city apartment complexes. Long-term ownership does not provide the flexibility required, nor do younger occupants have the high capital necessary to participate. At the same time, short-term UK leasing legislation and the current supply are inefficient in both space, operation, and capital reward.

In today's fast-moving digital economy, we are seeing a crossflow of knowledge across different property sectors with increasing velocity, and the problem posed above has a readily available solution already evolving in the commercial sector, namely "Co-," where a co-living environment represents a feeling of togetherness, being more than in a block of flats: it provides a home and a sense of closeness and friendship with fellow residents. These evolving characteristics and the way in which this concept works are explored further.

Co-living can be described as a way of living in cities that is focused on community, convenience, and well-being. This manifests itself as a small apartment with kitchen facilities akin to a mini studio apartment that is supported by larger communal areas that can include work areas, lounge areas, sundry services, storage, and leisure facilities. More often than not, these communal areas are also curated such that events and activities are hosted for the residents.

As we have seen from the changes occurring in the office sector driven by the co-working environment, the same evolving characteristics act as enabling agents, namely:

- the paradigm shift from landlord and tenant to customer and customer service provider;
- tech enabled property management and customer relationship systems;
- multiple revenue streams from services rather than rent from a FRI lease;
- a cash flow approach to valuation, with a drive to increased margins to compensate for potentially higher overall volatility.

The principal revenue for an operator is room rent which is usually on a fully inclusive and furnished basis, with the landlord managing all services such as rates, heating, lighting, etc. Additional services, such as Wi-Fi, workstations, gyms, etc., and their costs, are bundled together with a margin added. There may also be diversification of income with shops and leisure facilities incorporated into a development. Increasingly, property assets are the platform for opportunities to enhance and diversify revenue streams that should be valued accordingly. These incomes can usually then be netted down with provisions for voids, refurbishment, and capital expenditure ("cap-ex") and the resultant granular income stream discounted in the usual manner at an appropriate rate.

The discount rates for co-living show an interesting phenomenon in how capital markets are responding to this new asset class, which is allowing the asset class to grow. Institutional investors, normally being drawn to secure income streams to match long-term liabilities, are accepting the granular short-term nature of co-living, whether the arrangement with the occupiers is on a daily, monthly, or a quarterly basis. The focus is on the quality and business attributes of the manager, as without this, the new paradigm would not be possible.

Of critical interest is the evolution of co-working and co-living models and parallels between the two. The residential market has some fundamental differences to the commercial office market: occupiers are small, income is granular, and there has been much more limited scope for provision of shared services at the building level. We see co-living currently akin to the first generation in co-working, with a small but growing market driven by trailblazing progressive intermediaries with bold ideas and branding.

The risk transfer between shareholders and operational companies is similar to the module used by hotel operators. It is likely that, as the landlord knowledge base increases, the market matures; then the co-living sector will follow the co-working sector with funders seizing the opportunity to cut out the middleman and their share of the revenue streams. Fig. 3.4 demonstrates changes in apartment styles and service provider's income sources.

The need for new ways of accommodating younger generations, and changes to how communities choose to live, are being facilitated by co-living operators coupled with a tide of long-term capital. Institutional capital is focusing on anticipated growth areas and the fund managers' need for greater portfolio diversification into the residential sector. This sector is still evolving with new operating models, and the pace of change can only increase.

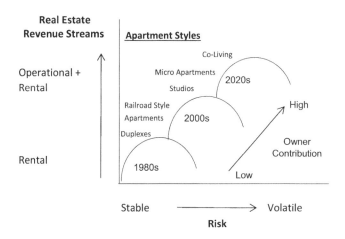

Fig. 3.4. Property Owners' Income: Co-living Space. *Source:* (Higgins & Wood, 2022).

Co-community Space: Owners and Investors

Driven by shifting demographics and digital connectivity, owners and investors can no longer be the passive supplier of real estate. The traditional property asset operational model is being replaced with engagement and flexibility in order to create new streams of revenue. Moving forward, these value-focused property owners will develop their offering to meet the rapidly-changing requirements of clients. A paradigm shift is occurring, where customer's on-demand experiences will be the focus for the flexible offering provided by the building owners and their appointed consultants.

In describing placemaking opportunities for building owners and investors, whether it is a coworking or a co-living offering, there is a requirement that the product can differentiate to those competing for the same space occupiers, essentially offering a best-in-class approach. Key themes can be grouped in three categories, namely: Amenities, Appeal, and Experience.

(1) Amenities: the ability to adapt and respond to customer's needs, by looking beyond the standard services offered by competing space providers. This could cover innovative health and well-being facilities alongside advanced digital offerings.
(2) Appeal: can be characterized by a themed design, aesthetics, and attraction to local values including cultural and environmental interests. Often, this can be created by the atmosphere and ambience which, in historical buildings, could include architectural features such as high vaulted ceiling and eccentric interiors.
(3) Experience: often the emphasis is on the personalized encounter within the individual and community space, for example, in providing social interaction and an active built environment atmosphere. These positive images often provide vivid memories and a catalyst to planned future events.

In identifying the attractions of co-community space, creating value for building owners and investors is now more than ever linked to the offering and the extraordinary attention to design detail and strong marketing appeal. This intimate and sophisticated approach can lead to ongoing strong demand and so provide value for successful building owners and investors beyond that which can be achieved with a passive real estate strategy.

Looking forward, traditional building owners and investors face a critical challenge. Whether providing living or working space, they need to recognize and actively tap into the changing target market, specifically the younger generation, identifying and providing for their needs and aspirations. This will require a deeper understanding of modern trends in social engagement, forward thinking on technology, and probably an increased focus on eco-friendly initiatives. To many senior property professionals, this would be like learning a foreign language, where even the structure of the sentence does not make sense.

The New Currency of Real Estate Investment

Planning for Change

To many industry observers, the traditional passive building owner and investor is being confined to history, as the real estate landscape is changing rapidly and requires ongoing active strategies to maintain and improve performance. This is most evident in the urban setting, where established conventional office and retail space is being seriously affected by new working and living trends, underpinned by three structural themes: environment, demographics, and technology. Building owners and investors who swiftly act with conviction can capture the potential performance uplift, although they need to examine both the asset and the surrounding locality as never before.

Thinking about the building as an asset, building owners and investors should consider four key elements in the current urban marketplace. There can be described as the open "DOOR" strategy – Diversify, Occupier, Operation, and Returns.

(1) Diversify: both structural changes and extreme risk events have changed the real estate marketplace, with increased occupier demand for shorter leases and flexible space offerings. To maintain some form of continuity of income, building owners and investors are diversifying by the traditional approach of location and property type, plus increasingly embracing inner-city locations, multiuse buildings, which can have many occupiers on short-term tenancies.
(2) Occupier: with an ever-changing business landscape, a central theme is the need to understand the demands of current and prospective tenants. This goes beyond the established lines of communication, with digital marketing strategies to both identify and create demand alongside retaining existing space occupiers.
(3) Operation: in managing space, there are the ongoing traditional requirements linked to the physical asset – cleaning, maintenance, etc. – plus more recent extensive sustainability compliance and reporting responsibilities. Added to this, the level of customer services that can be offered to the space occupiers is mushrooming. It is being built around enhancing the positive experience for the inhabitants. More often, this will be driven by digital devices offering everything from a virtual assistant to coordinating creative social activities.
(4) Returns: to many building owners and investors, financial viability is still the sole measure of real estate performance. While this blunt approach recognizes financial returns as the cornerstone of any investment, there is an increasing pyramid of emerging benchmarks (ESG scorecards, etc.) that need to be considered and achieved to create long-term value in a real estate asset. Increasingly, in today's environment, occupiers, financiers, and investors can have more indirect control on investor's real estate decisions than ever before.

So often overlooked, a missing variable to the real estate equation is the surrounding locality. Rather than the physical urban environment, which is easy to measure, the emphasis is increasingly on the residents and their community, both from taking space in local co-working enterprises to benefitting from the social offering as defined in a building owner's ESG contributions. Increasingly, in today's real estate environment, the local community will have an important part to play in the success of urban redevelopments. Placemaking is a core element of transforming spaces into meaningful places for local communities (Everfi, 2023).

To access the local community, building owners are realizing that they need to be part of the community, rather than acting as individuals. This can occur with engagement and collaboration particularly around social and economic inclusion of the local community. These values can lead to informed decisions benefiting all participants and so create – and manage – attractive places with a strong pulse and a vibrant identity.

Owner and Investor Awareness

In identifying the changing real estate landscape, the ability and continuity to generate income from buildings will be a key consideration for owners and investors. In many instances, this will relate less to lease terms and rather more to the credentials and ability of management to attract and retain space occupiers. In essence, building owners and investors are becoming part of the service industry rather than a manager of space or a physical asset. Likewise, building owners need to understand that they are providing an experience for which occupiers are willing to pay more. Achieving excellence relates to the quality of the services, amenities, and flexibility being provided.

Far from shying away from the flexible space offering, owners and investors may want to embrace the advantages it can bring to an asset, not only as a revenue generator but, in the wider context, from the traditional ground-floor business café lounge area offering, to promoting well-being and green spaces. Overall, these benefits can lead to a more positive environment for the occupiers, with increased productivity and greater financial success. The better the occupiers' experience, the higher will be the demand for leasing space (by new and current tenants) in the building, which will ultimately push up rents and associated income streams.

In detailing the changing marketplace, valuation models have to adjust when considering flexible space. A key issue is the management structure, as to what extent the building owner bears all the risk. If the building owner is seeking to sell hospitality-led services to the occupiers, being a broad range of amenities and flexibility, then placing a financial value on those services must be different from the yield-based valuation approach of the past. A value proposition for flexible space needs to account for fluctuating demand, rental structures, diverse revenue streams, and additional operational costs. In many areas, this requires the real estate industry to look beyond the traditional comparisons and source granular real-time building data.

As these changes occur, the ramifications for the real estate industry may initially be unclear: but it can be fairly certain that they will be both broad and significant. Those who are prepared will succeed, and those who look to the past may be replaced by a younger generation, more prepared to adapt and change to a forward-looking dynamic real estate market. Foremost, in rethinking and transforming real estate, a placemaking approach is required, in order to create vibrant and sustainable communities that will promote the local economy and provide a platform to increase real estate performance.

References

Climate Central. (2021). *Disaster fatigue*. Climate Central. https://www.climatecentral.org/climate-matters/disaster-fatigue

Everfi. (2023). *Everfi's guide to meaningful social impact*. Everfi from Blackbaud.

Forbes. (2021). Will the gig economy become the new working-class norm? *Forbes*. https://www.forbes.com/sites/forbesbusinesscouncil/2021/08/12/will-the-gig-economy-become-the-new-working-class-norm/?sh=49491e23aee6

Goldin, I., & Lee-Devlin, T. (2023). *Age of the city: Why our future will be won or lost together*. Bloomsbury.

Goodchild, R., & D'Arcy, E. (2019). An international overview of real estate markets: Similarities and differences. In B. MacGregor, R. Schulz, & R. Green (Eds.), *Routledge companion to real estate investment* (pp. 11–42). Routledge.

Higgins, D. (2017). Residential property market performance and extreme risk measures. *Pacific Rim Property Research, 22*(3), 21–32.

Higgins, D., & Wood, P. (2020, July 8). Making money, from offices – The next step. *Property Chronicle*. https://www.propertychronicle.com/smart-flexible-office-space-the-implication-for-property-income-returns/

Higgins, D., & Wood, P. (2021, November 11). Intergenerational diversity and the office workforce. *Property Chronicle*. https://www.propertychronicle.com/intergenerational-diversity-and-the-office-workforce/

Higgins, D., & Wood, P. (2022, February 14). Finding value in co-living space. *Property Chronicle*. https://www.propertychronicle.com/finding-value-in-co-living-space/

IPCC (Intergovernmental Panel on Climate Change). (2022). *Climate change 2022: Impacts, adaptation and vulnerability*. IPCC. https://www.ipcc.ch/report/ar6/wg2/

JLL (Jones Lang LaSalle). (2023). *A new employee value proposition for a new world of work*. JLL. https://www.jll.co.uk/en/solutions/workforce-advisory

McAfee, A., & Brynjolfsson, E. (2017). *Harnessing our digital future: Machine platform crowd*. Norton.

Raconteur. (2022). *The future workplace*. Raconteur. https://www.raconteur.net/report/future-workplace-2022

Ritche, H., & Roser, M. (2019). *Land use*. Our World in Data. https://ourworldindata.org/land-use

Schwebel, A., Root, J., Allen, J., Hazan, J., Almquist, E., Devlin, T., & Harris, K. (2021). *The working future: More human, not less*. Bain and Co. https://www.bain.com/insights/the-working-future-more-human-not-less-future-of-work-report/

Swiss Re. (2023). *Sigma: Natural catastrophes and inflation in 2022: A perfect storm*. Swiss Re.
Taleb, N. (2009). *The black swan: The impact of the highly improbable* (2nd ed.). Penguin.
WMO (World Meteorological Organisation). (2023). *State of the global climate 2022*. WMO.
World Bank. (2023). *Climate change overview*. World Bank. https://www.worldbank.org/en/topic/climatechange

Chapter 4

Placemaking, Nature, and the Promise of Digital Transformation

Mike Grace

Birmingham City University, UK

Abstract

The governance of our towns and cities requires an approach that connects people with nature and places. Digital technology can be the glue that does this, if it serves the needs of the various stakeholders, including urban communities. It means identifying the potential connections across people, digital, and place themes, examining successful approaches, and exploring some of the current practice (or lack of it) in spatial planning and smart cities. This can be considered using a range of Internet of Things (IoT) technologies with other methodologies which combine the use of socioeconomic and environmental data about the urban environment. This ambient domain sensing can provide the ecological and other data to show how digital connectivity is addressing the placemaking challenges alongside providing implications for urban governance and communities.

Keywords: Placemaking principles; local digital; Web 3.0; green infrastructure; land use

Making places is a complex business. Places constantly change as we continually impose more demands on where we live. This makes them even more complex to design, manage, and especially, to sustain. This chapter deals with how we go about the challenges of connecting people with nature in our increasingly urban and increasingly digital world. It explores whether the promise and practice of digitally enabled approaches can deliver smarter places and empowered people. Can it help to create sustainable, greener cities, and the governance tools to make the most effective use of our limited land resource? This is particularly an issue in the context of continual efforts to reform the UK spatial planning system and the shift to a digital world that envisages connected places. To paraphrase Stanislaw

Lec (1959), can it be progress if a placemaking cannibal now uses a digital knife and fork?

Urban Challenges

We know that we live in an increasingly urbanizing world. In 1950, 30% of the world's population resided in urban areas; in 2018, this was 55%, and by 2050, this is projected to be 68%. This would add 2.5 billion to the world's urban population, with almost 90% of this growth happening in Asia and Africa (United Nations, 2019). In 2018, 1.7 billion people (23% of the world's population) lived in a city with at least 1 million inhabitants. In 2030, this is projected to be 28% of people worldwide. Globally, the number of megacities (those with more than 10 million inhabitants) is projected to rise from 33 in 2018 to 43 in 2030 (Government Office for Science, 2021). The global building floor area is expected to double by 2060, the equivalent of adding an entire New York City to the world, every month, for 40 years. The impact and footprint will be huge; nearly 40% of global carbon dioxide emissions come from the real estate sector.

Trends in urbanization are variable, often linked to economic and other social cycles (Cortinovis et al., 2022). The recent experience of European cities shows that densification always happened in growing cities. In the United Kingdom, the COVID pandemic inspired something of a shift in population movements away from traditional urban areas to rural regions, motivated by the desire for access to a larger garden, to be closer to parks and green spaces (Marsh, 2020). Over the next decade, the population of most areas of the United Kingdom is set to continue growing, particularly in the south and Midlands. The proportion of people aged 65 years and over is projected to increase almost everywhere by 2028 (Nash, 2020).

Calls to integrate nature into our urban world have gathered pace. Climate and ecological emergencies have been declared internationally and, in the United Kingdom, at national and local levels (for example, BBC, 2019). Part of becoming net-zero carbon by 2030 is achieving a "just transition" to ensure that this transition addresses social inequalities, brings communities along, and connects people to nature for "inclusive and sustainable urbanization and the provision of ecosystem functions and services" (Convention on Biological Diversity, 2022, Target 12).

Similarly, the UK Environment Plan requires high-quality, accessible, natural spaces close to where people live and work, particularly in urban areas, and encourages more people to spend time in them to benefit their health and well-being (UK Government, 2018). To achieve these ambitions for the recovery of the natural environment, statutory targets for Biodiversity Net Gain, duties on public bodies to improve biodiversity, and voluntary standards for delivering more green infrastructure (GI) in urban areas are being set out (Environment Act, 2021; see Benyon, 2022). Ten goals for restoring nature and improving environmental quality have been set out in the Plan's 5-year review (UK Government, 2023c). Oversight to achieve the promised sustained environmental improvement in the United Kingdom will lie with the Office for Environmental Protection (OEP, 2022).

Yet, in the United Kingdom, successive studies have indicated that there are unrealistic expectations about the ability of the finite land resource to meet our multiple demands including for development, food production, leisure, and energy generation. The United Kingdom is also falling short of meeting its commitment of protecting one-third of English land and seas for nature by 2030 (Government Office for Science, 2010; House of Lords, 2022; Royal Society, 2023). Land is clearly a valuable and limited resource. The pressures on land from climate change, demographic shifts, and changing patterns of work and habitation are increasing. This urgently requires new land-use policies, and placemakers will have to decide how to resolve these competing pressures to meet the demands for greener urbanization.

Cities, towns, and villages will be at the heart of our response to the climate and ecological emergencies. The multifunctional role of urban GI is especially relevant as it helps in adapting cities to climate change (for cooling in hotter summers and manage increased risks from flood events), biodiversity, and nature recovery. Experiencing nature in cities supports national leveling-up, economic regeneration, and is good for our health (Green et al., 2022; Lovell et al., 2020; Turunen et al., 2023), even being labeled as "green care" (Mitchell et al., 2024). It is estimated that between US$16 billion and US$20.6 billion could be saved in global healthcare expenditure by 2050 by persuading people to be physically more active. The loss of the Haizhu (China) wetland natural areas was calculated to lead to an annual increase in mental health expenditures of US$2.90 million, with a net present value of US$44.6 million over 30 years (Guerry et al., 2023). Implementing green corridors throughout Barcelona suggests significant benefits that could reduce annual antidepressant use and visits to mental health specialists by 13% (Vidal Yáñez et al., 2023). More plainly, in popular surveys, the United Kingdom's happiest places are those that have access to beautiful green spaces and nature (Rightmove, 2023).

Nature and biodiversity restoration, carbon sequestration, new development and infrastructure, land for energy, access, and well-being are all taking on a greater priority (HM Treasury, 2022; House of Lords, 2022). Yet we remain some way off from delivering our ambitions (Office for Environmental Protection, 2024) and the benefits we get from urban nature is at risk through, for example, the surface urban heat island effect (Cai et al., 2023). The demands we make of our places will change as our communities change. It means taking opportunities for a new multifunctional and integrated approach if we are to achieve green, cool, and accessible urban places which equitably meet the needs of all sectors of urban communities for generations to come. Post-COVID-19, we have recognized the importance of sufficient green infrastructure provision and protection in new development and for maximum beneficial use to be made of it. It especially asks questions about how we know what is needed from governance through regulation, policy, and stewardship in placemaking.

Principles for Places

Local authorities are required to identify their strategic priorities and have planning policies to achieve sustainable development across economic, social, and environmental objectives. This is to meet the needs of present and future generations and by fostering well-designed, beautiful, and safe places, with accessible services and open spaces that reflect current and future needs and support communities' health, social, and cultural well-being (Department for Levelling-Up, Housing and Communities [DLUHC], 2023a, para 8). The UK Government is supporting this drive through initiatives such as the Office for Place (Office for Place, 2023a). The devolved UK Governments and third sector advocates have identified principles and the concept of a "place standard" (Design Commission for Wales, 2020; Scottish Government, 2022). This is to maximize the potential of the physical and social environment to support health, well-being, a high quality of life and community engagement and empowerment. It provides a framework for placemaking at all scales and for the improvement of new and existing places.

The common denominator within this multiplicity of guidance is the principle of empowering people and communities, with structured conversations through which communities, the public sector, private sector, and third sector work together to deliver high-quality places (Emery & Thrift, 2021). This is backed up by other principles:

- setting a clear vision well communicated;
- efficient use of land and resources;
- well designed;
- attractive and coherent development;
- accessible and well-connected through walking cycling and public transport;
- green spaces with nature enhanced.

The Government-backed design codes and standards for urban green infrastructure support the delivery of these inclusive approaches (DLUHC, 2021a; Natural England, 2023; Office for Place, 2023b). These are now helping to bridge sectoral and disciplinary divides as the engineering sector embraces nature-based solutions (Washbourne & Wansbury, 2023). The Biophilic Cities Network has drawn upon the collective activities of its members (including Los Angeles, Singapore, and Birmingham) to generate a table of biophilic city indicators (Brown, 2023). Birmingham City Council has identified 11 domains for shaping Health Action Zones, its version of the 15 Minute City. Other emerging standards will be relevant for placemakers; the net-zero carbon buildings national standard that is emerging for the construction industry (Cameron-Smith, 2023) sets out the default preference of taking a holistic view of the built stock that already exists, reusing and retaining it as much as possible. These approaches also aim to give some certainty to developers and communities as to what is expected from the delivery and management of new urban development or regeneration (Green et al., 2022; Natural England, 2023).

This is a complex agenda for placemakers. Its delivery is not without its challenges. In hard urban environments, ecological processes are artificial or largely absent. While in general terms, we know that there is strong evidence that more nature is better for us, the direct link between green places and actual health benefits can be hard to quantify. Even if delivery is achieved, maintaining it can be harder as resources for stewardship of the green assets diminish. Community involvement within traditional, top-down urban planning processes has long been criticized for its lack of inclusivity (Jian et al., 2020). Methods and practices vary, are often based on local expertise and initiatives, and can be tokenistic or aspirational (Kaehne et al., 2020). It is a decades-old concern (Altshuler, 1965; Morgan & Moseley, 1981), and the frustration continues to be seen in practice today. Response rates to a typical preplanning consultation are around 3% of those directly made aware of it, and in Local Plan consultations, this figure can fall to less than 1% of the population of a district (Manns, 2017). Community representatives at Local Plan Examinations formally complain in these public hearings that local authorities are just doing the regulatory minimum of consultation with electorates in their bid to meet self-imposed development targets (as the author observed at a hearing in Shropshire: Shropshire Council, 2022).

A Digital Fix?

The UK Government has acknowledged the problem of achieving meaningful engagement in proposals for reform of the planning system, not least because it views the erosion of trust in current plan-making and, by extension, placemaking as a barrier to growth. Proposals for planning reforms increasingly suggest a solution lies within the application of emerging technologies (DLUHC, 2023b).

There are parallels with Industry 4.0 (also called the Fourth Industrial Revolution) and the digitization of the manufacturing sector, driven by disruptive trends including the rise of data and connectivity, analytics, human–machine interaction, and improvements in robotics (McKinsey & Company, 2022). The efficiency benefits and improved customer experience sought by commercial businesses and industry (Erl & Stoffers, 2022) are increasingly being seen to apply equally to the evolution of smarter and greener urbanization.

Improved access to shared and increasing amounts of data assets is becoming possible through technology, and government is pushing the digitization of the planning system to speed up decisions and make it more efficient and engaging for stakeholders (Jenrick, 2021; UK Parliament, 2023).

Feedback from emerging practice strikes a positive note about the emerging potential of digital techniques and big data for changing the way in which it undertakes its placemaking role. Applications include Building Information Management (BIM), Geographical Information Systems (GIS), OpenStreetMap, the Internet of Things (IoT, as part of smart cities), and big data through social media. Using these kinds of data sources, the ambition is that digital transformation offers place shapers the opportunity to develop approaches which can align environmental, economic, and social outcomes. In turn, this can enhance the quality of urban living experienced by communities and help to engage them. And perhaps to fulfill that government expectation that if urban change is more beautiful and greener and shaped by local communities, then development will become more acceptable.

The DLUHC's PropTech Innovation Fund and Digital Planning programme report that local planning authorities that blended face-to-face citizen engagement with digital engagement reported some of the most positive outcomes. In addition to getting beyond business between 9 and 5, in many cases, it has increased the diversity of respondents, as groups such as younger, working, or time-poor residents, and encouraged groups typically under-represented in planning decisions – such as renters, young people, and those from Black and ethnic minority communities – to make their voices heard on planning in their area (DLUHC, 2023c; DLUHC, 2024).

Software developments such as "PlaceMaker" enable assembly of the evidence base for local plans through geospatial algorithms to automate the initial site data collection, processing, and analysis. Data analytics techniques create a "rules-based" approach to appraise the development potential of more and smaller sites based on their merits. This kind of refinement can evidently help to ensure the best use of land resources and has the potential to allow citizens to directly provide data at a site level. This may, perhaps, not be transformational but may help as a counterbalance to the allocation of land driven by the certainty of development or generation of financial benefits.

Some researchers and practitioners have called for fundamental changes, advocating a cyclical planning system informed by multidisciplinary evidence and empowered by data and digital technology (Batty & Yang, 2023). Their recommendations include:

- Developing a "common spatial data environment" based on national mapping and datasets to allow better simulation and modeling.
- Setting up a National Network of "Regional Data Observatories" – tasked with collecting and analyzing demographic, economic, social, and environmental data.
- Introducing planners to digital tools and techniques which can be employed and integrated in spatial planning.

The Geospatial Commission has looked to the bigger picture for how data science, technology, and innovation can address the challenges of managing finite land resources, to support local engagement and identify new opportunities for multi-functional land use. The Commission is ambitious, believing that through predictive and scenario-based land-use models that incorporate algorithms to demonstrate alternative futures "can help us to spatially assess a range of economic, environmental and social factors to support decisions about the best use of land" (Geospatial Commission, 2023, p. 6). The Royal Town Planning Institute (2020) has also proposed regional data observatories and advocates digital tools for inclusive and participatory planning that should complement traditional face-to-face methods. Collectively, these suggest that moving toward an integrated, digitally enabled approach to spatial planning can facilitate better access to data, improve evidence-based land-use decision-making, and enable faster and more inclusive planning processes.

Placemaking Isn't Just About Planning

Governmental agendas for reducing inequalities, engaging citizens, and communities in co-design, improving delivery, and placemaking reach across the breadth of public services. The DLUHC Futures Councils program has set out the challenge of overcoming working in siloes, including digital, to support local council-wide collaboration. It combines this with an expectation that they will incentivize the market to support effective service delivery in an ever-changing landscape (DLUHC, 2023d). The UK Government's (2023a) roadmap for a digital future identifies 6 categories for driving digital futures for central government and other public agencies, and notably, there is, often, a strong emphasis on transactional "service delivery" rather than places,

Community feedback will help many other public services learn about grassroots sentiment in their areas. Associated service delivery through the National Health Service (Public Health England, 2014, p. 13; Culpin, 2024) and the managers of the water environment (Environment Agency, 2020) both aim to use digital applications to deliver improvements. Innovations such as "lo-code" software are helping national government to develop nutrient mitigation systems (Shaw, 2023) and local authorities like Birmingham City Council and Wigan Metropolitan Borough Council (Jadu / Wigan MBC, 2023) to transfer and combine paper records, for example, on highways and customer experience, in digital format. More easily analyzed and shared, the expectation is that it improves the chances of coordinated service delivery. Stirling has declared itself the world's first fully Augmented Reality city with digital initiatives aimed at the visitor economy (Stirling Council, 2022).

This extends to commissioning technologies and ideas to improve services, such as housing, parks, and waste management in the city, that include a requirement to build citizen engagement and knowledge. This is to enable people to understand the decarbonization and green infrastructure commitments of the council and the steps required to deliver (Birmingham City Council, 2023).

The expanding number of projects to develop Digital Twins also often have multiple aims of building inclusive innovation and run simulations of local challenges, that accurately twin or mirror the physical environment to help deliver local solutions to net zero, pollution, and traffic congestion (Birmingham City Council, 2023; Say, 2023).

These parallel trends toward digital services can help contribute to integrated, connected places if there is a shift from optimizing disconnected service silos to integrated place-based systems. It has potential for transformational change (UK Government, 2018, p. 4) that is not constrained by vague definitions as to what constitutes "smart" and not limited by urban boundaries (Creese, 2023).

Digital Knives and Forks?

User cases for digital placemaking are driven by increasing amounts of data and enabled by appropriate digital technology. The Department for Environment, Food & Rural Affairs (DEFRA) "Top Ten" of these includes: Low Earth Satellites, IoT (linked data sources), computer visions (machine learning), outdoor location intelligence (geospatial), autonomous drones, BOTs (software robots; driven by algorithms for repetitive tasks), immersive workspace (virtual or augmented reality overlaying digital onto real word views), distributed ledger technology (synchronized databases), and Digital Twins that model the physical world and enable "what if?" scenarios to be queried (Defra, 2021a). To this could be added citizen science platforms and artificial intelligence. Hafferty et al. (2023) propose a comparable list for engaging people in nature based solutions to environmental challenges. There is insufficient space here to review the progress across these ten-plus digital approaches. We can illustrate a few.

- Tracking: using sensors, Chicago's Array of Things measures air and surface temperature, barometric pressure, light, vibration, carbon monoxide, nitrogen dioxide, sulfur dioxide, ozone, and ambient sound intensity, while cameras collect data on vehicle and pedestrian traffic, standing water, and cloud cover (Mitchum, 2016).
- Modeling: the Tallinn-Helsinki Dynamic Green Information Model project is a dynamic digital modeling of the green environment. It creates green elements for the Digital Twins of Tallinn and Helsinki and additionally creates a permanent hub for city planning in Tallinn center (Dembski, 2021). "Smart urban forest" projects identify open data and open-source mapping platforms as part of a package of monitoring techniques involving sensors and IoT technologies, citizen engagement via mobile devices and applications (Nitoslawski et al., 2019).
- Digital mapping: GIS has been used for identifying green locations to address urban heating, flood risk management, building shading, and biodiversity (Winkelman, 2017). More recently, Natural England (2023) has built on these initiatives, placing GIS mapping tools at the heart of the presentation of England's national green infrastructure standards framework.
- Platforms for inclusivity: Linz's participation platform allows citizens to participate on any topic from anywhere at any time and vote on what they would like to see the city take on (Cuau, 2020). Virtual and augmented reality tools give a "real world" perspective and allow people to experience what enhanced areas might look like in ways that other technologies simply cannot.
- Citizen scientists: the "DECIDE" project's DECIDE tool (ceh.ac.uk) uses data analytics to inform better targeting and engagement of citizen scientists in providing biological data in ways that can improve decision-making on land uses. It evolves citizen science beyond viewing "people as sensors" at the direction of scientists.
- The UK's DLUHC PropTech Innovation Fund (DLUHC, 2022a) has sponsored the development of multiple pilots for increasing the level and diversity of responses to planning consultations. This taps into a strong desire within local government for more inclusive approaches.

Getting There?

This developing context and practice sets up expectations and drivers for how and why new digitized futures can help create these beautiful, smart, integrated, inclusive, and greener places that will be sustained over time. Academic labels for "smarter cities" have been numerous for some time, including the "sentient city" that involves the management and analysis of big data through ubiquitous computing to map, understand, monitor, and inform the future use of city spaces (Boland et al., 2022). The uptake of digital technologies for planning and placemaking has been identified as the "planning–technology nexus," a global phenomenon. It begs the questions whether digital transformation will help to empower a smarter citizen, or will it simply enable a more efficient transactional relationship between citizens and service providers? In trying to cope with urban complexities and political processes of real places, will it be able to help make future-proofed decisions?

While decision-makers now recognize that local empowerment, beautiful places, and digital futures go hand in hand (DLUHC, 2022b), the research literature also suggests that in practice, we are clearly some way off from holistic, smart city, and digital approaches becoming the glue that overcomes current disintegrated, silo thinking. Reviews of the literature suggest that city practices do not currently integrate smart, sustainable, and green city thinking (Javidroozi et al., 2023). Big Data Analytics (BDA) in smart cities is frequently focused on economic growth, quality of life, and governance, while ignoring the most pressing issues and complicated challenges associated with sustainability. Indeed, many claims for facilitating sustainable development, enhancing citizen involvement, or protecting the environment are hypothetical (Lim et al., 2019). More research is needed, specifically in respect of the democratic deficit and the digital divide (Boland et al., 2022). There is also evidence that emerging smart solutions are incompatible with sustainability objectives, and sparse evidence exists for the alleged sustainability benefits of smart governance (Tomor et al., 2019; Wu et al., 2022; Yigitcanlar et al., 2019) or even that attention is paid to ecosystems.

Digital technology is shaping those futures, but at the macro level, the current indices for the smartness of cities are not holistic. They do not readily include nature and green infrastructure as common criteria (Alderete, 2020; Cavada et al., 2017). Urban greenspace which improves quality of life and reduces environmental impacts tends to be neglected in visions of smart cities (Martin et al., 2018). In practice, we find a range of issues associated with data and evidence. The lessons from Defra's Local Nature Recovery Strategy pilot authorities were that the presentation of data needs to be accessible enough to empower non-specialists to make informed suggestions about their priorities (Defra, 2021b).

Puchol-Salort et al. (2021) have advocated a systems-based master planning framework for a spatial representation of urban development in a GIS to create an operational link between design solutions and evaluation metrics. There are issues associated with the application of how GIS is used to represent real-world places. Techniques that recognize fuzzy boundaries – that is, those that integrate a gradual transition from neighborhood space to non-neighborhood space when the boundary is in a vague or indeterminate location – are rarely seen in the greenspace and health literature. This affects how the functional health benefits of greenspace can be assessed (Labib et al., 2020). Technical challenges will always be work in progress, not least in maintaining the connectedness within places. There are also social and governance issues to resolve, such as how to integrate health, climate and greenspace agendas. Birmingham' emerging Environmental Justice Index, developed through geospatial analysis, aims to create a dynamic map to help resolve some of these issues (Sultan et al., 2023).

There is power in combining digital techniques such as satellite imagery, data analytics, GIS and incorporating social media data into urban green space planning (Chen et al., 2021). Mobile apps and wallets are now being used to enable citizen participation (Marsal-Llacuna, 2020). Small-scale domains in which social media, used as near real-time data, are very helpful in the urban context. However, few if any of the studies report on how social media data were used in planning practice (Zabelskyte et al., 2022).

Digital Twins cannot be obtained "off the shelf ready to go"; they are dependent on and powered by data, so this starts with developing a data culture and treating data as an asset (Wray, 2022). These require data from a digital ecosystem of providers, a mix of internal departments, public sector organizations, the private sector, and with adequate permissions and privacy in place, citizens themselves (NIC, 2023; WEF, 2023).

Online political participation worldwide similarly remains timid both in quantity and quality in which only the privileged partake, while the majority remains silent: Santini and Carvalho (2019) identified the growth of a kind of "rhetorical participation" promoted by policymakers and the rise of a "participatory despotism." In smart cities, there is a lack of stakeholder participation in the assessment process, and that traditional citizen-centric smart city initiatives that rely on a top-down approach are often ineffective (Hajek et al., 2022).

While citizen participation platforms provide a central place for people to share their ideas with other citizens and local authorities online, they are not always fully inclusive. They require access to an internet connection and device, therefore excluding some marginalized groups. City dashboards, immersive technologies, and Digital Twins all require expertise and skills that many do not have. Data may need to be supported by immersive technologies to enable nonprofessionals to easily visualize their implications. Continuing measures to address skills gaps and digital poverty will be needed if these platforms are to fully succeed in enabling diverse participation.

Similarly, the promise offered by the advantages of social media data may be overestimated, and planners may lack the expertise and time to work with social media data. The complexity and limitations with data security issues suggest that applying social media data for urban planning may currently be too complex. Indeed, there is a significant shortfall in data, digital, ecological, and sustainability expertise available in both the private and public sectors (McKinsey & Company, 2022; The Planner, 2022). This may be the most severe drag on transformational change in placemaking.

Beyond these weaknesses, there have been calls for more radical reform. The National Audit Office (NAO, 2021) reports that the past 25 years of government digital projects show a consistent pattern of underperformance, fossilizing past processes that delays improvements in public services. Deloitte's 2022/23 State of the State report comments that the scale of the challenge for government and public services suggest a system that needs bold reform rather than incremental adjustments. Their view is that Government needs to think postdigital given the relentless progress of digital is changing the physical, social, and economic environment we live in. Additionally, to accelerate the future of government, trust needs to be prioritized and built by leaders with empathy (Deloitte LLP, 2022).

Web 3.0 and the Multiverse

The advent of Web 3.0 may be both the biggest disruptor and driver of that reform, for placemakers and communities alike. Web 3.0 is an umbrella term for disparate ideas all pointing in the direction of an iteration of the internet where new social networks, search engines, and marketplaces crop up (Allyn, 2021). These are decentralized and built upon a system known as the blockchain, where many computers at once host data that are searchable by anyone. It is operated by users collectively, rather than a corporation. As such, it eliminates the need for a central authority to manage transactions. In a Web 3.0 world, people control their own data and bounce around from social media to email to shopping using a single personalized account, creating a public record on the blockchain of all that activity. This is done through a multitude of small competing services on the blockchain. "Tokens" for participating can be used to vote on decisions and even accrue real value (Allyn, 2021).

If Web 3.0 is going to be all about experience, the blockchain technology can also be applied across service sectors such as transportation, health care, and education. This allows for the integration of current service silos for a more cohesive system in developing smart sustainable cities. It has the potential for creating a link between service providers and citizens (Khawaja & Javidroozi, 2023). The implication is that Web 3.0 could turn out to be a communal effort, part of the metaverse that turns the internet into a single, shared virtual space, enabling people to do things that are not possible in the physical world, suggesting that it might be a symbiosis between people and the digital and its collective knowledge (Essex et al., 2023). Consequently, the commercial world has recognized a role for "community managers" to help their brands arbitrate on safeguarding, rather than relying on external oversight or regulation. Brand stewardship and the curation of an experience will not be just about selling a product or service, rather more about creating engaged communities in real time (Fischer & Fittipaldi, 2023).

For placemakers, the shift to decentralized technologies can be seen in the difference between Web 2.0 tools, where communities may be asked for their suggestions or perspectives, and Web 3.0 decentralization in which communities draw on different information and communications technologies (ICTs) and their capabilities to enable self-organization, problem-solving, and action on urban issues. At the same time, in a data-rich, urban context, traditional approaches, such as the local plans and zoning for diverse communities, may not be seen as fit for purpose. The risk here is that organizations such as local planning or transport authorities, at least initially, simply ignore these opportunities or realities as too difficult and are unable to respond to the volume, velocity, and relational nature of the data being produced (Potts, 2020).

In response to the challenges of a digital future, some authors have already echoed the call for substantial reform to establish new, novel modes of governance for planning and placemaking. The call is for mechanisms for adaptive changes and structures, tools, and technologies that are agile rather than fixed (Devlin & Coaffee, 2021).

What do Placemaking and Smarter, Big Data-Enabled Technologies Need From Each Other for Success in a Digital Future?

Addressing Complexity

Improved governance is at the heart of addressing the complexity of urban challenges. Planning practitioners have long recognized that these are often addressed within separate sectoral "silos" leading to policy disintegration (Lennon, 2015; Scott et al., 2013) for places. Not least, there is the highly complex challenge in how placemaking contributes to the Government's plan (UK Government, 2023b) for delivering net zero in the decarbonization of industry, places, and development.

Holistic thinking and processes for placemaking can integrate digital design to capture the principles of placemaking or biophilic criteria that Governments and others have identified. This would help to degrade the silo thinking. This also needs to work across spatial scales, joining neighborhood to city strategy and, in turn, national ambitions. A holistic approach should lead to the generation of an integrated user case for placemaking to guide digital designers. It will include the challenge of reconciling the legislative and regulative requirements across the current raft of consultation processes with the new, constantly connected set of communities being recognized. In addition to establishing multifaceted dialogues, it is especially important to ensure an audit trail of decisions is visible to all. The perspective of users and proposed beneficiaries of existing and new places will be increasingly important as our opportunity to understand the complexity of places increases through flows of data and multiple channels of communication.

All of this suggests that consultation and engagement will, in future, become a continuous process for public and private sector alike. Pacemakers will need to cope with the data flows and show they have listened and responded, becoming agile points of contact. This goes well beyond congratulating ourselves that we have received comments after 5 p.m. or publishing Statements of Community Involvement that simply repeat regulatory requirements or just nod to neighborhood initiatives as if they had little strategic relevance (DLUHC & MHCLG, 2019, 2021b). Local government will look increasingly silly if it just replaces a consultation template with a virtual form which assembles feedback in ways that do not reflect these complexities.

Addressing Current and Future Value

Digital transformation for placemaking needs to be future-proofed and regret free. The principles ask for a vision, so digital designers need to "Think Like a Futurist" (Hagan, 2017). This means addressing the current and future value of places. In real estate terms, the application of ledger technology – blockchain – processes for seamless, accessible, transparent, unalterable, and verifiable transactions of property asset data can provide valuable information on property price, floor area, ownership, and identifying those involved in each development, if data protection issues can be resolved. This can help with efficiency and to create an "internet of value" (O'Boyle, 2017). Placemaking principles would expect the digital world to be able to answer wider questions of value of what and to whom.

The current and future value of greenspace for health is understood, as is the value added to property values. Nature-based solutions (NBS) (for example, see McPhearson et al., 2023; UK Green Building Council, 2022) are an exceptional solution for the challenges of the climate and biodiversity crises. However, the value of NBS is often not recognized and can result in private markets performing below their capacity. When NBS are omitted from a place-based approach due to the monetary cost of implementation, this fails to recognize their cost-effectiveness and the wider value that they can deliver (OECD, 2024). Mapping tools are becoming available to enable placemakers to understand the value of NBS (Nature Based Solutions Initiative, 2024).

The development of financial tools and packages for delivering net-zero neighborhoods (NZN) such as Somers Town in London (Somers Town Community Association, 2023) may be able to integrate local net-zero projects into attractive investment, blended finance propositions by creating scale and long-term certainty for investors. These may join up the different types of assets that are important to decarbonization and work toward transforming transportation, energy, housing, and waste services in a coordinated way (Cities Commission for Climate Investment, 2023). The design of NZNs may provide a specific user case for designing digital decarbonized places, but even here, it is worth noting that biodiversity and nature are not always mainstreamed and seen as nonfinancial returns, an additional benefit aligned with an NZN.

To be effective at maintaining and enhancing value of nature within spaces, the application of digital techniques will need to enable business models that can deliver better stewardship (Cavada et al, 2021; Mell, 2021) to These will need to be dynamic, addressing increasing urban densities, as communities age and as food or new urban bioresource products are grown. As land becomes a scarcer resource, from a qualitative perspective, digital models will have to generate data that embrace the perceptions of greenness and their value to people locally to help generate alternatives to commercially driven solutions. In this sense, technologies such as machine learning and artificial intelligence (AI) should support the delivery of circular bioeconomies that help the resilience of urban ecosystem services (Paes et al., 2022). Digital approaches can also help integrate "green finance" mechanisms with ensuring nature is embedded into an increasingly urbanized world, responding to demands for nature-related financial disclosures (TNFD, 2023). This may help to expose the future and long-term value of nature within cities.

It supports the need identified by WEF (2023) of fixing the paucity of local urban data. Smart, digital, and data-driven placemaking that reflects value at local, neighborhood, and city scales is collectively important for strategic decisions. In land-use terms, for example, a data-driven model can begin to integrate top-down health service designs for delivering "green care" with local needs and community preferences for their places. More broadly, it may inform the way we may think about the distinction between urban and rural and the structure of our cities within landscapes.

Aside from the influence on national, top-down policy, the principles are strong on the need for local distinctiveness. In the United Kingdom, for example, planting more fruit trees for food, birds, and pollinating insects is advocated strongly (see, for example, RHS, 2023). That said perhaps a future-proofed digital design will need to consider an ageing population that may not always welcome where fruit will fall and create a slippery surface (see Adams et al., 2023)? While in Banff and Canmore in British Columbia, GIS could instead be helpful in making efficient use of resources to cut down fruit trees. In this case, to help stop conflicts between people and bears looking for local food sources (The Rocky Outlook, 2023).

Addressing Transferability

Placemaking, by definition, looks to the future. This requires predictive modeling. The challenge is to assemble the data and design a machine learning model that draws together the varied forms and types of data into a decision support tool. Data on natural assets, local use of green spaces, accessibility, and property values can assist the decision-maker in, for example, designing the connected, varied, and accessible green network espoused by the national framework and standards for GI and which may enable the development of new circular bioeconomies.

To do this independently for every place is costly in terms of data collection and in design of the "Digital Twin" for each place. Here there is an implication for the governance of digital futures that can embed nature and the environment in placemaking. The Local Government Association's (LGA) recent White Paper on place-based public service reform joins these agendas together. It includes an explict call on the one hand, to protect and grow green and blue infrastructure, giving Local Nature Recovery Strategies the teeth to shape all public environment spending in places, and to review powers they hold to lead nature-based adaptation action, from managing floods to droughts, and, on the other hand, to establish a Local Government Centre for Digital Technology that would work across all councils (LGA, 2024). Digital designers will need to work with placemakers to develop the rules-based model that can be adapted to other urban places at lower cost. However, one size will not fit all, and the individuality of each place – landscapes, townscape, climate, economy, valued species, health needs such as incidences of dementia in increasingly elderly communities or play for younger communities – will need to be designed in. This suggests that common agreement on the rules (the algorithm) will be necessary.

Addressing Data

Data are a business treasure for commerce and government alike and are central to digital transformation. A vital challenge for urban planning practice is to translate information into knowledge and to make spatial sense of an increasing amount of information (Soeiro, 2020). Arts et al. (2015) used the term "digital conservation" as shorthand for the broad range of developments at the interface of digital technology and nature conservation. They identified five key dimensions: Data on Nature, on People, Data Integration and Analysis, Communication and Experience, and Participatory Governance. There are ever-increasing examples of sensor networks being installed in urban areas using schools, street furniture, and other assets (see City of Edinburgh Council, 2023; Department for Science, Innovation and Technology (DSIT), 2023) using schools and street furniture. Grace et al. (2021) suggested constructing a digital environment that systemically embeds the natural environment through a "network of networks." This would link, say, sensor networks codesigned by citizens with networks of other remote sensors at the local as well as the city scale.

Placemaking extends the list even further as it encompasses the multiple domains of, to give just one example, the 15-minute neighborhood. As has already been noted, the track record of smart cities for delivering sustainability has not been positive. Air and water quality is increasingly considered in city tracking, though nature and greenspace have often been left behind in favor of traffic counts or other easily measurable factors. Sörensen et al. (2021) have identified a need to improve the organisation of data management and the skills of trans-disciplinary cooperation to better understand and interpret different types of data to ensure efficient planning of GI. They call for closer interactions between development of strategic political goals and data collection. The risk for placemaking is that crucial data sets are not available as others are prioritized or the software is not developed that enables accurate analysis of data (such as habitat or species type). This concern becomes more acute as AI and Machine Learning evolve as techniques, given their requirement for a large set of training data for more accurate and precise decision-making processes (Ullah et al., 2020). To deliver connected placemaking, the question of who chooses priorities for data within the framework of placemaking principles becomes important.

Addressing Inclusivity

Ensuring the meaningful engagement of individuals and communities in determining the future of their places is crucial. This needs to be about the end-to-end process from policymaking to stewardship and securing the benefits from urban change.

The risks of failure are high, where, for example, logics of value devalue places and the people who inhabit them are targeted for new kinds of investment (Safransky, 2020), or there is a backlash over intrusive data collection (Vincent, 2021). Digital connectivity in places must address the crucial importance of trust and inclusivity of the placemaking process and it is encouraging that some research suggests that blockchain technology can help address transparency, inclusiveness and confidentiality (Ietto et al., 2023). However, the proposition that ICT can pave the way for more democratic forms of urban planning and governance has limitations; it is dealing with "wicked" problems that lack simplistic solutions (Colding et al., 2019). Issues of digital division, such as those highlighted in Bristol's smart city agenda (Lockwood, 2020), for Dorset's more rural communities (Dorset Council, n.d.) and by the House of Lords (2023) warn that to deliver the promise of smart cities, training and education for all ages is required so that everyone can gain the digital skills needed to participate fully. Inclusion rather than exclusion in the design process and research of digital technology is essential if technology is to fulfill the promise of improving well-being (Mannheim et al., 2019).

This requires "digital poverty" to be addressed within political, professional, and community spheres. Politicians will need to embrace Web 3.0. Using unskilled, weakly accountable, and under-resourced sectors such as parish councils that traditionally control formal channels of engagement will need significant support if not fundamental reform. The "soft" skill of being comfortable with change is critical for digital progress alongside developing communication and technical skills. Not least is an understanding of the importance and limitations of data and digital ethics.

Future Web 3.0–driven community or place managers can be pivotal in the development of "integrated use case briefs" as a means through which they can engage, gain trust, and enable the inclusion of disparate communities. Bellone et al. (2021) have suggested the application of sentiment analysis, to guarantee the identification of the real needs of the local communities upstream in consultations. This would use the vast amount of data found on blogs and social media to analyze the feelings (i.e., people's moods) on any chosen topic. It is therefore a system that might be capable of managing, interpreting, and synthesizing through a human behavior-centered set of logarithms. This engagement can be a means of integrating delivering across services as well as future-thinking development. They will require skills in avoiding polarization in communities, sharing data, and mixing the virtual with a face-to-face democratic process. Several studies have explored the strengths and limitations of digital engagement techniques as well as the challenges and benefits of blending digital with traditional engagement approaches (Wilson & Tewdwr-Jones, 2021; Hafferty et al., 2023, 2024). Some of this ground was explored by Murgante et al. (2013) who especially anticipated the need to align formal administrative processes with local knowledge and engagement. They developed a theory of knowledge structures for a more effective communication tool in order to improve dialogue and be used not only by analysts and external experts, but also by local technicians and by those who produce data, information and knowledge. Their question was how to make the ontology dynamic and able to self-update knowledge structures over time? Anticipating Web 3.0, through enough self-organization of users? Not least, the advancing impact of AI will mean that the public need reassurance that the technology is being designed with their personal information rights in mind (Information Commissioner's Office (ICO), 2023).

It is possible that other agents of change, such as Business Improvement District managers and developers, will exploit the opportunity of Web 3.0 to establish interactive conversations with affected communities. This enables developers to share their ideas at an early stage and create an interactive relationship. This raises the question of whether this will be aligned within a trusted common framework of placemaking principles. Which "brand" or "community manager" will be trusted most?

In Conclusion?

Some authors argue that smart sustainable cities are becoming knowable, controllable, and tractable in new dynamic ways thanks to urban science. This is responding to the data generated about their systems and domains, exploiting the enormous benefits of the emerging paradigm of big data computing (Bibri, 2019). Yet the research literature seems to suggest that the plethora of conceptual models about smart or digital cities is not transforming the practice of placemaking. It is evident that there is no systemic, transdisciplinary digital transformation under way. This means that it is not delivering integrated ecological, economic, or social benefits.

Yet it is a fast-moving world. There are, encouragingly, emerging initiatives that can become the building blocks for integrated approaches. The Natural History Museum's Urban Nature Project (Natural History Museum, n.d.) is developing a new public-facing biodiversity and environmental monitoring data ecosystem to help capture, share, and interpret urban nature data. AI and data sciences are being exploited to model the impact of different development scenarios on key outcomes for the city of Newcastle. Including a visualization tool to explore the trade-offs between scenarios, the modeling system will help evaluate the impact of high-level development options against policy priority indicators for air pollution, access to jobs and green space and house prices (Geospatial Commission, 2023).

Bolsover District Council's "PlaceBuilder" master planning tool aimed to encourage engagement particularly from young people who are most affected by future growth plans but are the least likely to turn up to traditional in-person events or respond to consultations, so increasing public engagement in land use choices (DLUHC, 2022a). Generic rules, standards, and improved transferability of models will be developed for tools such as Digital Twins that can then be adapted locally (see Alan Turing Institute, 2023).

The delivery of placemaking policy objectives is framed by its complexity and the need for inclusive approaches. It is clear there are yet no convincing models for addressing this wicked problem. Beyond weaknesses in data, for the development of truly "smart cities," Mora and Deakin (2019) concluded that there is a need for a collaborative environment based on a holistic interpretation of smarter city development. This is a matter for smart city design (Dessai & Javidroozi, 2021).

Those studies that do address integration of smart, sustainable, and green places suggest that the natural subsystem is more important than the social and economic subsystems (Feng et al., 2022), and urban greening is the cost-effective approach (Beatley & Brown, 2022) that needs greater priority. Nature and ecosystems, broader placemaking principles and the connections between them, the UN's Sustainable Development Goals (Castro et al., 2021), or the arts-based placemaking methodology meaning, approaches, and processes (MAP) (Arts and Humanities Research Council, 2023) are available to provide a framework – or vision – for the user case for defining the digital and technological applications for smarter, sustainable, and greener placemaking. Either way, the choices behind the design of the algorithms that drive machine learning and AI and their predictive power must be through a shared dialogue about city systems and governance. It must also be managed with the principle of engaged, inclusive communities in a world where the regulatory and governance context is being disrupted by Web 3.0.

In the meantime, the pace of digital opportunities for transformation will outstrip concepts and reforms of systems of governance. Placemaking will continue to rely on having a shared vision as well as the evolution of practice, skills, and the transferability of knowledge between researchers, practitioners, and communities. Most importantly, in a digital world shaped by digitally smart citizens, the vision for the creation of truly inclusive and liveable places will also need to be flexible enough to embrace changes in behavior and governance. In the context of the climate and nature emergencies and excluded communities, the question remains as to how committed we are to transforming placemaking and whether the digital knives and forks we now own can be used in truly transformative ways.

Acknowledgments

The author would like to thank Xi Gou and especially Sue Hand for their insightful comments on an early draft of this chapter.

References

Adams, D., Larkham, P. J., & Hardman, M. (2023). Edible garden cities: Rethinking boundaries and integrating hedges into scalable urban food systems. *Land, 12*, 1915. https://doi.org/10.3390/land12101915

Alan Turing Institute. (2023, June 22). The Alan Turing Institute secures £3 million to establish new digital twin research network. https://www.turing.ac.uk/news/alan-turing-institute-secures-ps3-million-establish-new-digital-twin-research-network

Alderete, M. V. (2020). Exploring the smart city indexes and the role of macro factors for measuring cities smartness. *Social Indicators Research, 147*(2), 567–589. https://doi.org/10.1007/s11205-019-02168-y

Allyn, B. (2021, November 21). People are talking about Web3. Is it the Internet of the future or just a buzzword? NPR. https://www.npr.org/2021/11/21/1056988346/web3-internet-jargon-or-future-visionllyn

Altshuler, A. (1965). The goals of comprehensive planning. *Journal of the American Institute of Planners, 31*(3), 186–194.

Arts and Humanities Research Council (AHRC). (2023). *Developing a people-centred, place-led approach: The value of the arts and humanities*. AHRC.

Arts, K., van der Wal, R., & Adams, W. M. (2015). Digital technology and the conservation of nature. *Ambio, 44*(Suppl. 4), 661–673.

Batty, M., & Yang, W. (2023, February). *A digital future for planning: Spatial planning reimagined*. Digital Task Force for Planning. https://digital4planning.com/a-digital-future-for-planning/

BBC. (2019, May 1). UK Parliament declares climate change emergency. *BBC News*. https://www.bbc.co.uk/news/uk-politics-48126677

Beatley, T., & Brown, J. D. (2022). *Greening cities – Integrating urban greening and ecology into city and neighborhood planning and connecting green infrastructure*. Cities4biodiversity. https://www.thegpsc.org/sites/gpsc/files/deep_dive_learning_session_1_summary_report_11-3-22.pdf

Bellone, C., Naselli, F., & Andreassi, F. (2021). New governance path through digital platforms and the old urban planning process in Italy. *Sustainability, 13*, 6911. https://doi.org/10.3390/su13126911

Benyon, L. (2022, December 16). *Final environmental targets under the Environment Act 2021* [Parliamentary statement]. House of Lords. https://questions-statements.parliament.uk/written-statements/detail/2022-12-16/hlws449

Bibri, S. E. (2019). The anatomy of the data-driven smart sustainable city: Instrumentation, datafication, computerization and related applications. *Journal of Big Data, 6*(1), 59. http://doi.org/10.1186/s40537-019-0221-4

Birmingham City Council. (2023, May 16). *Report to cabinet*. https://birmingham.cmis.uk.com/Birmingham/Document.ashx?czJKcaeAi5tUFL1DTL2UE4zNRBcoShgo=GH1bFk%2ft8eAOU3nxqIcubvz394lGpifzpXGqd%2fShx0yRFsrAC3wCKg%3d%3d&rUzwRPf%2bZ3zd4E7Ikn8Lyw%3d%3d=pwRE6AGJFLDNlh225F5QMaQWCtPHwdhUfCZ%2fLUQzgA2uL5jNRG4jdQ%3d%3d&mCTIbCubSFfXsDGW9IXnlg%3d%3d=hFflUdN3100%3d&kCx1AnS9%2fpWZQ40DXFvdEw%3d%3d=hFflUdN3100%3d&uJovDxwdjMPoYv%2bAJvYtyA%3d%3d=ctNJFf55vVA%3d&FgPllEJYlotS%2bYGoBi5olA%3d%3d=NHdURQburHA%3d&d9Qjj0ag1Pd993jsyOJqFvmyB7X0CSQK=ctNJFf55vVA%3d&WGewmoAfeNR9xqBux0r1Q8Za60lavYmz=ctNJFf55vVA%3d&WGewmoAfeNQ16B2MHuCpMRKZMwaG1PaO=ctNJFf55vVA%3d

Boland, P., Durrant, A., McHenry, J., McKay, S., & Wilson, A. (2022). A 'planning revolution' or an 'attack on planning' in England: Digitization, digitalization, and democratization. *International Planning Studies, 27*(2), 155–172. https://doi.org/10.1080/13563475.2021.1979942

Brown, J. D. (2023). Indicators of a biophilic city. *Biophilic Cities Journal, 5*(1), 46–47. https://static1.squarespace.com/static/5bbd32d6e66669016a6af7e2/t/645d364b9a4abe6d562edf2b/1683830347633/Indicators_Brown.pdf

Cai, Z., Chen, Y., La Sorte, F. A., & Wu, J. (2023). The surface urban heat island effect decreases bird diversity in Chinese cities. *Science of the Total Environment*. https://doi.org/10.1016/j.scitotenv.2023.166200

Cameron-Smith, A. (2023, May 2). Introducing the UK's first net zero carbon buildings standard. Unlock Net Zero. https://www.unlocknetzero.co.uk/home/introducing/introducing-the-uks-first-net-zero-carbon-buildings-standard?utm_campaign=737231_UNZ%20Newsletter%20100523&utm_medium=email&utm_source=unz_dotdigital&dm_i=6VTO,FSUN,1SW19Y,1YPEN,1

Castro, G. D. R., Fernández, M. C. G., & Colsa, Á. U. (2021). Unleashing the convergence amid digitalization and sustainability towards pursuing the Sustainable Development Goals (SDGs): A holistic review. *Journal of Cleaner Production, 280*(1), 122204. https://doi.org/10.1016/j.jclepro.2020.122204

Cavada, M., Bouch, C., Rogers, C., Grace, M., & Robertson, A. (2023). A soft systems methodology for business creation: The lost world at Tyseley, Birmingham. *Urban Planning and Green Infrastructure*, 6(1). https://www.cogitatiopress.com/urbanplanning/article/view/3499/3499

Cavada, M., Hunt, D., & Rogers, C. (2017). *The little book of Smart Cities*. Imagination Lancaster.

Chen, Y., Weng, Q., Tang, L., Liu, Q., Zhang, X., & Bilal, M. (2021). Automatic mapping of urban green spaces using a geospatial neural network. *GIScience and Remote Sensing*, 58(4), 624–642. https://doi.org/10.1080/15481603.2021.1933367

Cities Commission for Climate Investment (3Ci). (2023, June). *The case for a national net zero neighbourhoods programme*. 3Ci. https://www.3ci.org.uk/wp-content/uploads/2023/06/3Ci-NZN-Outline-Business-Case-June-2023-2-1.pdf

City of Edinburgh Council. (2023). *Our smart city programme*. https://www.edinburgh.gov.uk/council-planning-framework/smart-city-programme

Colding, J., Barthel, S., & Sörqvist, P. (2019). Wicked problems of smart cities. *Smart Cities*, 2(4), 512–521.

Convention on Biological Diversity (CBD). (2022). *The Kunming-Montréal Global Biodiversity Framework (GBF) adopted at the December 2022 United Nations Biodiversity Conference of the Parties to the UN Convention on Biological Diversity (COP 15)*. https://www.cbd.int/article/cop15-final-text-kunming-montreal-gbf-221222

Cortinovis, C., Geneletti, D., & Haase, D. (2022). Higher immigration and lower land take rates are driving a new densification wave in European cities. *Npj Urban Sustainability*, 2, 19. https://doi.org/10.1038/s42949-022-00062-0

Creese, J. (2023). *Public sector digital trends 2023 Summary*. Socitm Ltd. https://media.socitm.net/wp-content/uploads/2023/01/23123111/socitm-public-sector-digital-trends-2023-summary.pdf

Cuau, C. (2020, April 14). *Case study: Citizen proposals in Linz*. Citizenlab. https://www.citizenlab.co/blog/case-study/case-study-citizen-proposals-in-linz/

Culpin, M. (2024, April 11). *Championing local well-being: How we can create a blueprint for social prescribing*. https://dleaders.substack.com/p/championing-local-well-being-how

Deloitte LLP. (2022). *The State of the State report 2022/23: From the pandemic to a cost of living crisis*. Deloitte. https://www2.deloitte.com/uk/en/pages/public-sector/articles/the-state-of-the-state.html

Dembski, F. (2021). *Green twins Tallinn and Helsinki: Digital twins for more democratic, resilient and greener cities*. https://fabiandembski.com/2021/05/28/greentwins-tallinn-and-helsinki-digital-twins-for-more-democratic-resilient-and-greener-cities/

Department for Environment, Food and Rural Affairs (Defra). (2021a, October). *Top 10 emerging technologies for Defra [Video]*. YouTube. https://www.youtube.com/watch?v=2iNE2A0lIu8

Department for Environment, Food and Rural Affairs (Defra). (2021b). *Local nature recovery strategy pilots: Lessons learned*. Defra. https://www.gov.uk/government/publications/local-nature-recovery-strategy-pilots-lessons-learned/local-nature-recoveryvery-strategy-pilots-lessons-learned?utm_source=Green+Infrastructure+Partnership&utm_campaign=4007ad6dec-EMAIL_CAMPAIGN_2017_08_31_COPY_01&utm_medium=email&utm_term=0_f4eb0dc7a3-4007ad6dec-103375017

Department for Levelling Up, Housing and Communities (DLUHC). (2022a). *How the adoption of digital tools is improving the planning process for communities and* local planning authorities across England. DLUHC PropTech Innovation Fund. https://media.localdigital.gov.uk/uploads/2023/11/28105757/PropTech-Innovation-Fund-Combined-case-studies.pdf

Department for Levelling Up, Housing and Communities (DLUHC). (2022b). *Levelling-up and regeneration: Further information.* DLUHC. https://www.gov.uk/government/publications/levelling-up-and-regeneration-further-information/levelling-up-and-regeneration-further-information

Department for Levelling Up, Housing and Communities (DLUHC). (2023a). *National planning policy framework.* DLUHC. https://assets.publishing.service.gov.uk/media/64f991c99ee0f2000fb7c001/NPPF_Sept_23.pdf

Department for Levelling Up, Housing and Communities (DLUHC). (2023b). *Levelling-up and regeneration bill: Consultation on implementation of plan-making reforms.* DLUHC. https://www.gov.uk/government/consultations/plan-making-reforms-consultation-on-implementation/levelling-up-and-regeneration-bill-consultation-on-implementation-of-plan-making-reforms#scope-of-the-consultation

Department for Levelling Up, Housing and Communities (DLUHC). (2023c). *PropTech Innovation Fund Round 1 Summary Report.* DLUHC. https://paas-s3-broker-prod-lon-252c9c29-444d-4eae-8a79-75f7eef7a638.s3.eu-west-2.amazonaws.com/wp-content/uploads/2023/03/31160845/PropTech-Innovation-Fund-Round-1-Summary-Report.pdf

Department for Levelling Up, Housing and Communities (DLUHC). (2023d). *Future councils' problem statements.* DLUHC. https://www.localdigital.gov.uk/feedback-on-future-councils/

Department of Levelling Up, Housing & Communities. (2024). *Digital planning case studies.* Council-led digital planning projects funded through the DLUHC Digital Planning programme. https://www.localdigital.gov.uk/digital-planning/case-studies/. Accessed on July 2, 2024.

Department for Levelling Up, Housing and Communities and Ministry of Housing, Communities and Local Government. (2019). *Neighbourhood planning.* DLUHC. https://www.gov.uk/guidance/neighbourhood-planning-2#full-publication-update-history

Department for Levelling Up, Housing and Communities and Ministry of Housing, Communities and Local Government. (2021a). *National model design code.* DLUHC. https://www.gov.uk/government/publications/national-model-design-code

Department for Levelling Up, Housing and Communities and Ministry of Housing, Communities and Local Government. (2021b). *Planning practice guidance.* DLUHC. https://www.gov.uk/government/collections/planning-practice-guidance

Department for Science, Innovation and Technology (DSIT). (2023). *Smart infrastructure pilots programme: Successful projects.* DSIT.

Design Commission for Wales. (2020, September 23). *The Welsh Place-making Charter (2020); Six principles for shaping the built and natural environments.* Design Commission for Wales. http://dcfw.org/wp-content/uploads/2020/09/PlacemakingWales_A4Charter_ENG.jpg

Dessai, A., & Javidroozi, V. (2021). Cross-sectoral process modelling for smart city development. *Business Process Management Journal, 27*(7), 2051–2074. https://doi.org/10.1108/BPMJ-05-2021-0333

Devlin, C., & Coaffee, J. (2021). Planning and technological innovation: The governance challenges faced by English local authorities in adopting planning technologies. *International Journal on the Unity of the Sciences, 27*, 149–163. https://doi.org/10.1080/12265934.2021.1997632

Dorset Council. (n.d.). *Dorset's digital infrastructure and inclusion strategy 2023 to 2030*. https://moderngov.dorsetcouncil.gov.uk/documents/s36825/Dorset%20Council%20Infrastructure%20Strategy%20v1.0%20for%20ISSUE%20070723.pdf

Emery, T., & Thrift, J. (2021). *20-minute neighbourhoods – Creating healthier, active, prosperous communities: An introduction for council planners in England*. Town and Country Planning Association.

Environment Agency. (2020). *National flood and coastal erosion risk management strategy for England*. HMSO.

Erl, T., & Stoffers, R. (2022). *A field guide to digital transformation*. Addison-Wesley Professional.

Essex, D., Kerner, S. M., & Gillis, A. S. (2023). What is Web 3.0 (Web3)? Definition, guide and history. TechTarget. https://www.techtarget.com/whatis/definition/Web-30

Feng, Z., Chen, Z., Cai, H., & Yang, Z. (2022). Evaluation of the sustainable development of the social-economic-natural compound ecosystem in the Guangdong–Hong Kong–Macao Greater Bay Area Urban Agglomeration (China): Based on complex network analysis. *Frontiers of Environmental Science, 10*. https://doi.org/10.3389/fenvs.2022.938450

Fischer, J., & Fittipaldi, J. (2023, March 16). Web 3.0 and the dark side of community. *Digital Leaders*. https://digileaders.com/web-3-0-and-the-dark-side-of-community/?utm_source=Active+Campaign&utm_medium=Blog&utm_campaign=SHARE+Creative&utm_source=ActiveCampaign&utm_medium=email&utm_content=How+can+public+services+innovate+using+emerging+technologies%3F&utm_campaign=Weekly+Newsletter+17%2F3%2F2023&vgo_ee=EkT2UrXouOgqURrCfO2YqhsKG5iWwDdhGewBvPgbAzhxEjkhCclh%3A3jemVZWHx2ItitWJt1mAAUtOu1LMsa34

Geospatial Commission. (2023). *Finding common ground*. Geospatial Commission. https://assets.publishing.service.gov.uk/government/uploads/system/uploads/attachment_data/file/1163819/2023-05-23_FINAL_NLDP_report_compressed.pdf

Government Office for Science (GOS). (2010). *Land use futures: Making the most of land in the 21st century: Foresight report looking at the future of land use in the UK over the next 50 years*. GOS. https://www.gov.uk/government/publications/land-use-futures-making-the-most-of-land-in-the-21st-century

Government Office for Science (GOS). (2021). *Trend deck in urbanisation*. GOS. https://www.gov.uk/government/publications/trend-deck-2021-urbanisation

Grace, M., Scott, A. J., Sadler, J. P., Proverbs, D. P., & Grayson, N. (2021). Exploring the smart-natural city interface; re-imagining and re-integrating urban planning and governance. *Emerald Open Research, 2*(7). https://doi.org/10.1108/EOR-05-2023-0004

Green, L., Toner, S., Evans, L., Parry-Williams, L., Johnson, T., Christian, G., Williams, C., Azam, S., & Bellis, M. A. (2022). *Maximising health and well-being opportunities for spatial planning in the COVID-19 pandemic recovery*. Public Health Wales NHS Trust. https://phw.nhs.wales/publications/publications1/maximising-health-and-well-being-opportunities-for-spatial-planning-in-the-covid-19-pandemic-recovery/

Guerry, A. D., Lonsdorf, E. V., Nootenboom, C., Remme, R. P., Griffin, R., Waters, H., Polasky, S., Tong Wu, B. H., Janke, B. D., Meacham, M., Hamel, P., & Wang,

X. (2023). Mapping, measuring and valuing the benefits of nature-based solutions in cities. In T. McPhearson, N. Kabisch, & N. Frantzeskaki (Eds.), *Nature-based solutions for cities* (pp. 259–293). Edward Elgar.

Hafferty, C., Hirons, M., Tomude, E. S., & McDermot, C. (2023, November). *Nature-based solutions practitioner guidance agile Iiitiative*. Recipe-for-Engagement.pdf (ox.ac.uk).

Hafferty, C., Reed, M., Brockett, B., Orford, S., Berry, R., Short, C., & Davis, J (2024). Engagement in the digital age: Understanding "what works" for participatory technologies in environmental decision-making. *Journal of Environmental Management, 365*, 121365.

Hagan, J. (2017, April 13). Survey finds majority of Americans don't think about the future. Future Now. https://legacy.iftf.org/future-now/article-detail/survey-finds-majority-of-americans-dont-think-about-the-future/?p=future-now/article-detail/survey-finds-majority-of-americans-dont-think-about-the-future/

Hajek, P., Youssef, A., & Hajkova, V. (2022). Recent developments in smart city assessment: A bibliometric and content analysis-based literature review. *Cities, 126*, 103709. https://doi.org/10.1016/j.cities.2022.103709

HM Treasury. (2022). *The growth plan 2022*. Command Paper 743. HM Treasury. https://assets.publishing.service.gov.uk/government/uploads/system/uploads/attachment_data/file/1105989/CCS207_CCS0822746402-001_SECURE_HMT_Autumn_Statement_2022_BOOK_Web_Accessible.pdf

House of Lords. (2022). *Land use in England committee: Report of Session 2022–23. HL Paper 105*. Making the most out of England's land. House of Lords. https://publications.parliament.uk/pa/ld5803/ldselect/ldland/105/105.pdf

House of Lords. (2023, June 29). *Communications and Digital Committee: 3rd Report of Session 2022–23. HL Paper 219*. Digital Exclusion. https://publications.parliament.uk/pa/ld5803/ldselect/ldcomm/219/21902.htm

Ietto, B., Rabe, J., Muth, R., & Pascucci, F. (2023). Blockchain for citizens' participation in urban planning: The case of the city of Berlin. A value sensitive design approach. *Cities, 140*, 104382. https://doi.org/10.1016/j.cities.2023.104382

Information Commissioner's Office (ICO). (2023, October 3). *Data Practitioners' Conference*. ICO. https://ico.org.uk/about-the-ico/data-protection-practitioners-conference/

Jadu/Wigan MBC. (2023). Wigan Council: Innovate & Thrive [Video]. YouTube. https://www.youtube.com/playlist?list=PLXnKjAZhh8hOlRa1TOprmKblLHIatgVMJ

Javidroozi, V., Carter, C., Grace, M., & Shah, H. (2023). Smart, sustainable, green cities: A state-of-the-art review. *Sustainability, 15*(6), 5353. https://doi.org/10.3390/su15065353

Jenrick, R. (2021, July 21). *Speech on the launch of the office for place*. https://www.gov.uk/government/speeches/office-for-place-launch

Jian, I., Luo, J., & Chan, E. (2020). Spatial justice in public open space planning: Accessibility and inclusivity. *Habitat International, 97*, 102122.

Kaehne, A., Bray, L., & Horowicz, E. (2020). Co-producing health care – pragmatic principles and an illustration. *Emerald Open Research, 2*(10). https://doi.org/10.35241/emeraldopenres.13475.2

Khawaja, S., & Javidroozi, V. (2023). Blockchain technology as an enabler for cross-sectoral systems integration for developing smart sustainable cities. *IET Smart Cities, 5*(3), 151–172. https://doi.org/10.1049/smc2.12059

Labib, S. M., Lindley, S., & Huck, J. J. (2020). Spatial dimensions of the influence of urban green-blue spaces on human health: A systematic review. *Environmental Research*, *180*, 108869. https://doi.org/10.1016/j.envres.2019.108869

Lec, S. J. (1959). *Myśli nieuczesane* (Translated by J. Galazka (1962) as *Unkempt thoughts*). St Martin's Press.

Lennon, M. (2015). Green infrastructure and planning policy: A critical assessment. *Local Environment*, *20*(8), 957–980.

Lim, Y., Edelenbos, J., & Gianoli, A. (2019). Identifying the results of smart city development: Findings from systematic literature review. *Cities*, *95*, 102397. https://doi.org/10.1016/j.cities.2019.102397

Local Government Association (LGA). (2024, June 7). *Local government white paper*. https://www.local.gov.uk/publications/local-government-white-paper. Accessed on July 2, 2024.

Lockwood, F. (2020). Bristol's smart city agenda: Vision, strategy, challenges and implementation. *IET Smart Cities*, *2*, 208–214.

Lovell, R., White, M. P., Wheeler, B., Taylor, T., & Elliott, L. (2020). *A rapid scoping review of health and wellbeing evidence for the Green Infrastructure Standards*. European Centre for Environment and Human Health. University of Exeter Medical School.

Mannheim, I., Schwartz, E., & Xi, W. (2019). Inclusion of older adults in the research and design of digital technology. *International Journal of Environmental Research and Public Health*, *16*(19), 3718. https://doi.org/10.3390/ijerph16193718

Manns, S. (2017, May 10). Planning and public engagement: The truth and the challenge. Royal Town Planning Institute blog. https://www.rtpi.org.uk/blog/2017/may/planning-and-public-engagement-the-truth-and-the-challenge/

Marsal-Llacuna, M.-L. (2020). The people's smart city dashboard (PSCD): Delivering on community-led governance with blockchain. *Technological Forecasting and Social Change*, *158*, 120150. https://doi.org/10.1016/j.techfore.2020.120150

Marsh, S. (2020, September 26). Escape to the country: How Covid is driving an exodus from Britain's cities. *The Guardian*. https://www.theguardian.com/world/2020/sep/26/escape-country-covid-exodus-britain-cities-pandemic-urban-green-space

Martin, C. J., Evans, J., & Karvonen, A. (2018). Smart and sustainable? Five tensions in the visions and practices of the smart-sustainable city in Europe and North America. *Technological Forecasting and Social Change*, *133*, 269–278.

McKinsey and Company. (2022, August 17). *What are Industry 4.0, the Fourth Industrial Revolution, and 4IR?* McKinsey & Company. https://www.mckinsey.com/featured-insights/mckinsey-explainers/what-are-industry-4-0-the-fourth-industrial-revolution-and-4ir

McPhearson, T., Kabisch, N., & Frantzeskaki, N. (Eds.). (2023). *Nature-based solutions for cities*. Edward Elgar.

Mell, I. (2021). 'But who's going to pay for it?' Contemporary approaches to green infrastructure financing, development and governance in London, UK. *Journal of Environmental Policy & Planning*, *23*, 628–645. https://doi.org/10.1080/1523908X.2021.1931064

Mitchell, L. M., Hardman, M., Howarth, M. L., & Cook, P. A. (2024). Mind, body and blood: Advancing green care through innovative methodologies within the field of health geography. *Cities & Health.* https://doi.org/10.1080/23748834.2023. 2290904

Mitchum, R. (2016, August 29). Chicago becomes first city to launch Array of Things. *UChicago News.* https://news.uchicago.edu/story/chicago-becomes-first-city-launch-array-things

Mora, L., & Deakin, M. (2019). *Untangling smart cities: From utopian dreams to innovation systems for a technology enabled urban sustainability.* Elsevier.

Morgan, D., & Moseley, S. (1981). Community development companies in the implementation of local planning. In *Conference papers of the Education for Planning Association (EPA), Annual Conference, May 1981* (pp. 32–45). Department of Town and Country Planning, Gloucestershire College of Arts and Technology.

Murgante, B., & Garramone, V. (2013). Web 3.0 and knowledge management: Opportunities for spatial planning and decision making. In B. Murgante, S. Misra, M. Carlini, C. M. Torre, H.-Q. Nguyen, D. Taniar, B. O. Apduhan, & O. Gervasi (Eds.), *Computational science and Its applications – ICCSA 2013* (pp. 606–621). Springer. https://doi.org/10.1007/978-3-642-39646-5_44

Nash, A. (2020). *Population and Household Projections.* Office for National Statistics. https://www.ons.gov.uk/peoplepopulationandcommunity/populationandmigration/populationprojections/bulletins/subnationalpopulationprojectionsforengland/2018based

National Audit Office (NAO). (2021). *The challenges in implementing digital change.* NAO Insight – Good practice guides. NAO. https://www.nao.org.uk/insights/the-challenges-in-implementing-digital-change/

National Infrastructure Commission (NIC). (2023, April). *Delivering net zero, climate resilience and growth Improving nationally significant infrastructure planning.* NIC. https://nic.org.uk/app/uploads/NIC-Planning-Study-Final-Report.pdf

Natural England. (2023). *Introduction to the Green Infrastructure Framework – Principles and standards for England.* Natural England. https://designatedsites.naturalengland.org.uk/GreenInfrastructure/Home.aspx

Natural History Museum. (n.d.). *Urban nature project.* https://www.nhm.ac.uk/about-us/urban-nature-project.html

Nature Based Solutions Initiative. (2024). *Mapping opportunities: NbS Knowledge Hub.* https://nbshub.naturebasedsolutionsinitiative.org/mapping-nbs-opportunities/

Nitoslawski, S. A., Galle, N. J., Van Den Bosch, C. K., & Steenberg, J. W. N. (2019). Smarter ecosystems for smarter cities? A review of trends, technologies, and turning points for smart urban forestry. *Sustainable Cities and Society, 51,* 101770. https://doi.org/10.1016/j.scs.2019.101770

O'Boyle, R. (2017, June). Block capital. *The Planner,* 18–21.

Office for Environmental Protection (OEP). (2022). *Our strategy.* OEP. https://www.theoep.org.uk/report/our-strategy-and-enforcement-policy

Office for Environmental Protection (OEP). (2024). *Annual report.* https://www.theoep.org.uk/report/government-remains-largely-track-meet-its-environmental-ambitions-finds-oep-annual-progress

Office for Place. (2023a). *Our vision and principles.* Office for Place. https://www.gov.uk/guidance/office-for-place-our-vision-and-principles

Office for Place. (2023b). *10 criteria for effective design coding.* Office for Place. https://www.gov.uk/guidance/10-criteria-for-effective-design-coding

Organisation for Economic Cooperation and Development (OECD). (2024, April 9). *Infrastructure for a climate-resilient future*. OECD. https://doi.org/10.1787/a74a45b0-en

Paes, L. A. B., Bezerra, B. S., Jugend, D., & Agudo, F. L. (2022). Prospects for a circular bioeconomy in urban ecosystems: Proposal for a theoretical framework. *Journal of Cleaner Production, 380*(1), 134939. https://doi.org/10.1016/j.jclepro.2022.134939

Potts, R. (2020). Is a new 'planning 3.0' paradigm emerging? Exploring the relationship between digital technologies and planning theory and practice. *Planning Theory & Practice, 21*(2), 272–289. https://doi.org/10.1080/14649357.2020.1748699

Public Health England. (2014). *Five year forward view*. Public Health England. https://www.england.nhs.uk/wp-content/uploads/2014/10/5yfv-web.pdf

Puchol-Salort, P., O'Keeffe, J., van Reeuwijk, M., & Mijic, A. (2021). An urban planning sustainability framework: Systems approach to blue green urban design. *Sustainable Cities and Society, 66*, 102677. https://doi.org/10.1016/j.scs.2020.102677

Rightmove. (2023, December 12). *The 10 happiest places to live*. https://www.londonworld.com/read-this/the-10-happiest-places-to-live-according-to-rightmove-4437989?page=3. Accessed on December 12, 2023.

Royal Horticultural Society. (2023). *The Garden, 148*(12).

Royal Society. (2023). *Multifunctional landscapes*. Royal Society. https://royalsociety.org/topics-policy/projects/living-landscapes/multifunctional-land-use/

Royal Town Planning Institute. (2020). *Plan the world we need: The contribution of planning to a sustainable, resilient and inclusive recovery*. RTPI. https://www.rtpi.org.uk/research/2020/june/plan-the-world-we-need/

Safransky, S. (2020). Geographies of algorithmic violence: Redlining the smart city. *International Journal of Urban and Regional Research, 44*(2), 200–218.

Santini, R. M., & Carvalho, H. (2019). The rise of participatory despotism: A systematic review of online platforms for political engagement. *Journal of Information, Communication and Ethics in Society, 17*(4), 422–437. https://doi.org/10.1108/JICES-02-2019-0016

Say, M. (2023, March 24). Calderdale Council to use digital twin for local area energy plan. *UKAuthority*. https://www.ukauthority.com/articles/calderdale-council-to-use-digital-twin-for-local-area-energy-plan/

Scott, A. J., Carter, C., Reed, M. R., Larkham, P., Adams, D., Morton, N., Waters, R., Collier, D., Crean, C., Curzon, R., Forster, R., Gibbs, P., Grayson, N., Hardman, M., Hearle, A., Jarvis, D., Kennet, M., Leach, K., Middleton, M., ... Coles, R. (2013). Disintegrated development at the rural–urban fringe: Re-Connecting spatial planning theory and practice. *Progress in Planning, 83*, 1–52. https://doi.org/10.1016/j.progress.2012.09.001

Scottish Government. (2022). *Our place: Place standard tool*. https://www.ourplace.scot/About-Place-Standard

Shaw, E. (2023, June 23). Unlocking the power of low code in Defra. https://defradigital.blog.gov.uk/2023/06/23/unlocking-the-power-of-low-code-in-defra/

Shropshire Council. (2022, July 5). *Examination stage documents: Hearing session*. Shropshire Council. https://www.shropshire.gov.uk/planning-policy/local-planning/local-plan-review/draft-shropshire-local-plan-2016-2038-examination/examination-library/examination-stage-documents/

Soeiro, D. (2020). Smart cities, well-being and good business: The 2030 Agenda and the role of knowledge in the era of Industry 4.0. In Matos, F., Vairinhos, V.,

Salavisa, I., Edvinsson, L., Massaro, M. (Eds.). *Knowledge, people, and digital transformation* (pp 55–67). Springer.

Somers Town Community Association. (2023). Somers town future neighbourhoods 2030 – Somers town area based strategy 2023–2030. http://www.somerstown.org.uk. https://www.somerstown.org.uk/wp-content/uploads/2024/04/STFN-2030-Area-Based-Strategy-final-1-1.pdf. Accessed on June 30, 2024.

Sörensen, J., Persson, A. S., & Olsson, J. A. (2021). A data management framework for strategic urban planning using blue-green infrastructure. *Journal of Environmental Management, 299*, 113658. https://doi.org/10.1016/j.jenvman.2021.113658

Stirling Council. (2022). *Stirling to become world's first fully augmented reality city.* Stirling Council. https://www.stirling.gov.uk/news/stirling-to-become-world-s-first-fully-augmented-reality-city/

Sultan, H., Grayson, N., Jones, S., Pike, D., Greenham, S., Needle, D., Sadler, J., & Frew, E. (2023). Green space and environmental justice – A new metric to guide resource allocation. *Town & Country Planning, 92*, 410–418.

Task Force for Nature-related Financial Disclosures (TNFD). (2023). *Executive summary of the recommendations of the TNFD.* https://tnfd.global/wp-content/uploads/2023/09/Executive_summary_of_the_TNFD_recommendations.pdf?v=1695117009

The Planner. (2022, August). Placemakers in the public sector. *The Planner,* 22–23.

The Rocky Outlook. (2023, August 10). *The Rocky Outlook, 23*(32). http://www.Rmoutlook.com

Tomor, Z., Meijer, A., Michels, A., & Geertman, S. (2019). Smart governance for sustainable cities: Findings from a systematic literature review. *Journal of Urban Technology, 26*(4), 3–27. https://doi.org/10.1080/10630732.2019.1651178

Turunen, A. W., Halonen, J., Korpela, K., Ojala, A., Pasanen, T., Siponen, T., Tittanen, P., Tyrväinen, L., Yli-Tuomi, T., & Lanki, T. (2023). Cross-sectional associations of different types of nature exposure with psychotropic, antihypertensive and asthma medication. *Occupational and Environmental Medicine, 80*, 111–118. https://doi.org/10.1136/oemed-2022-108491

UK Government. (2018). *A green future: Our 25-year plan to improve the environment.* Defra. https://assets.publishing.service.gov.uk/government/uploads/system/uploads/attachment_data/file/693158/25-year-environment-plan.pdf

UK Government. (2023a, October). *Transforming for a digital future: government's 2022 to 25 roadmap for digital and data.* https://www.gov.uk/government/publications/transforming-for-a-digital-future-governments-2022-to-25-roadmap-for-digital-and-data?utm_medium=email&utm_campaign=govuk-notifications-topic&utm_source=2e5a7991-cd51-4409-a667-29d9cfcb7481&utm_content=immediately

UK Government. (2023b). *Powering up Britain: Net Zero Growth Plan Policy paper.* https://www.gov.uk/government/publications/powering-up-britain/powering-up-britain-net-zero-growth-plan

UK Government. (2023c). *Environmental improvement plan 2023.* https://assets.publishing.service.gov.uk/media/64a6d9c1c531eb000c64fffa/environmental-improvement-plan-2023.pdf

UK Green Building Council (UKGBC). (2022, May). *The value of urban nature-based solutions.* UKGBC. https://ukgbc.org/wp-content/uploads/2022/05/UKGBC_WIP-Report_V09-LR.pdf

UK Parliament. (2023). *Levelling-up and Regeneration Act 2023*. UK Parliament. https://bills.parliament.uk/bills/3155

Ullah, Z., Al-Turjman, F., Mostarda, L., & Gagliardi, R. (2020). Applications of artificial intelligence and machine learning in smart cities. *Computer Communications, 154*, 313–323. https://doi.org/10.1016/j.comcom.2020.02.069

United Nations. (2019). *World Urbanization Prospects 2018: Highlights*. United Nations, Department of Economic and Social Affairs, Population Division. https://population.un.org/wup/Publications/Files/WUP2018-Highlights.pdf

Vidal Yáñez, D., Pereira, E., Cirach, M., Daher, C., Nieuwenhuijsen, M., & Mueller, N. (2023). An urban green space intervention with benefits for mental health: A health impact assessment of the Barcelona 'Eixos Verds' Plan. *Environment International, 174*, 197880. https://doi.org/10.1016/j.envint.2023.107880

Vincent, D. (2021, March 10). Waterfront Toronto launches post-Sidewalk Labs chapter in the development of Quayside property. *Toronto Star*. https://www.thestar.com/news/gta/waterfront-toronto-launches-post-sidewalk-labs-chapter-in-the-development-of-quayside-property/article_0d85770d-39a8-5311-9729-309e40c88f44.html

Washbourne, C. L., & Wansbury, C. (Eds.). (2023). *ICE Manual of Blue-Green Infrastructure*. ICE Publishing.

Wilson, A., & Tewdwr-Jones, M. (2021). *Digital participatory planning: Citizen engagement, democracy, and design*. Routledge.

Winkelman, S. (2017, September 18). *Blue green infrastructure: Example and benefits* (Conference presentation). Liveable Cities Forum, Victoria, BC.

World Economic Forum (WEF). (2023, June). *Data for the city of tomorrow: Developing the capabilities and capacity to guide better urban futures*. WEF. https://www.weforum.org/reports/data-for-the-city-of-tomorrow-developing-the-capabilities-and-capacity-to-guide-better-urban-futures

Wray, S. (2022, June 29). *Digital twins are finding their place*. Connected Places Catapult. https://cp.catapult.org.uk/article/digital-twins-are-finding-their-place/

Wu, M., Yan, B., Huang, Y., & Sarker, M. N. I. (2022). Big data-driven urban management: Potential for urban sustainability. *Land, 11*(5), 680. https://doi.org/10.3390/land11050680

Yigitcanlar, T., Kamruzzaman, M., Foth, M., Sabatini-Marques, E., da Costa, E., & Ioppolo, G. (2019). Can cities become smart without being sustainable? A systematic review of the literature. *Sustainable Cities and Society, 45*, 348–365. https://doi.org/10.1016/j.scs.2018.11.033

Zabelskyte, G., Kabisch, N., & Stasiskiene, Z. (2022). Patterns of urban green space use applying social media data: A systematic literature review. *Land, 11*(2), 238. https://doi.org/10.3390/land11020238

Chapter 5

The City as a System of Places: Smart Placemaking for Future Living

Vahid Javidroozi

Birmingham City University, UK

Abstract

Placemaking plays a crucial role in enhancing the quality of life in cities, necessitating a holistic approach and the incorporation of smart strategies. This study addresses the gap in existing research by exploring the integration of systems thinking and systems integration in smart placemaking within cities to make the placemaking more resilient, connected, and smart. The city is viewed as a system of interconnected and integrated smart places, where attractions, communication hubs, public spaces, and infrastructures seamlessly connect. The outcomes of smart placemaking include economic prosperity, environmental sustainability, health and well-being, safety and security, cultural preservation, innovation, and resilience. The research develops a framework that highlights the interconnectedness and interdependencies between systems thinking, systems integration, and smart placemaking. The framework provides guidance for city planners, urban designers, and policymakers in implementing effective strategies for creating vibrant, inclusive, and sustainable public spaces within the broader context of a smart and interconnected city.

Keywords: Smart city; system of systems; systems thinking; systems integration; smart places; smart placemaking

Introduction

Placemaking has emerged as a fundamental approach to the transformation of urban spaces into vibrant, inclusive, and more livable environments. It emphasizes the importance of designing and managing public spaces that promote social interaction, cultural expression, and a sense of identity and belonging (Khemri et al., 2020). As cities face increasing challenges in terms of population growth, environmental sustainability, and technological advances, there is a growing need to adopt a holistic view and incorporate smartness in placemaking strategies (Javidroozi et al., 2015). This is crucial in order to create cities that are enjoyable, healthy, secure, safe, sustainable, and resilient for their residents and visitors.

While extensive research has been conducted on placemaking, the integration of systems thinking and systems integration with the placemaking agenda remains relatively limited. There is a gap in understanding how these concepts can be effectively applied to create smart and connected public spaces within cities. Therefore, this chapter aims to bridge this gap by exploring the connections between systems thinking, systems integration, and placemaking in the context of smart cities.

This chapter therefore reviews the existing literature on three core concepts: systems theory, systems thinking, and systems integration, along with the emerging field of smart cities. In examining these concepts, they are connected to the practice of placemaking, and the concept of "smart placemaking" is developed. This concept considers the city as a system of interconnected and integrated smart places, where technology, sustainability, community engagement, and systems thinking converge to create vibrant, inclusive, and resilient urban spaces.

The aim of this research is to develop a framework that highlights the relationships and interdependencies between systems thinking, systems integration, and smart placemaking. By synthesizing the findings from the literature review, the research provides a comprehensive understanding of the key components and principles necessary to create smart and connected public spaces within the larger urban system. This framework will serve as a guide for city planners, urban designers, and policymakers in more effectively implementing smart placemaking strategies and contributing to the overall well-being and sustainability of cities.

In the following sections, the literature on systems theory, systems thinking, systems integration, and smart cities will be reviewed. This chapter then connects these concepts to the practice of placemaking, exploring how they can be integrated to create the concept of "smart placemaking" within the broader framework of a city as a system of interconnected and integrated smart places. Through this research, I aim to contribute to the development of knowledge and practices in urban design and planning, paving the way for the creation of smarter, more livable cities in the future.

Background

Systems Theory

There are numerous definitions of the term "system." For instance, Machol (1965), Emery (1969), Checkland (1981, 1999), Laszlo and Krippner (1998), Backlund (2000), and Stichweh (2011) have all provided definitions of the term. For example, Machol (1965) conceptualizes a system as an operational entity that undergoes varying states over time in response to both external and internal forces, employing the Markov chain theory to describe its continuous evolution. Emery (1969) defines a system as a collection of interdependent components forming an integrated whole, emphasizing their interaction and interrelation within the entirety. Similarly, Checkland (1981, 1999) centralizes the idea of a system around interconnected elements that collectively exhibit properties distinct from those of their individual parts, reflecting properties inherent to the whole. Laszlo and Krippner (1998) view a system as a complex interplay of components and their relationships, forming a boundary-maintaining entity or process. Backlund (2000) characterizes a system as an assembly of interacting elements held together by relationships. Stichweh (2011) extends the understanding, framing "system" as the subject of a scientific discipline concerned with the comparative study of various systems. This indicates that the concept of "system" has been studied and analyzed extensively, and that there is no single, universally accepted definition of the term. Each of these authors has contributed to the understanding of systems and how they operate, and their definitions are useful in different contexts and applications. Overall, the varying definitions of "system" reflect the complexity and versatility of the concept, which can be applied in a broad range of fields, including engineering, biology, social sciences, and management.

Nevertheless, the various definitions of the term "system" all share a common thread. They view a system as a collection of interconnected components that work together dynamically toward a common goal or purpose. This aspect of interconnectivity is seen as a defining feature that sets a system apart from a mere collection of individual components. This concept is also supported by the principles of systems thinking and systems theories, particularly General Systems Theory (GST) (Bertalanffy, 1968). The GST proposes that a system is an entity composed of interrelated components that exhibit properties and behaviors that cannot be understood by examining each component in isolation. Instead, understanding a system requires analyzing the relationships and interactions between its components.

Based on GST, which is a transdisciplinary approach for understanding complex systems, all systems, regardless of their domain, share common features and can be studied as an entity. GST proposes that systems are made up of interrelated components, and their emergent properties and behaviors cannot be comprehended by analyzing each part in isolation. Instead, the entire system must be examined, taking into account the relationships and interactions between its parts. GST also highlights that systems exist in a hierarchy of nested systems, with each level possessing its own unique emergent properties and behaviors. For instance, an organism can be viewed as a system composed of cells, which are systems made up of molecules and so on. Furthermore, GST asserts that systems are open, which implies that they interact with their environment and exchange matter and energy with it. This interaction with the environment can result in feedback loops, where the system's output influences its input, affecting the system's behavior over time. Feedback loops can either be positive or negative, resulting in either reinforcing or balancing behaviors within the system (Bertalanffy, 1968; Checkland, 1981, 1999).

This way of thinking provides a useful framework for understanding the complex, interdependent systems that exist in cities, such as transportation, health care, education, energy, and communication networks, as well as efficient, attractive, modern, and interconnected places within cities, which facilitate social interaction, improve public health, enhance local economies, and provide a greater sense of community pride and identity.

Systems Thinking

Systems thinking is an interdisciplinary approach to understanding complex problems by recognizing the interconnectedness and relationships between various components of a system. It emphasizes the system's behavior as a whole and involves identifying feedback loops and behavioral patterns that can influence the system's overall behavior. In other words, systems thinking is a process of thinking that emphasizes the interconnection and interrelatedness of various components of a system (Checkland, 1999). This approach suggests that changes or improvements made to one part of a system can affect other parts of the system, and therefore, the components of a system cannot be considered separately. Many studies have utilized systems thinking to study various systems such as information systems, enterprise systems, and change management (e.g., Antonelli et al., 2013; Cordeiro De Paula & Pereira Dos Santos, 2019; Kettinger et al., 1997; Mingers & White, 2010; Pahl-Wostl, 2002; Setiawansyah et al., 2021). It has also been used to develop organizational change theory (Deming, 2000; Seddon, 2008).

There are four fundamental concepts in systems thinking: emergent properties, layered structure, communication processes, and control. Emergent properties refer to the phenomenon where the whole entity generated by the aggregation of unique properties has something more than the mere sum of its components. It is the relationship between the elements that generates a whole entity that can achieve the observer's goal, which cannot be achieved by the collection of parts. For instance, the departments of an organization have their own properties, but when they link and work together, the emergent properties of the entire enterprise emerge. The integration of this interconnection provides seamless exchange of information and business processes. This same concept can also be applied to cities. Currently, city services cannot be delivered by discrete agents, organizations, or sectors because the systems within cities are closely interrelated. Therefore, many factors must be considered to provide and deliver services to citizens (Javidroozi et al., 2019a). For instance, although it can be in favor of the citizens, a municipality should not suddenly decide to bring in new amenities such as playgrounds, benches, and public art in a low-income neighborhood to revitalize a public space, without understanding the inhabitants' concerns and priorities. To appropriately reach such a decision, a large amount of data and considerations from numerous departments such as transport, health care, security, energy, as well as the community, need to be considered to allow the usefulness and impact of the new developments to be effectively assessed. This uncomplicated instance exemplifies the importance of the correlation and amalgamation required between the city sectors and their corresponding systems. The second fundamental concept of systems thinking is a stratified arrangement, implying that the "whole" entity, such as the enterprise and the city, comprises smaller "wholes" within them. As a system of systems, the city evidently encompasses multiple sectors, comprising several organizations and departments that are considered smaller "wholes." Consequently, the idea of stratified arrangement is pertinent to both the city and the enterprise. The final two core tenets of systems thinking are also indispensable in both the enterprise and the city to adapt and endure in the contemporary dynamic business and living milieu. The capacity to control change and adaptability in cities can only be accomplished by transforming the method of city operations to a modern and integrated approach that enables access to real-time data, effective communication among all departments, and timely decision-making (Checkland, 1999).

Systems Integration

An entity that is composed of interrelated components is referred to as "intercommunicated" and/or "interconnected" but not necessarily "integrated" (Davenport, 1998; Davenport et al., 2004). This means that the subsystems or departments of a system can impact each other without being integrated as a whole, due to the absence of smooth information and process flow among them (Ackoff, 1981; Laszlo & Krippner, 1998). Therefore, an integrated entity, such as a city, must have subsystems or components that interact seamlessly with each other, allowing them to be viewed as a single entity. As a result, an integrated system should be defined based on the principles of systems thinking and systems theory, particularly GST. Achieving this requires integrating subsystems at both the information and process levels. Systems integration, therefore, is the process of enabling seamless intercommunication throughout the subsystems of an entity. By using systems thinking, planners and designers can develop holistic solutions that take into account the interconnectivity and dynamic behavior of these systems, ultimately leading to more effective and sustainable outcomes (Chen et al., 2008; Grabot et al., 2008).

Javidroozi et al. (2014) assert that successful systems integration requires consideration of the three key elements of people, process, and technology, which have been identified as integral components of a system (Fig. 5.1). They support their argument by referencing Singleton's (1974) definition of a system and Grover et al.'s (1995) identification of these elements as organizational subsystems. In addition to these components, data alignment and sharing among various systems components is another aspect that would be enhanced through the systems integration process.

Given that systems integration can significantly enhance performance, a sufficient and appropriate change in all aspects of the entity, such as a city, is required. Therefore, the key elements of systems integration are the main components that require change and improvement. To facilitate successful implementation of this change, entities need to have prepared and enthusiastic people, supported by appropriate technology (Ramamoorthy et al., 1992). Importantly, during the systems integration process, all operations and circumstances of

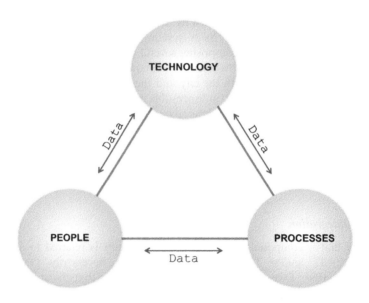

Fig. 5.1. Key Elements of Systems Integration.

business strategy, which are created by business processes, are subject to change. Business processes, which are systematic rules connecting inputs to outputs in an organization to address business issues, are a crucial component of systems integration. Other components, such as people, management, roles, tasks, information flow, and technology, add value to inputs and generate outputs, such as products and services, for customers (Javidroozi et al., 2019b).

Smart Cities: Smart Everything

Cities consist of many interconnected subsystems, such as health care and transport, that cannot function separately. These components must be connected to each other to improve the overall quality of public spaces and livability. Even if each component operates flawlessly, without interconnection and interrelatedness, the entity as a whole cannot provide efficient and effective services. Managing changes in a city requires managing the entity as a system so that changes can be adaptive and integrated rather than reactive and distributed.

Hence, cross-sectoral collaboration is essential in the development of smart cities. While technology plays a crucial role in the transition from traditional services to smart city services, it is important to recognize that technology alone is not sufficient. Liu and Peng (2013) and Marciniak and Owoc (2013) emphasize that technology is merely an enabler. In the development of a smart city, every aspect of the city should embrace smartness. This includes the involvement of people, businesses, technology, processes, data, infrastructures, consumption, spaces, energy, strategies, and management. These components should be interconnected, leveraging each other's data, supporting one another, and minimizing waste. This concept, often referred to as "smart everything," is highlighted in earlier research such as Townsend (2013) and Medina-Borja (2015). To achieve this interconnectedness and maximize the benefits of smart city initiatives, a systems thinking approach is necessary.

A systems thinking approach recognizes the interconnectedness and interdependencies within a system. As Checkland (1981, 1999) suggests, everything within a system is related to everything else. Therefore, to bring about improvements and changes in the whole system, it is crucial to ensure that all components are connected and aligned. This principle applies to the city as a "system of systems," where various sectors and systems within the city need to be interconnected and coordinated. Davidson and Venning (2011) emphasize the importance of systems thinking in comprehending the complexities of a city and viewing it as a system of systems. This perspective acknowledges that a city comprises multiple systems (sectors) that operate together, utilizing their own data, processes, technologies, and human resources to improve performance and achieve shared goals.

Smart Placemaking

The notion of placemaking is fully covered in other chapters, where it is identified that placemaking plays a crucial role in creating vibrant and livable cities, and its significance becomes even more pronounced in the context of smart and sustainable cities (Courage, 2020). Placemaking involves the intentional design and development of public spaces that reflect the needs and aspirations of the community. It aims to create places that foster social interaction, cultural expression, and a sense of identity and belonging (Toolis, 2017).

In the context of smart and sustainable cities, placemaking becomes essential for several reasons. First, following the requirement of smart cities explained above, placemaking ensures that technology is integrated thoughtfully into public spaces, creating an environment that is not only technologically advanced but also functional, inclusive, and aesthetically pleasing. By incorporating smart features such as interactive displays, smart lighting, and Wi-Fi connectivity, placemaking can enhance the user experience and provide valuable services to the community (Freeman et al., 2019; Sanaeipoor & Emami, 2020). Secondly, placemaking can contribute to sustainability goals by incorporating eco-friendly design principles and promoting sustainable practices. This may include incorporating green spaces, integrating renewable energy sources, implementing rainwater harvesting systems, and designing for efficient use of resources (Ghavampour & Vale, 2019). By creating sustainable public spaces, placemaking encourages environmentally responsible behavior and contributes to the overall sustainability of the city.

Furthermore, placemaking in smart and sustainable cities promotes social equity and inclusivity. Enabled by digital technology, it ensures that public spaces are accessible and welcoming to people of all ages, abilities, and backgrounds. Considerations such as universal design, equitable access to amenities, and the integration of diverse cultural elements can help to create an inclusive environment that fosters social cohesion and equal opportunities for all community members.

Additionally, placemaking in smart and sustainable cities recognizes the importance of community engagement and participatory processes. It involves actively involving residents, businesses, and other stakeholders in the decision-making and design processes. By engaging with the community and considering their input and feedback, placemaking can address local needs and aspirations, resulting in public spaces that truly reflect the identity and character of the city.

Hence, in the context of smart and sustainable cities, placemaking becomes even more crucial for creating vibrant, inclusive, and functional public spaces. It ensures that technology is integrated appropriately, promotes sustainability, fosters social equity, and engages the community in the process. By prioritizing placemaking in smart and sustainable city development, we can create cities that are not only technologically advanced but also livable, resilient, and harmonious for their residents and visitors and at the same time contributing toward developing a holistic view for a city from all aspects of livability including smart, sustainable, and green agenda, using the systems thinking approach (Javidroozi et al., 2023).

Accordingly, placemaking in a city should also be smart, meaning that it works as an integral part of the whole city to create an intentional and inclusive design and management of public spaces within the context of a smart city. In smart placemaking, the focus is on leveraging technology as an enabler to improve the functionality, accessibility, and overall experience of public spaces. This includes incorporating features such as smart lighting, interactive displays, Wi-Fi connectivity, and real-time data to enhance user convenience, safety, and engagement.

Moreover, smart placemaking embraces a systems thinking approach, recognizing the interconnectedness of various components within a public space and their influence on the larger urban system. It seeks to align the design and management of public spaces with the broader goals and strategies of the smart city, promoting integration, collaboration, and optimization. It provides a holistic approach to the design and management of public spaces. By considering the interconnectedness of elements in a system, systems thinking helps to create public spaces that are designed and managed in a way that considers the interplay between the physical environment, social dynamics, and technology.

Emergent properties, layered structure, communication processes, and control are fundamental concepts of systems thinking that can be applied to placemaking. Placemaking, as an application of systems thinking, recognizes that a city is a complex system composed of interconnected sectors and departments. The concept of emergent properties highlights that the whole city system has properties and behaviors that go beyond the sum of its individual components. Similarly, in placemaking, the design and management of physical spaces must consider the interconnections and integration of various factors and sectors within the city (Henshaw, 2019; Mingers & White, 2010).

Placemaking acknowledges the need to address the specific needs and characteristics of these smaller systems within the larger urban context. For example, different organizations within a city play distinct roles in the development and maintenance of public spaces, and placemaking requires coordination and collaboration among these entities. The concepts of communication processes and control in systems thinking emphasize the importance of effective information exchange and decision-making within a system (Checkland, 1999). In placemaking, this means facilitating seamless communication and collaboration among different city sectors, departments, and stakeholders. It involves leveraging real-time data, enabling efficient decision-making, and adapting to changing conditions.

By applying systems thinking concepts, placemaking can effectively address the interconnectedness, integration, and adaptive capacity required in the design and management of public spaces. The application of systems thinking recognizes the need for holistic approaches that consider the emergent properties of the city system, the layered structure of its subsystems, and the necessity of effective communication and control processes. Ultimately, systems thinking supports the principles of placemaking and the integration of various components and systems to create vibrant, inclusive, and sustainable urban environments.

Hence, drawing upon the foundational principles of systems thinking, the application of these principles can yield a multitude of favorable outcomes within the domain of placemaking, encompassing various key aspects as follows:

- Holistic perspective: systems thinking provides a comprehensive view of public spaces as complex systems, rather than just physical locations. This holistic perspective helps to identify and understand the interrelated components of a public space and how they affect each other.
- Sustainability: systems thinking helps to create public spaces that are sustainable by considering the impact of human activities on the environment and the interplay between the environment and technology. For example, systems thinking can help to design public spaces that use renewable energy sources, reduce waste, and conserve resources.
- Community engagement: systems thinking recognizes the importance of community engagement in the design and management of public spaces. By considering the social dynamics of a public space, systems thinking can help to create spaces that are inclusive and foster positive social interactions.
- Resilience: systems thinking helps to design and manage public spaces that are resilient in the face of change and disruption. By considering the interplay between the physical environment, social dynamics, and technology, systems thinking helps to create public spaces that can adapt to change and continue to meet the needs of users.
- Technology integration: systems thinking can help to integrate technology into public spaces in a way that enhances the user experience and fosters positive social dynamics, while also considering the potential impacts on privacy and the environment. This is the main point that connects smart city requirements and placemaking.

These are the main emergent properties when systems thinking is applied for placemaking. Hence, the sustainability, smartness, and citizens' experience will be enhanced, and the city will become more livable, responsive, and resilient to changes.

The City as a System of Smart Places

Smart placemaking is crucial for creating vibrant, inclusive, and sustainable public spaces within a city, as discussed above. These smart places are designed and managed in a way that leverages technology, sustainability, community engagement, and resilience to enhance the overall urban experience. However, it is important to know that a city is not just a collection of individual smart places but should be viewed as a system of interconnected and integrated smart places.

A city as a system of smart places means that each individual smart place within the city, whether a park, a transportation hub, a cultural center, or a commercial district, is connected and integrated with other places and systems in the urban environment. This connectivity and integration are achieved through systems integration, which involves bringing together key components and elements (Javidroozi et al., 2014, 2023).

Systems integration in the context of a city encompasses various aspects. First, it involves the integration of technology across different smart places, enabling seamless connectivity and data exchange. This could include the integration of smart sensors, Internet of Things (IoT) devices, and data platforms that facilitate real-time information sharing and analysis (Abdel-Aziz et al., 2016). Secondly, systems integration considers the integration of processes and operations across smart places. It involves coordinating and aligning activities, services, and resources among different places to ensure efficient and optimized functionality. For example, transportation systems can be integrated with public spaces to enable convenient and sustainable mobility options for residents and visitors (Javidroozi et al., 2019a). Thirdly, systems integration encompasses the integration of stakeholders and communities. It involves fostering collaboration and engagement among various actors, such as government entities, businesses, community organizations, and residents. This integration ensures that the diverse needs, perspectives, and aspirations of different stakeholders are considered in the development and management of smart places. Furthermore, systems integration addresses the importance of data integration and interoperability. It involves harmonizing data from different sources and systems within smart places, allowing for holistic insights and analysis. This integration of data supports informed decision-making, performance monitoring, and the delivery of efficient and effective services across the city (Javidroozi et al., 2015).

Hence, a city can be viewed as a "system of smart places" that highlights the interconnectedness and integration of various elements and systems within the urban environment. Systems integration plays a crucial role in connecting and integrating smart places, enabling seamless communication, data exchange, and collaboration. By embracing systems integration, cities can achieve the full potential of smart placemaking, creating a cohesive and dynamic urban system that enhances the quality of life for its residents and visitors. In addition, systems integration offers a seamless connectivity, coordination, and integration of various physical city places, including attractions, communication hubs, infrastructures, and other key places (Couper et al., 2023; Dai et al., 2017; Lew, 2017).

It involves bringing together these diverse elements to create a cohesive and efficient urban environment:

- Attractions and Cultural Centers: systems integration ensures that attractions and cultural centers within the city, such as museums, theaters, and art galleries, are connected with other places and systems. This can involve integrating ticketing and scheduling systems, providing real-time information on events and exhibitions, and facilitating collaborative programs and initiatives between different cultural entities.
- Transportation Hubs: systems integration plays a crucial role in transportation hubs like airports, train stations, and bus terminals. It involves integrating various transportation systems, including ticketing systems, scheduling systems, and real-time information displays, to ensure seamless connectivity and efficient passenger flow. Additionally, integrating these hubs with surrounding attractions and services can provide convenient and integrated mobility options for residents and visitors.
- Public Spaces and Parks: systems integration in public spaces and parks involves connecting various systems and amenities. This can include integrating smart lighting systems, surveillance systems, and environmental monitoring systems to enhance safety and security. Integration can also involve providing real-time information on park events, activities, and facilities through digital platforms or interactive displays, enhancing the user experience and engagement.
- Communication Hubs: places within the city that serve as communication hubs, such as community centers, libraries, and information centers, can benefit from systems integration. This may involve integrating communication technologies, digital information systems, and interactive displays to provide access to information, services, and resources. Integration can also facilitate community engagement, allowing residents to participate in decision-making processes and access civic services.
- Infrastructure: while infrastructure itself may not be considered a place, systems integration plays a vital role in ensuring that infrastructural elements, such as smart grids, transportation networks, and utility systems, operate in a coordinated and efficient manner. While systems integration enables real-time monitoring, data exchange, and decision-making to optimize the performance, sustainability, and resilience of the city's infrastructure, it should also help integrate all other places across the city to be seamlessly connected, use each other's data, and integrate their processes to provide efficient and on-time services for citizens and visitors.

This discussion leads to the development of a conceptual framework for smart placemaking (Fig. 5.2):

This framework represents smart placemaking and requires the application of both systems integration and systems thinking. Systems integration ensures the seamless connectivity and coordination of various elements within a city, such as

86 Vahid Javidroozi

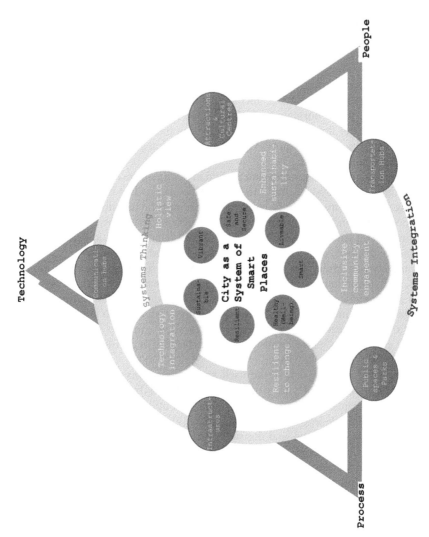

Fig. 5.2.   A Framework for the City as a System of Smart Places.

attractions, communication hubs, public spaces, and infrastructures. It involves integrating technologies, processes, people, using flows of data among them to create a cohesive and efficient urban environment. Systems thinking provides a holistic and interdisciplinary approach to understand the interconnectedness and relationships between these elements. It considers the interplay between the physical environment, social dynamics, technology, and sustainability. By combining systems integration and systems thinking, smart placemaking can create vibrant, inclusive, and sustainable public spaces that enhance the quality of life for residents and visitors, while fostering resilience, safety, security, social cohesion, and efficient resource utilization within the larger urban system.

Conclusion

This chapter has explored the integration of systems thinking and systems integration in the context of smart placemaking within cities. By reviewing the literature on systems theory, systems thinking, systems integration, and smart cities, a framework was developed that highlights the interconnectedness and interdependencies between these concepts. Through this investigation, several key findings and contributions have emerged.

First, the concept of smart placemaking emphasizes the importance of considering the holistic view of cities and integrating technology, sustainability, community engagement, and systems thinking in the design and management of public spaces. This approach promotes enjoyable, healthy, secure, safe, sustainable, and resilient cities.

Secondly, the city can be viewed as a system of interconnected and integrated smart places, where various elements, such as attractions, communication hubs, public spaces, and infrastructures, are seamlessly connected and integrated. This understanding highlights the significance of systems integration in creating cohesive and efficient urban environments.

Furthermore, the framework provides a comprehensive understanding of the relationships between systems thinking, systems integration, and smart placemaking. It serves as a valuable guide for city planners, urban designers, and policymakers to implement effective strategies for creating vibrant, inclusive, and sustainable public spaces within the broader context of a smart and interconnected city.

However, this research has certain limitations. The exploration of systems thinking and systems integration in the context of smart placemaking is a relatively new field, and further empirical research and case studies are needed to validate and refine the framework proposed. Additionally, the practical implementation of smart placemaking strategies may face challenges related to funding, stakeholder engagement, and regulatory frameworks, which require further investigation and analysis.

To advance this field of research, future studies should focus on empirically evaluating the effectiveness of the framework in real-world settings. Case studies and comparative analyses can provide valuable insights into the practical application and outcomes of smart placemaking initiatives. Moreover, exploring the social and cultural dimensions of smart placemaking, as well as the long-term impacts on community well-being and urban sustainability, would be valuable areas for further research.

References

Abdel-Aziz, A. A., Abdel-Salam, H., & El-Sayad, Z. (2016). The role of ICTs in creating the new social public place of the digital era. *Alexandria Engineering Journal, 55*(1), 487–493. https://doi.org/10.1016/J.AEJ.2015.12.019

Ackoff, R. L. (1981). *Creating the corporate future: Plan or be planned for.* Wiley.

Antonelli, D., Chiabert, P., & Romagnoli, V. (2013). Information system and systems thinking: A compulsory marriage? *IFAC Proceedings Volumes, 46*(9), 1780–1785. https://doi.org/10.3182/20130619-3-RU-3018.00612

Backlund, A. (2000). The definition of system. *Kybernetes, 29*(4), 444–451. https://doi.org/10.1108/03684920010322055

Bertalanffy, L. V. (1968). *General system theory: Foundations, development, applications.* G. Braziller.

Checkland, P. (1981). *Systems thinking, systems practice.* Wiley.

Checkland, P. (1999). Systems thinking. In *Rethinking management information systems: An interdisciplinary perspective* (p. 528). Oxford University Press.

Chen, D., Doumeingts, G., & Vernadat, F. (2008). Architectures for enterprise integration and interoperability: Past, present and future. *Computers in Industry, 59*(7), 647–659.

Cordeiro De Paula, F., & Pereira Dos Santos, R. (2019). Systems thinking as a resource for supporting accountability in system-of-information-systems: Exploring a Brazilian school case. In *Proceedings - 2019 IEEE/ACM 7th International Workshop on Software Engineering for Systems-of-Systems and 13th Workshop on Distributed Software Development, Software Ecosystems and Systems-of-Systems, SESoS-WDES 2019* (pp. 42–49). https://doi.org/10.1109/SESOS/WDES.2019.00014

Couper, I., Jaques, K., Reid, A., & Harris, P. (2023). Placemaking and infrastructure through the lens of levelling up for health equity: A scoping review. *Health & Place, 80*, 102975. https://doi.org/10.1016/J.HEALTHPLACE.2023.102975

Courage, C. (2020). Introduction: What really matters: Moving placemaking into a new epoch. In C. Courage, T. Borrup, M. R. Jackson, K. Legge (Eds.), *The Routledge handbook of placemaking* (pp. 1–8). https://doi.org/10.4324/9780429270482-1

Dai, G., De Vries, J., Dai, G., & De Vries, J. (2017). Place making in Shanghai Hongqiao business district: An institutional capacity perspective. *Urban Policy and Research, 36*(1), 97–113. https://doi.org/10.1080/08111146.2017.1294536

Davenport, T. H. (1998). Putting the enterprise into the enterprise system. *Harvard Business Review, 76*(4), 121–131.

Davenport, T. H., Harris, J. G., & Cantrell, S. (2004). Enterprise systems and ongoing process change. *Business Process Management Journal, 10*(1), 16–26.

Davidson, K. M., & Venning, J. (2011). Sustainability decision-making frameworks and the application of systems thinking: An urban context. *Local Environment, 16*(3), 213–228. https://doi.org/10.1080/13549839.2011.565464

Deming, W. E. (2000). *Out of the crisis.* MIT Press.
Emery, F. E. (1969). *Systems thinking: Selected readings.* Penguin.
Freeman, G., Liu, S.-Y., Bardzell, J., Lu, X., Bardzell, S., & Cao, D. (2019). Smart and fermented cities: An approach to placemaking in urban informatics. In *Proceedings of the 2019 CHI Conference on Human Factors in Computing Systems* (p. 13). https://doi.org/10.1145/3290605
Ghavampour, E., & Vale, B. (2019). Revisiting the "Model of place": A comparative study of placemaking and sustainability. *Urban Planning, 4*(2), 196–206. https://doi.org/10.17645/UP.V4I2.2015
Grabot, B., Mayère, A., & Bazet, I. (2008). *ERP systems and organisational change: A socio-technical insight* (1st ed.). Springer.
Grover, V., Jeong, S. R., Kettinger, W. J., & Teng, J. T. C. (1995). The implementation of business process reengineering. *Journal of Management Information Systems, 12*(1), 109–144.
Henshaw, J. L. (2019). Systems thinking for systems making: Joining systems of thought and action. *Systemic Practice and Action Research, 32*(1), 63–91. https://doi.org/10.1007/S11213-018-9450-2/FIGURES/10
Javidroozi, V., Carter, C., Grace, M., & Shah, H. (2023). Smart, sustainable, green cities: A state-of-the-art review. *Sustainability, 15*(6), 5353. https://doi.org/10.3390/SU15065353
Javidroozi, V., Shah, H., Amini, A., & Cole, A. (2014). Smart city as an integrated enterprise: A business process centric framework addressing challenges in systems integration. In L. Patrono (Ed.), *3rd International Conference on Smart Systems, Devices and Technologies* (pp. 55–59). International Academy, Research, and Industry Association (IARIA). https://doi.org/10.13140/RG.2.1.2561.1921
Javidroozi, V., Shah, H., Cole, A., & Amini, A. (2015). Towards a city's systems integration model for smart city development: A conceptualization. In H. Arabnia, L. Deligiannidis, & Q.-N. Tran (Eds.), *2015 International Conference on Computational Science and Computational Intelligence (CSCI)* (pp. 312–317). IEEE Computer Society. https://doi.org/10.1109/CSCI.2015.10
Javidroozi, V., Shah, H., & Feldman, G. (2019a). Smart city development: A business process-centric conceptualisation. In G. H. Parlier, F. Liberatore, & M. Demange (Eds.), *Proceedings of the 8th International Conference on Operations Research and Enterprise Systems* (pp. 346–353). Springer.
Javidroozi, V., Shah, H., & Feldman, G. (2019b). Urban computing and smart cities: Towards changing city processes by applying enterprise systems integration practices. *IEEE Access, 7*, 108023–108034. https://doi.org/10.1109/access.2019.2933045
Kettinger, W. J., Teng, J. T. C., & Guha, S. (1997). Business process change: A study of methodologies, techniques, and tools. *MIS Quarterly, 21*(1), 55–80.
Khemri, M. Y., Melis, A., & Caputo, S. (2020). Sustaining the liveliness of public spaces in El Houma through placemaking. *The Journal of Public Space, 5*(1), 129–152. https://doi.org/10.32891/JPS.V5I1.1254
Laszlo, A., & Krippner, S. (1998). Systems theories: Their origins, foundations, and development. *Advances in Psychology, 126*, 47–74.
Lew, A. A. (2017). Tourism planning and place making: Place-making or placemaking? *Tourism Geographies, 19*(3), 448–466. https://doi.org/10.1080/14616688.2017.1282007
Liu, P., & Peng, Z. (2013). Smart cities in China. *Computer, 47*, 72–81.

Machol, R. E. (1965). *System engineering handbook*. McGraw-Hill.
Marciniak, K. & Owoc, M. L. (2013). Usability of knowledge grid in smart city concepts. In S. Hammoudi, L. Maciaszek, J. Cordeiro & J. Dietz (Eds.), *15th International Conference on Enterprise Information Systems* (pp. 341–346). SCITEPRESS (Science and Technology Publications, Lda).
Medina-Borja, A. (2015). Editorial column—Smart Things as service providers: A call for convergence of disciplines to build a research agenda for the service systems of the future. *Service Science*, 7(1).
Mingers, J., & White, L. (2010). A review of the recent contribution of systems thinking to operational research and management science. *European Journal of Operational Research*, 207(3), 1147–1161. https://doi.org/10.1016/j.ejor.2009.12.019
Pahl-Wostl, C. (2002). Towards sustainability in the water sector – The importance of human actors and processes of social learning. *Aquatic Sciences*, 64(4), 394–411. https://doi.org/10.1007/PL00012594
Ramamoorthy, C. V., Chandra, C., Kim, H. G., Shim, Y. C., & Vij, V. (1992). Systems integration: Problems and approaches. In P. A. Ng (Ed.), *Proceedings of the Second International Conference on Systems Integration* (pp. 522–529). IEEE Comput. Soc. Press. https://doi.org/10.1109/ICSI.1992.217311
Sanaeipoor, S., & Emami, K. H. (2020). Smart city: Exploring the role of augmented reality in placemaking. In *Proceeding of 4th International Conference on Smart Cities, Internet of Things and Applications, SCIoT 2020* (pp. 91–98). https://doi.org/10.1109/SCIOT50840.2020.9250204
Seddon, J. (2008). *Systems thinking in the public sector: The failure of the reform regime... and a manifesto for a better way*. Triarchy Press Limited.
Setiawansyah, S., Parjito, P., Megawaty, D. A., Nuralia, N., & Rahmanto, Y. (2021). Implementation of the framework for the application of system thinking for school financial information systems. *Tech-E*, 5(1), 1–10. https://doi.org/10.31253/TE.V5I1.619
Singleton, W. T. (1974). *Man-machine systems*. Penguin.
Stichweh, R. (2011). Systems theory. In B. Badie, D. Berg-Schlosser, & L. Morlino (Eds.), *International encyclopedia of political science* (pp. 2579–2588). SAGE Publications Ltd.
Toolis, E. E. (2017). Theorizing critical placemaking as a tool for reclaiming public space. *American Journal of Community Psychology*, 59(1–2), 184–199. https://doi.org/10.1002/AJCP.12118
Townsend, A. M. (2013). *Smart cities: Big data, civic hackers, and the quest for a new utopia*. Norton, New York.

Chapter 6

Placemaking and Sustainability: Moving from Rhetoric to Transformative Sustainability Policies, Mindsets, and Actions

Claudia E. Carter

Birmingham City University, UK

Abstract

Sustainability features in the national and local policies of many countries, but there is often a lack of clarity about what it means in practice. Interpretations of sustainable development (or sustainable cities and places) vary widely between different countries and social, economic, political, and environmental actors and interest groups influenced by underlying values and specific contexts. Considering the already-felt impacts of rapid climate change and ecological breakdown, continuing with business as usual will add more pollution, resource depletion, and lead to economic and societal turmoil under a massive shift or collapse in ecological and climate systems. A significant factor in past and current policy failures is that "weak" rather than "strong" sustainability models have been adopted laced with a voter-enticing rhetoric yet delaying painful (to the current status quo), but essential, changes in production and consumption and a shift in focus away from profit toward human and ecological well-being. This requires clear and ambitious legal, regulatory, and policy frameworks, yet also flexible approaches and "agency" of citizens, employees, employers, and politicians for transformation across different geographical and institutional levels, moving away from competition and greed, making room for experimentation and creativity and old and new forms of collaboration and sharing. Relevant concepts, principles, examples and critiques can be gleaned from the ecological economic, social–ecological transformation, and planning literature, offering direction for the kinds of shifts in placemaking to achieve social and environmental justice and well-being.

Keywords: Greenwashing; weak sustainability; strong sustainability; sustainability indicators; placemaking; transformative practices; social–ecological systems; collaborative approaches; sufficiency; quality of life

The Push for Sustainability

This chapter focuses on examining what different interpretations of becoming sustainable means for informing policies and actions relating to placemaking. Enabling sustainable development, and adopting sustainability as the focus for policy- and decision-making, requires clarity of rationale and underlying principles as well as some understanding of the origin and spectrum of interpretations and representations of the concepts.

In the late-20th century, many countries committed to "sustainable development" after the publication of *Our common future* (World Commission on Environment and Development (WCED), 1987), also called "the Brundtland Report," which advocated intergenerational equity. The 1992 United Nations (UN) Conference on Environment and Development held in Rio added influential conventions on climate change and biodiversity spurring new policies and actions. Other outputs included "Agenda 21" (United Nations Conference on Environment and Development, 1992), which was adopted by 178 governments across the world, aiming to achieve sustainable development by 2000. Its Chapter 28 focuses on "Local Agenda 21," recognizing that many problems and solutions are rooted in local activities and the role of local governments in devising, supporting, or overseeing economic, social, and environmental policies and actions, thus being directly relevant to strategic and local planning and efforts in placemaking.

The concept of "sustainability" also emerged in academic and policy circles around that time, introduced by the International Union for Conservation of Nature (IUCN) in 1969 and discussed by the UN conference in Stockholm in 1972 (Adams, 2006). Among the several hundred definitions of "sustainability" and "sustainable development" that have emerged since (Dobson, 1996; Johnston et al., 2007), the definition from the Brundtland Report, stating that sustainable development "meets the needs of the present without compromising the ability of future generations to meet their own needs" (WCED, 1987, p. 8), is one of the most frequently used or adapted. This is so general that it is not particularly helpful other than emphasizing attention on human needs (rather than wants) now and into the long term. However, looking beyond the generic definition, four principles were highlighted by Davies (2013, p. 112) as embedded in this influential WCED publication which have direct relevance for good spatial planning and creating sustainable places: (1) holistic planning and strategy making, (2) preservation of ecological processes, (3) protection of heritage and biodiversity and (4) development that can be sustained for future years. These signal an emphasis on holistic or integrated approaches and natural systems dependency – and therefore the need to maintain and pay attention to these.

Regarding the urban placemaking context, the 10 Melbourne Principles for Sustainable Cities developed in April 2002 (United Nations Environment

Program (UNEP) and International Environmental Technology Centre (IETC), 2002) were endorsed by local governments at the Johannesburg Earth Summit in June 2002. These principles "have become the touchstone for the urban sustainability movement" (Campbell, Bouman, et al., 2023, p. 4) providing specific guidance to towns and cities for their sustainability trajectory. Each principle is elaborated with a few paragraphs to help explain the rationale, actions, and desired outcomes (see Table 6.1 for an overview of the focus and principles).

Table 6.1. The 10 Melbourne Principles for Sustainable Cities.

Focus	No.	Principle
Vision	1	Provide a long-term vision for cities based on sustainability; intergenerational, social, economic, and political equity and their individuality.
Economy and society	2	Achieve long-term economic and social security.
Biodiversity	3	Recognize the intrinsic value of biodiversity and natural ecosystems and protect and restore them.
Ecological footprint	4	Enable communities to minimize their ecological footprint.
Model cities on ecosystems	5	Build on the characteristics of ecosystems in the development and nurturing of healthy and sustainable cities.
Sense of place	6	Recognize and build on the distinctive characteristics of cities, including their human and cultural values, history, and natural systems.
Empowerment	7	Empower people and foster participation.
Partnership	8	Expand and enable cooperative networks to work toward a common, sustainable future.
Sustainable production and consumption	9	Promote sustainable production and consumption, through appropriate use of environmentally sound technologies and effective demand management.
Governance and hope	10	Enable continual improvement, based on accountability, transparency, and good governance.

Source: Newman and Jennings (2008, Table 0.1, p. 4); United Nations Environment Program (UNEP) and International Environmental Technology Centre (IETC) (2002).

While both sustainability and sustainable development continue to be widely used and familiar terms, their meaning is still ambiguous and their interpretations certainly wide-ranging. Differences in interpretation of what sustainable development means largely relate to the underlying worldview, associated economic, social–ecological paradigms, and associated ethical perspectives (Barr, 2008; Davies, 2013). Attention to these differences is the focus of this chapter, highlighting how they affect policies, decisions, and actions.

Are (We Making) Countries and Places Sustainable?

The looseness in definition of what sustainable development means is seen as a significant reason for its ineffectiveness in driving change at the scale required (Ghavampour & Vale, 2019), whether that is in local placemaking or national and international endeavors. Globally, the 17 UN Sustainable Development Goals (SDGs; UN, 2015) have gained traction, and, nationally and locally, these are often used alongside governmental policies and commitments arising from international efforts and negotiations such as the Paris Agreement and the Convention on Biological Diversity, among others. Based on research and trends worldwide, it is apparent that, to date, no developed and few developing nations can prove that they are being sustainable or even on a sustainable pathway (e.g., UN, 2023; Voulvoulis et al., 2022). In fact, the opposite has been observed. Signs of this include a persisting strong push for global economic growth with rising production and consumption, as well as recreational behaviors that are largely reliant on fossil fuels. This economic growth policy and decision-making mantra also has led to the continued exploitation and decline of natural resources (e.g., Brondizio et al., 2019; Pörtner et al., 2022, especially chapter 8) and destruction, degradation or threat to the livelihoods of low-impact societies under the banner of "progress." It has also increased local to global thermal, physical, and chemical pollution of fresh and saline waters, air, and soil (see, for example, Almond et al., 2022).

Around 55% of the world's population currently lives in cities, and substantial urban growth is forecast to continue. While cities cover around 2%–3% of land surface across the globe and contribute around 80% of gross domestic product (GDP), they consume 60%–80% of the world's primary energy and 75% of natural resources (Clement et al., 2023; World Economic Forum (WEF), 2021). On the energy/carbon front alone, huge efficiencies and reductions are thus required by the construction, housing, power generation, and transport sectors, as well as in advancing and supporting energy efficiency (retrofit) measures. The environmental footprint of cities is large, especially when accounting for their consumption needs that extend well beyond their city boundaries (see, for example, the case study of Brussels, Belgium, in Athanassiadis et al., 2018). Even cities marketing themselves as being sustainable tend to be so only in parts, such as Copenhagen in Denmark, Vancouver, Toronto and Montreal in Canada, or Melbourne in Australia, which have put sustainability at the top of their policy agendas and boast many public and private sector sustainability schemes to reduce waste, improve infrastructure efficiency and resilience, extending and improving greenspaces and urban woodland, creating attractive civic spaces and safe active travel routes. However, ultimately, even those cities and other urban areas still consume more than is produced, and currently, they are neither carbon neutral (one aspect of becoming sustainable) nor ecologically, socially, or economically sustainable in the long term (Shmelev & Shmeleva, 2018; Zhang et al., 2018). However, these urban transformative efforts still serve as examples of attempts to make places sustainable in terms of their physical provisions such as green, blue, and gray infrastructure (transport, energy, water, nature-rich habitats, digital, etc.), public spaces and (mixed-use) developments; but also in terms of their social–cultural and socioeconomic justice goals and inclusivity efforts in shaping urban planning and placemaking.

Sustainability is often interpreted as the goal of sustainable development, although some disagree with this simplistic explanation and point to the different origins and associated worldviews of these concepts. Hector et al. (2014), for example, argue that the concept of sustainability was influenced by philosophical thinking and values of the eighteenth-century Romantic Movement which saw Nature as more than providing useful services and materials for humans. Nature carries a sacral, or beyond human, significance which in policy- and decision-making leads to provisions and actions of environmental protection. Sustainable development, on the other hand, has its origin in conservationism, with humans standing above Nature and managing it according to human needs. This distinction thus places the attention on underlying beliefs values, and moral interests of individuals, groups, and societies.

What Kind of Sustainable Development?

This section focuses on the kind of values and principles that inform different interpretations of what "sustainable" placemaking means. It represents, explains, and critiques existing commonly found ways of conceptualizing sustainable development and highlights the differences for policy- and decision-making between weak and strong interpretations. The following sections then provide further explanation of what sustainable placemaking could or should look like and specific examples to illustrate different interpretations in informing and shaping local planning and placemaking in practice.

Common Representations of Sustainability and Sustainable Development

Representations of sustainable development, as captured in Fig. 6.1, include the widely used Venn diagram representing environmental, social, and economic interests (Fig. 6.1a) with alternative labels used, such as People–Planet–Profit or Prosperity, and in the middle where they all intersect signaling the locus of sustainability; this is sometimes also referred to as the triple bottom line. The three-legged chair or three pillars to a building are variations of this where the three legs or pillars of sustainability need to be balanced to reach sustainability (represented by the seat and the roof, respectively). Especially in applications for urban and historic environments, the

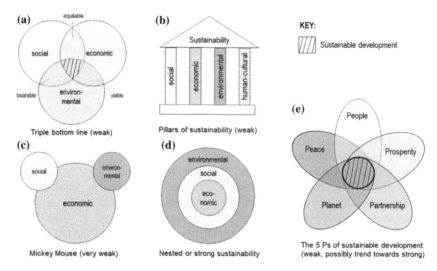

Fig. 6.1. Commonly Used Generic Representations of Various Weak and Strong Sustainability. *Source:* Drawn by Claudia Carter based on publicly available images.

three pillars may extend to include a fourth, human-cultural, pillar (Fig. 6.1b). A further expansion of this is the 5P version which, in addition to People, Planet, and Prosperity, also includes Partnership and Peace. This model draws on the UN SDGs, and specifically the preamble of its formal launch document *Transforming our world: The 2030 agenda for sustainable development* (UN, 2015) which explains the 5 Ps; Fig. 6.1e is based on a 5Ps diagram made popular by Wayne Visser in the same year (waynevisser, 2015). Economic-centric presentations include the so-called Mickey Mouse version as illustrated in Fig. 6.1c; here, the economic realm is central and largest, and social and environmental aspects are represented as the "ears," both being significantly smaller in focus compared to the large economic "face" with little or no space for integration (no or small intersections between the three parts).

A different iteration of representing sustainable development, and in fact sustainability, as shown in Fig. 6.1d, uses a nested hierarchy. Here, the environment provides the base and must be protected and maintained for society to flourish and economic systems to operate. This nested structure signals strong sustainability, whereas the other representations all symbolize weak sustainability as explained in more detail next.

Weak and Strong Sustainability

As illustrated in Fig. 6.1, a key distinction can be made between weak and strong sustainability, some also including very weak and very strong categories (see Table 6.2). To fully appreciate the differences between them, one needs to understand the different underlying values and theories.

Table 6.2. Characterizing Different Forms (or Stages) of Sustainable Development.

Stages and Transformation	Policy	Economy	Society	Environment	Discourse
Very weak sustainability	Lip service to policy integration; no or vague delivery targets	Neoliberal economic tools to support economic growth; minor adjustments	Superficially aware; little media coverage	Biodiversity loss, habitat losses; product-oriented management	Polarized debate; superficial consultations; rhetoric
Weak sustainability	Some policy integration and delivery targets	Market-based tools; microeconomic incentives; niche markets; recycling; innovation	Sustainability project opportunities and education	Biodiversity loss; habitat fragmentation; targeted (un-coordinated) efforts	Parliamentary surveillance; voice through stakeholder groups; intentions
Strong sustainability	Binding policy integration; strong international agreements	Green accounts alongside national accounts; full costing; partnership approaches	Curriculum integration; local initiatives; collaborative efforts; innovation	Net balance of natural capital; catchment/habitat targets and management plans	Parliamentary accountability; community actions; "glocal" information and debates
Very strong sustainability	International commitments and targets; duty of care; precautionary; statutory and cultural support	Formal and effective adoption of sustainability accounting, reduce, reuse, and repair	Sustainability literate and skilled; plurality and diversity of projects and communities	Ecological recovery; integrated management practices; long-term goals and support	Community-led or supported initiatives become the norm; ethics and values made explicit

(Continued)

Placemaking and Sustainability 97

Table 6.2. (Continued)

Stages and Transformation	Policy	Economy	Society	Environment	Discourse
Holistic transformation	Strong local to global commitment with monitoring and accountability; multi-scalar; proactive	Focus on social–ecological well-being, sharing and repairing; sufficiency; within planetary boundaries	Embedded sustainability literacy and skills; beyond-human communitarian	Regenerative management; some rewilding; connected and long-term planning and actions	Human and ecological well-being supported by economy; shared responsibility

Source: Claudia Carter, inspired by, and partially based on, Carter (2001, Table 8.1, p. 201) who acknowledges O'Riordan (1996).

Weak sustainability is grounded in neoclassical economic theory of capital, postulating that the total capital (whether that is social, economic, or environmental) needs to stay constant or at least nondeclining; it thus assumes that all parts are commensurate. Under this paradigm, human-made capital (such as wealth created through technological innovation or urban development) can substitute natural capital. Berkes and Folke (1992, p. 2) explain that natural capital is a collective term for (1) nonrenewable/exhaustible resources (such as fossil fuels), (2) renewable resources (such as food crops, fish, wood), and (3) regulating ecosystem services functions (such as the hydrological and soil cycles). In reality, there is no such clear demarcation between natural or human because the geo-hydro-ecological and human systems and processes are intrinsically intertwined. However, while Nature can survive without humans, humans cannot survive without Nature (or, as expressed in economic terminology, without natural capital from which ecosystem services are derived). In weak sustainability, the decline of exhaustible resources can be compensated with human-made alternatives. Weak sustainability protagonists typically put money and faith into science and technology to develop technical fixes, push for economic growth, and accommodate (but not prioritize) environmental issues within development decisions (Carrosio, 2024). A utilitarian stance is evident in which Nature is being commodified and marketed to produce profit and happiness; any negative impacts are labeled "externalities" that could be internalized with appropriate policies or regulations (Gómez-Baggethun & Muradian, 2015).

Strong sustainability, on the other hand, recognizes incommensurability (O'Neill, 2017). A strongly sustainable stance prioritizes attention to environmental objectives with a clear awareness of environmental functions and limits when advancing economic and social development. Using commonly found economic-influenced thinking and terminology, strong sustainability requires that natural capital is kept constant or nondeclining, over time. According to Barr (2008), natural capital includes three dimensions: critical, constant, and tradeable natural capital. Critical natural capital is vital to life, such as the composition of the atmosphere and ozone layer; constant natural capital is important but not essential and means that while the overall stock of natural capital should remain constant over time, changes in composition through substitution is possible (e.g., a park instead of an area of woodland); tradable capital indicates a low value and hence can be replaced (e.g., natural capital that is very common, of low quality, and in a location where other land cover and land use is desirable). Valued capital is a further category which includes, for example, rare species (Davies, 2013). Strong sustainability poses definitive limits on consumption of natural resources and aims to halt and reverse ecological degradation, such as the loss of species and biodiversity or the undermining of integrity of natural (water, climatic, and air) cycles. Nature, or natural capital, is seen as key to a good life and any deterioration or loss in habitats and species as potentially irreversible. Attention to the environmental and ecological integrity of both local and global systems is important. Thus, the Earth is understood as a complex system with thresholds and finite elements and a system that is nearing several tipping points due to massive land-use changes that have caused irreversible global warming and pollution (Lenton et al., 2023; Trisos et al., 2020). Development goals under a strong sustainability paradigm focus on human and environmental well-being and explore degrowth as a new political–economic paradigm (Buch-Hansen & Nesterova, 2023; Kallis, 2018; Latouche, 2009). The strong sustainability perspective is sometimes labeled as spiritual or eco-centric, whereas weak sustainability as anthropocentric.

Defined with reference to economic theory, weak sustainability is grounded in neoclassical theory of capital accumulation and economic growth, whereas strong sustainability adopts a steady-state paradigm anchored in the laws of thermodynamics and biophysical principles (see Hediger, 2006). Thus, different visions and interests exist as to what, or what kinds of capital, should be sustained. As the different theoretical foundations imply, it would be naïve to conceive of sustainable and weak sustainability as a simple continuum; their ideologies, reasoning, and associated policies and actions are only in parts progressive and, in several ways, substantially different, as is outlined in Table 6.2. Even so, some authors have tried to create bridges and attempted to argue that economic growth and environmental protection, or sustainability more generally, do not have to be mutually exclusive (Hediger, 2006) or that these two paradigms are, in fact, reconcilable, and a middle ground would be the most probable hope for a trajectory toward sustainability (e.g., Davies, 2013). Others are less convinced, based on recent efforts to halt or reverse climate and ecological crises but which are falling a long way short (see, for example, Bonnedahl & Heikkurinen, 2018).

Discourses, Investments, and Mindsets

Recent decades have seen fast-paced progress and innovation and associated (often neoliberal thinking infused) educational models, enabling for many citizens a lifestyle of convenience. These developments are generally viewed as superior to what we had before. Associated dominant political discourses, public distractedness, and wishful siloed thinking are, therefore, not easily challenged or changed, despite some contrary evidence of long-term detrimental impacts on political stability, human well-being, the environment, and the global economy (Bihouix, 2020). Neoclassical economic assumptions and narrow analysis of costs and benefits have become mainstream and misled policy- and decision-makers in underestimating the severity of environmental (and social) negative impacts of economic growth, as Keen (2022), for example, argues and illustrates in relation to climate change economics.

While a change in political–economic orientation, mindset, and processes that are anchored in strong rather than weak sustainability has been advocated, it is certainly not visible or on the horizon for most countries (Buch-Hansen & Nesterova, 2023; Carter, 2024; Hickel, 2019; Spash, 2024; Spash & Smith, 2019). Societies that show strongly sustainable characteristics are largely indigenous or traditional societies with cultures or policies aligned to ecological/natural cycles and culturally embedded moral–ethical principles of respect and care for others. Chet A. Bowers, for example, was a strong advocate within the education sector who highlighted such cultures as worthy of learning from and emulating (e.g., Bowers, 1993, 2001). This in some ways runs counter to the strong influence by Freire (1970) in educational contexts with the move away from traditional educational systems and an emphasis on liberation and freeing oneself from cultural shackles. Communities and societies foregoing technological development and global information platforms are commonly seen to be in need of educating and development support (see, for example, the role of and dilemmas encountered by anthropologists working in developing countries: Lewis, 2005). Any project proposals or person advocating low/traditional-tech or no-tech solutions may receive labels such as primitive, outdated, backward, Neo-Luddite, or nostalgic because the world has moved on. Such a perspective highlights the liberating aspects of modernization and the assumptions that technological progress is implicitly equated with social progress, and that economic growth is synonymous with progress (Schmelzer, 2023).

A current example is the investment and drive, politically and economically, to provide "smart" digital and increasingly now also artificial intelligence (AI) solutions for almost any societal challenge and some fundamental changes to most areas of life. Massive investment has been provided by both governments and a super-rich elite to facilitate this. However, some of these developments cause ethical concern yet largely fail to investigate and discuss those technologies' own human, social, and environmental negative impacts explicitly and transparently. These include known impacts such as environmentally damaging, unsafe and exploitative mining operations; exploitation of rare metals and materials (e.g., McKie, 2021, 2023; Penke, 2021) and high energy use where gains in efficiency improvements are quickly outweighed by more widespread demand and intensive uses (e.g., Bertics, 2024; Kettle, 2021; Williams et al., 2022, chapter 4). They also include many unknown impacts especially considering rapid AI development and the push for ever-faster and pervasive digital connectivity, such as 5G which uses higher waveband frequencies. Computer processing and cloud-based storage systems also need cooling and maintaining. Furthermore, installations, hardware, and software need frequent upgrading to accommodate innovation but also due to their vulnerability to public and private security risks and disruptions (International Energy Agency, 2017), resulting in a race for ever-faster changes to protect against potential misuses of digital systems and data, as well as to stay competitive in the market. These factors drive up waste generation and the costs of digital solutions; they also highlight the limited or failing resilience of these services and infrastructures. A sustainable approach would be to transparently scope alternatives (including low and no-tech known methods; Bihouix, 2020) and apply integrated digital approaches to placemaking and planning where they offer reductions in cost and materials/energy and improve socially just outcomes (see Chapter 5).

Increasing the Focus on Social Sustainability

Interestingly, the distinction between weak and strong sustainability has largely been based on distinguishing between a primary concern for economic development and a primary concern for the preservation of the environment and ecological recovery. While the economy is anthropocentric and social welfare gain assumed, issues surrounding the distribution of the economic system's benefits and disbenefits, access to nature and infrastructure, distribution and enjoyment of environmental quality, equity and other social sustainability related concerns generally seem to receive less explicit attention in those debates (see Chapter 8). According to Atalay and Gülersoy (2023), a significant reason for current urban problems is this comparative neglect of social sustainability in urban areas and interventions. They argue that "social sustainability is still largely unexplored and undertheorized" (Atalay & Gülersoy, 2023, p. 19). To them, a holistic approach to measuring and evaluating social sustainability through qualitative and quantitative indicators relates to the following top 10 criteria:

(1) *population* (balanced distribution, poverty prevention, and employment);
(2) *accessibility* to social and blue-green-gray infrastructure and services;
(3) *education* and *skills*;
(4) physical and mental *health*;
(5) adequate and affordable *housing*;
(6) *security* in public spaces and private areas;
(7) social and spatial *belonging*;
(8) *participation* in policy- and decision-making and projects/actions;
(9) *social capital* and *social cohesion* (while ensuring cultural diversity and integration); and
(10) *urban life quality satisfaction* and *adequacy of services* (sufficient, fair, and balanced).

Social sustainability includes a strong focus on participation in decision-making (see criterion 8) and access or opportunities to meeting fundamental physical, psychological, social–cultural, and economic needs (criteria 1–7, 9–10). Voice and agency in urban planning and placemaking is widely recognized as a key ingredient (e.g., Healey, 1997, 2010) and advocated by some as a fundamental right (see Chapters 8 and 9 discussing the "right to the city"). Some disagreement and conflicting interests are a given, but through dialogue and inclusive planning, a more holistic approach is possible and meaningful projects and plans appropriate for the specific context(s) can be cocreated to benefit the many (humans and beyond human) in the longer term and not just a privileged few (Healey, 2010). In a nutshell, social (and environmental and economic) sustainability requires planning *with*, not just *for*, people.

While advocating that more attention to researching and improving social sustainability should not lead to neglecting any of the other interacting and important principles, goals, and factors of sustainable development overall (see Fig. 6.2), Campbell, Bouman, et al. (2023) provide evidence that social infrastructure needs attention first to enable the success of green infrastructure. In this vein, neglecting social sustainability may in fact undermine ecological and economic well-being, and hence, attention to social sustainability in urban

Placemaking and Sustainability 103

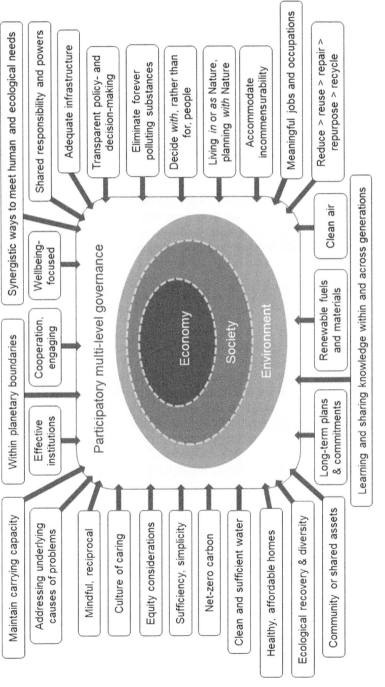

Fig. 6.2. Principles and Goals for (Strong) Sustainable Development Which Seek to Create and Maintain Healthy Economies and Societies Both of Which Are Intricately Linked With and Reliant on the Environment With Its Ecosystems.
Source: Claudia Carter.

placemaking may be a necessary starting point from which agency to aid ecological recovery and economic benefits can be catalyzed.

Sustainable Placemaking

Sustainable placemaking draws together theory and thinking from both sustainability and placemaking: it has received some explicit attention and provides useful principles and suggestions for its visioning and collaborative translation into practice (Goosen & Cilliers, 2020; Healey, 2010). Prevalent urban development has been characterized as being centered on profit-driven consumption and dependence on substantial investment in real estate and technology akin to weak sustainability, which caters for and favors affluent sections of society, rather than creating high quality-of-life urban designs which serve the wider socioeconomic diverse population (Nassar, 2013). However, alternative urban development and planning models are evident and perceived to be more holistic and environmental- and social-justice orientated. Fig. 6.2 captures goals and principles that are typical across strong sustainable development and placemaking, most of which are mentioned or discussed above and below to provide more explanation and reasoning.

Lively Planning

According to the Lively Planning perspective, an integrated approach to address complex urban realities is necessary (Cilliers et al., 2014). Whether focusing on public spaces or placemaking more generally, attention needs to focus on "creating versatile, diverse and integrative functions, elements and linkages" to attract people and activities and create unique places (Goosen & Cilliers, 2020, p. 848). These considerations can then link or lead to research and marketing (researching community needs for quality of space) to elicit functional (practical and useful), environmental (green designs, nature-based solutions), social (interaction opportunities), visual and aesthetic (appealing), movement (pedestrian flow), compatibility (layout in context), and psychological (mental and emotional) dimensions of placemaking (Goosen & Cilliers, 2020, Table 6.3).

Ahirrao and Khan (2021) developed an analytical framework of the Lively Planning Integrative Perspective (LPIP) to critically examine planned and spontaneous, active and passive uses of public open spaces (POS) at the city, neighborhood, and site scales. They included seven aspects – green planning intervention, livability, new urbanism, placemaking, public realm, successful spaces, and sustainability – and these seven aspects are further split into 16 variables and 39 items in their LPIP index to evaluate two POS in the form of urban parks in the city of Nagpur, India. Their developing country case study identified strengths and weaknesses of POS provision at the three scales (city, neighborhood, and site) and provided scale-related recommendations to enable existing and new POS to be "more inclusive, meaningful, functional and aesthetically appealing to a wide range of users" (Ahirrao & Khan, 2021, p. 5253).

The results for this case study showed that, depending on the chosen scale, different aspects of the lively planning integrated approach were important and performing well. This zooming in and out for their evaluation of existing POS then led to specific meaningful recommendations for different actors and stakeholders.

Green Urbanism

As part of sustainable cities, a focus on Green Urbanism emerged as an important approach in the built environment which emphasizes connectivity and interconnectedness (see Chapter 4). According to Beatley (2000), green cities are centered upon urban and environmental sustainability, living within ecological limits, nature-based or inspired solutions, local and regional self-sufficiency (food, energy, and economy), and healthy lifestyles facilitated as part of highly livable neighborhoods. Their urban design and planning characteristics include the integration of multifunctional environmental elements of vegetation and habitats at multiple scales (human, neighborhood, urban, and city region) emphasizing diversity, sustainability, and adaptability, requiring inter- and transdisciplinary working for its design and implementation (Goosen & Cilliers, 2020, pp. 848–852). "Green" is also sometimes interpreted as a synonym for net-zero-carbon designs and moving toward zero-waste living (e.g., Nassar, 2013), but this seems a rather narrow and partial interpretation. Increasingly, green, sustainable, and smart are considered in combination, highlighting the need for a more holistic lens in city planning when framing primary and wider challenges and pursuing integrated approaches to developing responses and solutions (see Javidroozi et al., 2023 for a state-of-the-art literature review on this).

Examples of Weak and Strong Placemaking

To illustrate what strong versus weak sustainability may look like in placemaking, this is approached first in a generic way (Table 6.3) and then by using two case studies: one at a regional level, being an area of largely countryside with small towns but situated within easy reach of large conurbations, and the other at the urban neighborhood level. Table 6.3 presents a selection of commonly found suggestions for urban improvements toward becoming sustainable, derived from the author's reading, contact with practitioners, teaching, and reflective practice. The examples help illustrate that the move from weak to strong sustainability requires a holistic framing and diverse perspectives. Probing into actual, intended, and unintended connections and connectivity across scales, sectors, and different individuals and communities is an important part of policy- and decision-making. Strong sustainability builds on critical awareness of self and culture(s) with an outlook toward achieving societal and beyond-human well-being.

Plural approaches and diversity (within and across social, economic, and environmental interests and realms) are a given and necessary to strengthen resilience and adaptability, and with these come potential conflict and the need for

Table 6.3. Characterizing Typical Urban Sustainability Elements and Goals From a Weak and Strong Sustainability Perspective.

Specific Elements	Weak Sustainability	Strong Sustainability
Green infrastructure	Approached as beneficial site-specific additions to fulfill specific needs (e.g., playing field, (pocket) parks, burial grounds, adventure/nature playgrounds)	Approached as networks of connected linear and areal habitats with different levels of management (from rewilding to targeted biodiversity gains and climate change adaptation measures); quality, size and multifunctionality are explicitly considered and inform the design and maintenance (e.g., for biodiversity, food-growing, recreation, active transport, mental health, climate change mitigation and adaptation)
Sustainable Urban Drainage systems (SUDs)	Designed for the relevant local capacity to reduce and mitigate flood risk	Designed with multifunctional benefits in line with local needs and opportunities to mitigate flood risk, increase biodiversity, provide recreational space and/or aesthetic pleasure
Digitalization	Competitive approach (that quickly makes products and services obsolete)	Targeted to where no low-tech alternatives exist, able to reduce energy and resource use, and encourage or improve sustainable behaviors; designed to be lasting and locally maintained

Goals	Weak Sustainability	Strong Sustainability
Access to amenities and essential services	Largely market-driven and planned by experts; some community-based initiatives	Proactive planning and provision for any new developments and collaborative planning for areas of regeneration and renewal; mixture of commercial, shared, gifted, etc.,

Placemaking and Sustainability 107

Clean, affordable, accessible public transport	Renewal of fleet to lower emission technologies; active travel provision	social–economic models; experimentation; cater for local needs Reducing the need to travel/access services; priority given to active travel road or shared space users; joined up local low-carbon travel provision and connectivity across scales (local, regional, national, and international); locally publicly subsidized fares for all; free fare for young, elderly, and unemployed
Affordable, healthy housing	Below market price housing offers and low-interest loans	Adaptable living spaces; local and sustainably sourced materials; well insulated and easy to ventilate buildings with natural light; range of tenures and co-living/housing options; provision of diverse, functional and attractive communal indoor and outdoor spaces; appliances/tools swap and loan facilities
Energy conservation	Efficient engineering and digital technologies; switch from high to low/no carbon and renewable fuels	Focus on reduction of need for energy use, then energy efficiency, greener energy sources, shorter supply distances; improving renewable energy generation and storage capacity and resilience of all energy infrastructure; low-tech and heat-recovery solutions
Improving air quality	Cleaner technology for manufacturing, chemical, recycling, and transport sectors; electric private cars and local fleet vans	Lean and circular economy; less choice but better quality longer lasting energy efficient products; less need to transport and travel (fast) by air; shared electric cars and switch to active and reliable public transport for commuting and most journeys; separate/safe

(*Continued*)

Table 6.3. (Continued)

Specific Elements	Weak Sustainability	Strong Sustainability
		and green local and regional active travel network; phasing out coal power stations; reduced and high welfare quality meat production
Waste reduction	Provision and use of recycling schemes; waste to energy; composting of organic waste; processing of food waste for animal feed, etc.	Waste hierarchy prioritizes reduction of material consumption, then reuse and repair of goods and materials, then separation and recycling of waste and finally safe disposal of or energy-generation from remaining waste; phasing out single use plastics for fast/microwave food and bottled drinks; reusable bags and containers; left-over materials exchange markets
Water purification and conservation	Garden water butts; water efficient equipment and appliances; water meters	Rainwater harvesting; graywater use for nonpotable water needs; ban of forever chemicals; swales and buffers alongside busy roads and polluting agricultural, industrial and commercial activities
Soil remediation and conservation	Remove, detox, or seal polluted brownfield soils	On-site remediation and conservation practices; avoid removal, compaction and pollution; vegetative soil cover practices to reduce soil erosion
Social justice/equity	Voluntary-, public- and private-sector support structures; living wages	Commercial and community clothes/goods repair and swap shops or places; narrowing of pay gaps within and across sectors; focus on removal of barriers and addressing causes of inequality or injustice

Source: Claudia Carter.

deliberation, negotiation, and social learning (Healey, 2010). How decision- and policy-making processes are structured and operating is important for joint-up collaborative efforts to achieve worthy outcomes and meaningful outputs. In relation to 21st century complex challenges, adaptive multilevel governance with shared responsibility and accountability is widely suggested for defining sustainability trajectories, making necessary adjustments, and taking the desired actions across sectors and local to global scales (Allen et al., 2023; Buch-Hansen & Nesterova, 2023; Carter, 2024).

Example: Integrated Plan-Making and Policies With Natural Capital and Ecosystem Services at the Core

In terms of using an explicit social–ecological systems approach in their plan-making process and Local Plan, the South Downs National Park Authority (SDNPA) in South-East England provides an interesting example at the local and regional scales; this case study mainly draws on Scott et al. (2018) and SDNPA (2019) which provide more detailed information. Formed in 2011, the SDNPA is a public body and the formal planning authority for the National Park. The South Downs National Park comprises 15 local authorities across the counties of Hampshire, West Sussex, and East Sussex and has over 50 neighborhood plans. It is the United Kingdom's most populated National Park and has over 2 million people living within 5 km of its boundary. The SDNPA put "ecosystem services" (and natural capital) as one of its three core policies for its local development plan for 2014–2022, alongside "sustainable development" and "major development" (SDNPA, 2019, pp. 33–41).

The Plan draws on the National Planning Policy Framework which, in its first version of 2012, mentioned "recognising the wider benefits of ecosystem services" (Department for Communities and Local Government (DCLG), 2012) and in later versions stated "recognising the intrinsic character and beauty of the countryside, and the wider benefits from natural capital and ecosystem services – including the economic and other benefits of the best and most versatile agricultural land, and of trees and woodland" (Department for Leveling Up, Housing and Communities [DLUCH], 2021, 2023, para 174 b; Ministry of Housing, Communities and Local Government [MHCLG], 2019, para 170 b). The adopted South Downs Local Plan pays attention to ecosystem services throughout the whole plan, explaining different types and linking their benefits and relevance to economic and social, and not just environmental policies and goals within the Plan. The SDNPA thus adopted an ecosystem-approach-led way of thinking, planning, and decision-making and, as part of that journey, developed its own research and collaborative explorations to help mainstream this ecosystem-services-centric approach internally (with its board members) and externally (public-, private-, and third-sector stakeholders, residents, tourists, etc.). Contributing factors to their success included being bold in their visioning, transparent in their learning and policymaking processes, inclusive in their evidence gathering and consultations, and specific in formulating their ecosystem approach principles (Scott et al., 2018, Box 1, p. 241). Most goals and principles outlined in Fig. 6.2 are being embedded within such local and regional planning and placemaking efforts.

Example: Bottom-Up Placemaking Through Creating a Neighborhood Venue

A second example of sustainable placemaking relates to the neighborhood and street level, triggered by the uncertainties and changes around 2016 (Trump presidency; Brexit; climate change emergency; ecological emergency; rise of AI; poly-crises; rise of populism and misinformation) and the lack of community spaces for meeting and critical debate. This specific initiative, *Zwischenraum* [in-between-room], is the brainchild of a private creative and entrepreneur who used their café-bar in Hamburg to bring people together, discuss, socialize, and laugh (See Fig. 6.3) (Heine, 2019). Perceiving a need to have more ad hoc and cross-cutting encounters of different people from across the neighborhood and beyond, as well as opportunities to discuss diverse topical societal issues, led to the café-bar offering regular (weekly/monthly) discourse sessions to foster informed debate, cultural exchange, and social learning alongside cultural and culinary offers.

This beyond-profit thinking brought into focus the many different connections that can be established and made with the people living locally, visiting, or in transit, and through the host's and participants' professional and social network being able to offer relevant debate, reflection and the opportunity to make new connections in understanding and connecting with people and places. The venture uses a STEAM approach (Science, Technology, Engineering, Arts, and Mathematics: see below), making connections between art, culture, and the sciences to consider, debate, and engage with neighborhood, urban, and regional development and planning, fostering attentive listening, interdisciplinary conversations,

Weekly debates and events are held in Hamburg's Hadley's Bar, a local-and-beyond initiative to make connections and hear about and discuss with experts and community members a wide range of contemporary and often complex societal issues, including sustainability, peace and security, digitalisation, AI, amongst others. Left: A 'Morgen.Salon' (morning salon) event hosted by author Elly Oldenburg. Right: Tina Heine (left), founder and owner of Hadley's and ideator of the 'Zwischenraum'; guest speaker Prof Dr Maja Göpel (middle); Elly Oldenburg (right). Photos by Xenia Bluhm.

Fig. 6.3. Hadley's Bar, Hamburg Which Hosts the Zwischenraum Regular Debates and Events. *Source:* With kind permission from Tina Heine.

and sparking ideas and connections for action. As highlighted earlier, a greater focus on social sustainability can act as a catalyst of greater resilience and motivate to actively help shape and create strong sustainability mindsets, practices, and contexts, rather than enduring greenwash or feeling clueless or powerless.

Measures, Concepts, and Skills to Aid the Transformation to Sustainable Places, Economies, and Societies

Progressing actions to satisfy human needs, to ensure social equity and respect environmental limits, will benefit from having specific time-bound goals and indicators to help drive holistic, sustainable changes, and accountability (Holden et al., 2017). Since different sectors, structures, and processes are intricately connected and interdependent, any measures and actions will have consequences beyond their immediate or primary goal. Ideally, goals and actions should trigger so-called "win-win" situations where, for example, an environmental project also brings positive impacts for advancing social and economic health and well-being into the future. However, realistically within a pluralistic society and complex systems, there will always be winners and losers, and a benefit in one area (in its beyond-spatial meaning) may prove a disbenefit in another and affect different people in different ways.

This section first considers the UN's SDGs and choosing and using sustainability indicators. Both measures are popular and widely discussed and applied, but not without their challenges and inadequacies. Furthermore, an integrative planning approach (Quality of Life Planning) and a new guiding mantra (sufficiency) are discussed with respect to their propensity to enable and advance strong sustainability.

The UN's SDGs

The 17 SDGs have generally been accepted globally as a holistic set of goal-focused principles for organizations, governments, settlements, production, and consumption systems to become sustainable by 2030, guided by the 169 associated aspirational targets. While widely referenced and discussed in academic and policy publications, there are also inherent tensions and gaps within them that give rise to concern, especially when advancing strong sustainability.

Hickel (2019), for example, examined the crux of tensions between achieving economic growth (rather than well-being) in SDG 8, on the one hand, and protecting the planet from degradation and living harmoniously with nature (e.g., SDGs 6 and 12–15), on the other hand. Essentially, an implicit assumption is that economic growth is necessary for (sustainable) development and is instrumental in overcoming hunger and poverty (as in SDGs 1–4). Furthermore, the assumption is that economic growth can happen within the carbon budget estimated to keep the world at or below 2 degrees Celsius warming compared to preindustrial levels. Jason Hickel's analysis showed that it is, in fact, not feasible to pursue all these goals simultaneously, and achieving continued economic growth as well as achieving "two key ecological indicators" of "resource use and greenhouse gas emission" is specifically problematic (Hickel, 2019, p. 874). Essentially, the rhetoric of economic growth in harmony with earth's land, water, and air systems and capacity is greenwash rather than feasible reality, based on existing data and empirical models. SDG 8 may benefit from being reconfigured into economic well-being and flows of benefits, at least to some extent, being dematerialized.

Another critique of the SDGs, discussed by Poole (2018), arises from a gap rather than an inherent contradiction or incompatibility, namely that drivers of unsustainable land-use practices and development as well as cultural diversity are insufficiently addressed. Issues such as explicit attention to subsistence-based cultures, biocultural, and linguistic diversity are largely ignored; yet relational and intrinsic values that people and communities have with Nature are important and constitute indirect drivers for land-use decisions and management. Alexandria Poole argues that since "values underlying the sustainable management of non-human resources" (Poole, 2018, p. 57) are absent, "threats to cultural diversity and alternative forms of economies will remain a blind spot in development discourse" (p. 58). She argues that attention to biocultural heritage should form the currently missing SDG 18.

Sustainability Indicators

Identifying appropriate proxies that are meaningfully measurable, be that qualitatively or quantitatively, and for which relevant data will be cost-effective to collect, can be challenging. Such indicators may be derived from and linked to the SDGs or decided and defined through other relevant drivers such as public policies or reference points from planning theory and good practice standards or guidance. While ideally such indicators will be comprehensive, reliable, and user-friendly, limited knowledge, lack of investment in data gathering/processing, and a political vacuum or manipulation may weaken or distort their development, use, and effectiveness (Gillen & Scanlan, 2004; Healey, 1997; Lyytimäki et al., 2020). Furthermore, the range of multiple scales (microscopic to global) and potential data at disaggregate and aggregate levels can prove challenging. Data at the disaggregate level, for example, include individual provisions, sightings, events, or activities at specific locations; whereas data at the aggregate level may relate to whole neighborhoods or cities or the national census (Singleton et al., 2017). Despite most likely being imperfect, in danger of nonuse, misuse, or overuse, sustainability indicators can be beneficial if associated risks and challenges are brought into focus and, as far as possible, mitigated (Lyytimäki et al., 2020).

While a wide range of indicators are possible, existing sets of sustainability indicators and standards are largely drawing on empirical or measured data that are already compiled or easily obtainable. Like the distinction between weak and strong sustainability, the choice of indicators and their measurement depends on the normative perspective adopted (Halla & Binder, 2020) – i.e., the worldview of those influencing and deciding what is monitored and measured. Thus, choices must be made between indicators for which the necessary data already exist or are cheap to obtain versus possibly more meaningful but more expensive or complex indicators, drawing on a wide range of heterogeneous sources and ways of measuring or calculating data points and trends.

Sets of indicators can be used to help compare performance across a wide range of neighborhoods, cities, or countries (Massaro et al., 2020) and/or to highlight endemic and situational specific characteristics over a period of time in a specific location. The balance between different aspects of sustainability, and especially attention to meaningful and accurate measures of impacts and change on society as well as specific groups thereof, also needs attention. An ethical holistic perspective having in focus planet and people and their long-term prosperity is key.

Quality of Life (QoL)

QoL is an important concept for planners; and, like sustainable development, it is multifaceted and has attracted various definitions and methods when used as an indicator for human well-being within built and natural environments (Massam, 2002). It is also a concept suitable for assessments at a range of scales from the street and neighborhood level to the national and global levels. QoL indicators have comprised objective and subjective measures of well-being, such as life expectancy, infant mortality, literacy and educational levels, economic status, physical and mental health, social capital, neighborhood satisfaction, and a wide range of other factors pertaining to the social, economic, and environmental (actual and perceived) qualities experienced in a place as well as relating to self. The variety of and connections between relevant factors are potentially huge.

Planning to enhance QoL has been shaped by policy, research, and practice and gained traction over recent decades. Myers (1988) proposed an early community- and trend-based approach for QoL-focused urban planning, highlighting the need for selecting an approach and measures that are accurate, appropriate, and meaningful within a policy-driven urban development and political planning context. More recently, a group of US-based social scientists developed QoL Planning as a methodology to enable rapid assessment, reflection, and consensus-building on community priorities and actions based around community assets (Campbell, Jarrett, et al., 2023). Their proposal arose from a context of removing barriers between communities and nature conservation goals, but its steps and principles are more widely relevant and applicable. Aligned with discussions in Chapter 9, this methodology takes a rights-based approach centered on working with communities and their life-supporting and wider connections with their natural and built environment. Hence, QoL Planning is highly relevant to sustainable placemaking, taking a strong social sustainability starting point in addressing environmental conservation issues and being mindful of the linkages between people and nature (as opposed to creating hard boundaries around biodiversity and ecological conservation areas and adopting siloed approaches).

The core tenets of QoL Planning come from multiple theoretical and methodological origins emphasizing (1) collaborating with and empowering marginalized communities through an asset-based approach, (2) giving communities in planning room for self-defined well-being processes, and (3) insisting on a holistic and biocultural approach to environmental conservation (Campbell, Jarrett, et al., 2023). While not universally relevant, such a QoL-oriented planning approach appears capable of dealing with some thorny and widespread sustainability challenges in current urban and urbanization contexts of the global North and South.

Similar to other approaches, QoL Planning has key principles which are outlined in Table 6.4. These show similarities in underlying values and principles as discussed in previous sections, notably the focus on being community-centric and participative, the importance of building and maintaining trust, holistic thinking and framing, the need for adaptability and flexibility, and considering strategic aspects. The seven QoL Planning principles also provide a useful prompt sheet, and their more detailed explanations in Campbell, Jarrett, et al. (2023) offer a practical methodology for planning and placemaking. Results from 54 QoL Planning projects in Peru and the United States show that this approach helped communities to become committed to nature conservation and improve the working relationship between policy/decision-makers and communities. It also helped to institutionalize integrated approaches to sustainable development, becoming more collaborative in the design and delivery of sustainability policies and actions than was previously the case (Campbell, Jarrett, et al., 2023).

Sankofa and Sufficiency

As argued above, current mainstream thinking tends to overlook traditional sustainable practices that have stood the test of time and are accessible and simple to use for most. Taking inspiration from them could help reduce resource consumption, human and Nature exploitation, as well as conflict and pollution. *Sankofa* is a movement, symbol, and word that is worthy of attention in this context. *Sankofa* is usually translated as "to retrieve," and the movement takes its steer from a Ghanian proverb which has been translated as "it is not wrong to reach back for that which you have forgotten" (Campbell, Bouman, et al., 2023, p. 2). In other words, learn from the past. It would be foolish to ignore, deny, and destroy knowledge and practices that have proven to be of low or no negative environmental impact yet able to satisfy human (and economic) well-being.

To become sustainable, the scale and efficiency of local to global economies and the (re)distribution of resources and benefits need attention. A political and economic shift away from growth or profit and realignment toward moral wisdom and good lives (Kekes, 1995) seems necessary. Proposals include an economy focused on human livelihood such as Polanyi's (1957) substantive economy or a sufficiency-based economy (Mongsawad, 2010). Such resituating of policies and actions toward everyday practices, basic respect for all life and efforts grounded in the physical reality and place could help overcome alienation between humans

Table 6.4. Seven Key Principles of QoL Planning.

Principle	Description
Asset-based	The approach draws from community strengths, rather than starting with problems or deficiencies. These positive aspects of social organisation, cultural practices, values, and environmental knowledge are explicitly identified and emphasised throughout the process.
Community-centered	The community is the central actor and driver of the process. Planning occurs through the facilitation of community reflection, debate, discussion, and priority-setting.
Holistic	Community well-being is understood as multidimensional and rooted in the understanding that healthy ecosystems and biodiversity underlie quality of life. QoL Planning always addresses economic, cultural, political, social, and environmental aspects of community health.
Pluralistic	QoL Planning begins with the assumption that communities are not monoliths. For this reason, the process is designed to bring in many partners, voices, and perspectives, and to identify shared understanding and goals before outlining priorities.
Trusting	A successful outcome depends on building and maintaining strong relationships and trust among all participants. This is a major factor in determining how much time to take and the order of phases as trust-building imbues all phases.
Flexible	The process is flexible in its phasing, duration, and particular activities because we have found differences across communities require an adaptive approach to create an agreed-upon, shared pathway for community priorities to inform conservation initiatives.
Strategically focused	One of the hardest but most important elements of the process is setting a few realistic and actionable priorities that clearly build on the particular assets of a given community.

Source: Campbell, Jarrett, et al. (2023, Table 1, p. 51).

and Nature, redress an elite and expert-driven development model, and catalyze inclusive local development and planning, leading to sustainable livelihoods, communities, and places. This would also shift the focus toward connectivity and relations rather than monetary valuation and a commensurating rationality (O'Neill, 2017) and producing and consuming what is needed rather than all that which is possible with current technologies or financially affordable by some. Both subsistence and sufficiency economies are socially embedded models with strong virtues-anchored philosophical rationales. The definition (and perceived values) of Nature then also moves away from Western science-centric notions and definitions with more holistic and pluralistic governance proposals (Raymond et al., 2023).

Sustainability Skills and STEAM

What kind of sustainability skills are needed for a sufficiency-oriented and community-based approach? According to the *Handbook of Sustainability Literacy* (Stibbe, 2009), the range of skills and attributes needed for transformation include, among others: grounded economic awareness; materials awareness; advertising awareness; technology appraisal; creative and cultural commons thinking; systems thinking; and practical skills such as woodland crafts, building crafts, field crafts, workshop crafts, textile crafts, and domestic crafts; community gardening; permaculture design; ecological intelligence; and mental/emotional well-being research, reflection, and practice.

This contrasts with the widespread current secondary and tertiary educational focus on STEM subjects (sciences, technology, engineering and maths) without placing them in their planetary boundaries context or taking an interdisciplinary STEAM approach which pays attention to critical framing and cultural-historic contexts embedding the humanities, arts, and creative-based disciplines as equals to STEM disciplines (see, for example, Carter et al., 2021). While innovation and new technological developments have their place in current societies and economies across the globe, the way these are driven and developed is neither reflecting a holistic or sustainable approach nor social and environmental justice goals. Drawing on Heidegger's work, technology may also create distance to Nature; it may block access to truth and neglect knowing through being (Diederich, 2023). Thus, we find the counter-currents to Enlightenment induced dualistic thinking in politics, economic systems, and society. Facing high uncertainties over political and social stability and with environmental and ecological systems' thresholds reached, we urgently need to accept more pluralistic approaches and a morally sound grounding as argued all the way through this chapter. STEAM-type inter- and transdisciplinary education and emphasis on practical skills as well as governance systems and institutions that anchor themselves in virtues/ethical principles to make moderated and prudent decisions would create some hope and scope for a strong(er) sustainability trajectory, be that in placemaking efforts or more generally.

Conclusions

The above sections and Fig. 6.1 and Table 6.1 clarified the different conceptions and associated definitions of sustainable development and their attributes.

Importantly, when bearing in mind the actual state of the environment and current decision-making processes for people and places, the need to shift from weak to strong sustainability becomes apparent (Tables 6.2 and 6.3). Interpretations of and efforts toward sustainable development to date largely fall into the category of "weak" sustainability and greenwashing, taking partial or ineffective approaches which lack (i) a holistic and realistic representation of the current state of the world and (ii) collaborative and integrated ways of change and transformation. Common viewpoints either emphasize economic or environmental considerations or superficially address the different, but closely connected, strands of environmental, social, and economic sustainability. In terms of urban sustainability, considering the push for zero-carbon neighborhoods as equivalent to creating sustainable communities and places is dangerous, as the urban carbon footprint is but one element among many other environmental, economic, and social sustainable development aspects, as is illustrated in Fig. 6.2.

The complexity of the connected factors and interdependent relationships from the microscopic to the global scale require ethically grounded inter- and transdisciplinary approaches, striving for collaboration rather than submitting to competition or the political and financial pressures levied to protect the current status quo. We need critical debate and more transparent, social–ecological grounded criteria to negotiate and decide the adoption/rejection of development and technological pathways and their likely social and environmental justice outcomes. We need wise and appropriate (long-lasting, reliant, equitable, etc.) solutions rather than unquestioningly jumping onto the bandwagon of smart and AI technologies. The need for a sustainability transformation in developed and developing countries, urban and rural areas, rather than a (linear) transition, is increasingly evident and highlighted (e.g., Carter, 2024; Marsden & Farioli, 2015; Martin et al., 2020; Raymond et al., 2023; Spash, 2024).

In placemaking, a crucial aspect highlighted for many years is the need for participatory planning, in which not only a wide range of experts, statutory stakeholders, and accepted interest groups are invited (often to inform or comment rather than "collaborate") but also those affected and living locally (Healey, 1997, 2010). While a focus on nature conservation of selected areas and species was and to a degree still is important, planning has to happen *with* rather than *for* people and with people *as* (part of) nature rather than *in* (making decision for) nature (Raymond et al., 2023). Such social–ecological systems awareness will help moving from putting Nature in designated spaces to Nature being a vital part of urban life (Campbell, Jarrett, et al., 2023, p. 4). Participatory, inclusive, integrated, climate- and biodiversity-aware spatial planning (Raymond et al., 2023, pp. 4–5) could and must happen across urban, peri-urban, and rural areas. Social infrastructure and green infrastructure become intertwined, integrating biodiversity and other environmental, economic, and social functions into sustainable placemaking.

This chapter suggests that sustainable placemaking focused around QoL and sufficiency looks promising, offering some flexibility and adaptability in the focus of specific goals and indicators, yet anchored in a physical reality and past-present-future context to coproduce aspirational futures and define necessary policies and actions. While there is no shortage of guiding principles (as discussed in this chapter and also Chapter 4) and relevant laws and policies (see Chapter 3) for placemaking projects and local planning, the actual specifics will be case-by-case dependent. None of these concepts and paths are ready-made. Placemaking must be negotiated between communities, stakeholders, and planners within its political context and societal, economic, and environmental trends; interpretations of policies will need to be negotiated and actions and responsibilities agreed and shared (Myers, 1988). Planning always involves political elements and needs to make space for local narratives and views. Different needs, wants, and interests should be made explicit and included in placemaking endeavors; they cannot just focus on the individual but must consider the community level (Myers, 1988, p. 355) and how local placemaking processes link or fit within wider strategic goals, social–ecological–economic requirements, processes, and impacts.

Human and planetary health is intricately connected and, as Hickel (2019, p. 873) put it: "human flourishing cannot be achieved and sustained on a planet in ecological crisis." Sustaining the current mainstream economic system rather than focusing on economic sustainability of communities and individuals is one elephant in the room. We have the knowledge, principles, tools, and examples for strongly sustainable placemaking; however, on the whole, we lack the political support and mindset to make the move from weak to strong sustainability. Until we do, environmental, economic, and social challenges and decline are likely to worsen.

References

Adams, W. M. (2006). *The future of sustainability re-thinking environment and development in the twenty-first century*. https://portals.iucn.org/library/sites/library/files/documents/Rep 2006 002.pdf

Ahirrao, P., & Khan, S. (2021). Evaluating public open spaces through the lively planning integrative perspective: A developing country context. *Environment, Development and Sustainability*, 24, 5225–5257.

Allen, C., Malekpour, S., & Mintsrom, M. (2023). Cross-scale, cross-level and multi-actor governance of transformations toward the Sustainable Development Goals: A review of common challenges and solutions. *Sustainable Development*, 31, 1250–1267. https://doi.org/10.1002/sd.2495

Almond, R. E. A., Grooten, M., Juffe Bignoli, D., & Petersen, T. (Eds.). (2022). *Living planet report 2022: Building a nature-positive society*. World Wildlife Fund.

Atalay, H., & Gülersoy, N. Z. (2023). Developing social sustainability criteria and indicators in urban planning: A holistic and integrated perspective. *ICONARP, International Journal of Architecture and Planning*, 11(1), 1–23. https://doi.org/10.15320/ICONARP.2023.230

Athanassiadis, A., Christis, M., Bouillard, P., Vercalsteren, A., Crawford, R. H., & Khan, A. Z. (2018). Comparing a territorial-based and a consumption-based approach to assess the local and global environmental performance of cities. *Cleaner Production*, 173, 112–123. https://doi.org/10.1016/j.jclepro.2016.10.068

Barr, S. (2008). *Environment and society: Sustainability, policy and the citizen.* Ashgate.
Beatley, T. (2000). *Green urbanism: Learning from European cities.* Island Press.
Berkes, F., & Folke, C. (1992). A systems perspective on the interrelations between natural, human-made and cultural capital. *Ecological Economics, 5*(1), 1–8.
Bertics, A. (2024, 3 February). Where the internet lives. *The Economist – Technology Quarterly.* https://www.economist.com/technology-quarterly/2024-02-03
Bihouix, P. (2020). *The age of low tech: Towards a technologically sustainable civilization* (C. McMahon, translator, originally published in French, 2014). Bristol University Press.
Bonnedahl, K. J., & Heikkurinen, P. (2018). The case for strong sustainability. In K. J. Bonnedahl & P. Heikkurinen (Eds.), *Strongly sustainable societies: Organising human activities on a hot and full earth* (Chapter 1). Routledge.
Bowers, C. A. (1993). *Education, cultural myths, and the ecological crisis: Toward deep changes.* State University of New York Press.
Bowers, C. A. (2001). *Educating for eco-justice and community.* University of Georgia Press.
Brondizio, E. S., Settele, J., Díaz, S., & Ngo, H. T. (Eds.). (2019). *Global assessment report on biodiversity and ecosystem services of the Intergovernmental Science-Policy Platform on Biodiversity and Ecosystem Services.* Intergovernmental Science-Policy Platform on Biodiversity and Ecosystem Services.
Buch-Hansen, H., & Nesterova, I. (2023). Less and more: Conceptualising degrowth transformations. *Ecological Economics, 205,* 107731. https://doi.org/10.1016/j.ecolecon.2022.107731
Campbell, J., Bouman, M., Crawford, A., & Derby Lewis, A. (2023). Sankofa urbanism: Retrieval, resilience, and cultural heritage in cities through time. *Frontiers in Ecology and Evolution.* http://doi.org/10.3389/fevo.2023.1219336
Campbell, J., Jarrett, C., Wali, A., Rosenthal, A., Alvira, D., Lemos, A., Longoni, M., Winter, A., & Lopez, L. (2023). Centering communities in conservation through asset-based quality of life planning. *Conservation and Society, 21*(1), 48–60.
Carrosio, G. (2024). Framing sustainability. In S. Fantoni, N. Casagli, C. Solidoro, & M. Cobal (Eds.), *Quantitative sustainability: Interdisciplinary research for Sustainable Development Goals* (pp. 139–150). Springer. https://doi.org/10.1007/978-3-031-39311-2_9
Carter, N. (2001). *The politics of the environment: Ideas, activism, policy.* Cambridge University Press.
Carter, C. E. (2024). Reconnecting with the social-political and ecological-economic reality. *Environmental Values, 33*(2). Special issue: Ecological Economics and the Plurality of Values: Engaging with the Work of Clive L. Spash.
Carter, C. E., Barnett, H., Burns, K., Cohen, N., Durall, E., Lordick, D., Nack, F., Newman, A., & Ussher, S. (2021). Defining STEAM approaches for Higher Education. *European Journal of STEM Education, 6*(1), 13. https://doi.org/10.20897/ejsteme/11354
Cilliers, E. J., Timmermans, W., Van den Goorbergh, F., & Slijkhuis, J. S. A. (2014). Designing public spaces through the lively planning integrative perspective. *Environment, Development and Sustainability, 17*(6), 1367–1380.

Clement, J., Ruysschaert, B., & Crutzen, N. (2023). Smart city strategies – A driver for the localization of the sustainable development goals? *Ecological Economics, 213*, 107941. https://doi.org/10.1016/j.ecolecon.2023.107941

Davies, G. R. (2013). Appraising weak and strong sustainability: Searching for a middle ground. *Consilience: Journal of Sustainable Development, 10*(1), 111–124.

Department for Levelling Up, Housing and Communities (DLUHC). (2023). *National planning policy framework.* DLUHC. https://assets.publishing.service.gov.uk/media/65a11af7e8f5ec000f1f8c46/NPPF_December_2023.pdf

Department for Communities and Local Government (DCLG). (2012). *National planning policy framework.* DCLG.

Department for Levelling Up, Housing and Communities (DLUHC). (2021). *National planning policy framework.* DLUHC.

Diederich, J. (2023, 11 March). Philosophical aspects of a resistance to artificial intelligence. *PsyArXiv.* https://doi.org/10.31234/osf.io/ru425

Dobson, A. (1996). Environmental sustainabilities: An analysis and a typology. *Environmental Politics, 5*, 401–428.

Freire, P. (1970). *Pedagogy of the oppressed.* Continuum.

Ghavampour, E., & Vale, B. (2019). Revisioning the 'Model of Place': A comparative study of placemaking and sustainability. *Urban Planning, 4*(2), 196–206. https://doi.org/10.17645/up.v4i2.2015

Gillen, M., & Scanlan, J. (2004). Sustainability indicators for measuring planning outcomes. *Australian Planner, 41*(2), 61–67. https://doi.org/10.1080/07293682.2004.9982355

Gómez-Baggethun, E., & Muradian, R. (2015). In markets we trust? Setting the boundaries of market-based-instruments in ecosystem services governance. *Ecological Economics, 117*, 217–224.

Goosen, Z., & Cilliers, E. J. (2020). Enhancing social sustainability through the planning of third places: A theory-based framework. *Social Indicators Research, 150*, 835–866.

Halla, P., & Binder, C. R. (2020). Sustainability assessment: Introduction and framework. In C. R. Binder, E. Massaro, & R. Wyss (Eds.), *Sustainability assessment in urban systems* (pp. 7–29). Cambridge University Press.

Healey, P. (1997). *Collaborative planning: Shaping places in fragmented societies.* UBC Press.

Healey, P. (2010). *Making better places: The planning project in the twenty-first century.* Palgrave Macmillan.

Hector, D. C., Christensen, C. B., & Petrie, J. (2014). Sustainability and sustainable development: Philosophical distinctions and practical implications. *Environmental Values, 23*(1), 7–28. https://doi.org/10.3197/096327114x13851122268963

Hediger, W. (2006). Weak and strong sustainability, environmental conservation and economic growth. *Natural Resource Modeling, 19*(3), 359–394. https://doi.org/10.1111/j.1939-7445.2006.tb00185.x

Heine, T. (2019). Hadley's zwischenraum. https://tina-heine.de/portfolio/hadleys-salon/

Hickel, J. (2019). The contradiction of the sustainable development goals: Growth versus ecology on a finite planet. *Sustainable Development, 27*, 873–884.

Holden, E., Linnerud, K., & Banister, D. (2017). The imperatives of sustainable development. *Sustainable Development, 25*, 213–226. https://doi.org/10.1002/sd. 1647

International Energy Agency. (2017). *Digitalization & Energy.* IEA.

Javidroozi, V., Carter, C., Grace, M., & Shah, H. (2023). Smart, sustainable, green cities: A state-of-the-art review. *Sustainability, 15*(6), 5353. https://doi.org/10.3390/su15065353

Johnston, P., Everard, M., Santillo, D., & Robert, K. (2007). Reclaiming the definition of sustainability. *Environmental Science Pollution Research, 14*, 60–66.

Kallis, G. (2018). *Degrowth.* Agenda Publishing.

Keen, S. (2022). The appallingly bad neoclassical economics of climate change. In B. Gills & J. Morgan (Eds.), *Economics and climate emergency* (pp. 79–107). Routledge.

Kekes, J. (1995). *Moral wisdom and good lives.* Cornell University Press.

Kettle, J. (2021, 9 June). The internet consumes extraordinary amounts of energy. Here's how we can make it more sustainable. *The Conversation.* https://theconversation.com/the-internet-consumes-extraordinary-amounts-of-energy-heres-how-we-can-make-it-more-sustainable-160639

Latouche, S. (2009). *Farewell to growth.* Polity Press.

Lenton, T. M., Laybourn, L., Armstrong McKay, D. I., Loriani, S., Abrams, J. F., Lade, S. J., Donges, J. F., Milkoreit, M., Smith, S. R., Bailey, E., Powell, T., Fesenfeld, L., Zimm, C., Boulton, C. A., Buxton, J. E., Dyke, J. G., & Ghadiali, A. (2023). *Global tipping points: Summary report 2023.* University of Exeter.

Lewis, D. (2005). Anthropology and development: The uneasy relationship. In J. G. Carrier (Ed.), *A handbook of economic anthropology* (pp. 472–486). Edward Elgar.

Lyytimäki, J., Salo, H., Lepenies, R., Büttner, L., & Mustajoki, J. (2020). Risks of producing and using indicators of sustainable development goals. *Sustainable Development, 28*, 1528–1538.

Marsden, T., & Farioli, F. (2015). Natural powers: From the bio-economy to the eco-economy and sustainable placemaking. *Sustainability Science, 10*, 331–344. https://doi.org/10.1007/s11625-014-0287-z

Martin, A., Armijos, M. T., Coolsaet, B., Dawson, N., Edwards, G. A. S., Few, R., Gross-Camp, N., Rodriguez, I., Schroeder, H., Tebboth, M. G. L., & White, C. S. (2020). Environmental justice and transformations to sustainability. *Environment: Science and Policy for Sustainable Development, 62*(6), 19–30. https://doi.org/10.1080/00139157.2020.1820294

Massam, B. H. (2002). Review article: Quality of life: Public planning and private living. *Progress in Planning, 58*(3), 141–227.

Massaro, E., Athanassiadis, A., Psyllidis, A., & Binder, C. (2020). Ontology-based integration of urban sustainability indicators. In C. R. Binder, E. Massaro, & R. Wyss (Eds.), *Sustainability assessment in urban systems* (pp. 332–350). Cambridge University Press.

McKie, R. (2021, 3 January). Child labour, toxic leaks: The price we could pay for a greener future. *The Guardian.* https://www.theguardian.com/environment/2021/jan/03/child-labour-toxic-leaks-the-price-we-could-pay-for-a-greener-future

McKie, R. (2023, 26 March). Deep-sea mining for rare metals will destroy ecosystems, say scientists. *The Guardian.* https://www.theguardian.com/environment/2023/mar/26/deep-sea-mining-for-rare-metals-will-destroy-ecosystems-say-scientists

Ministry of Housing, Communities and Local Government (MHCLG). (2019). *National planning policy framework*. MHCLG.
Mongsawad, P. (2010). The philosophy of the sufficiency economy: A contribution to the theory of development. *Asia-Pacific Development Journal, 17*(1), 123–143.
Myers, D. (1988). Building knowledge about quality of life for urban planning. *Journal of the American Planning Association, 54*(3), 347–358.
Nassar, U. (2013). Principles of green urbanism: The absent value in Cairo, Egypt. *International Journal of Social Science and Humanities, 3*(4), 339–343.
Newman, P., & Jennings, I. (2008). *Cities as sustainable ecosystems: Principles and practices*. Island Press.
O'Neill, J. (2017). Pluralism and incommensurability. In C. L. Spash (Ed.), *Routledge handbook of ecological economics: Nature and society* (pp. 227–236). Routledge.
O'Riordan, T. (1996). Democracy and the sustainability transition. In W. Lafferty & J. Meadowcroft (Eds.), *Democracy and the environment* (pp. 140–156). Edward Elgar.
Penke, M. (2021, 13 April). The toxic damage from mining rare elements. *DW (Deutsche Welle)*. https://www.dw.com/en/toxic-and-radioactive-the-damage-from-mining-rare-elements/a-57148185
Polanyi, K. (1957). The economy as institutional process. In K. Polanyi, C. M. Arensberg, & H. W. Pearson (Eds.), *Trade and market in the early empires* (pp. 243–269). Henry Regnery.
Poole, A. K. (2018). Where is goal 18? The need for biocultural heritage in the sustainable development goals. *Environmental Values, 27*(1), 55–80. https://doi.org/10.3197/096327118X15144698637522
Pörtner, H.-O., Roberts, D. C., Tignor, M., Poloczanska, E. S., Mintenbeck, K., Alegría, A., Craig, M., Langsdorf, S., Löschke, S., Möller, V., Okem, A., & Rama, B. (Eds.). (2022). *Climate change 2022: Impacts, adaptation and vulnerability. Contribution of Working Group II to the Sixth Assessment Report of the Intergovernmental Panel on Climate Change*. Cambridge University Press.
Raymond, C. M., Anderson, C. B., Athayde, S., Vatn, A., Amin, A. M., Arias-Arévalo, P., Christie, M., Cantú-Fernández, M., Gould, R., Himes, A., Kenter, J. O., Lenzi, D., Muraca, B., Murali, R., O'Connor, S., Pascual, U., Sachdeva, S., Samakov, A., & Zent, E. (2023). An inclusive typology of values for navigating transformations towards a just and sustainable future. *Current Opinion in Environmental Sustainability, 64*, 101301. https://doi.org/10.1016/j.cosust.2023.101301
Schmelzer, M. (2023). From Luddites to limits? Towards a systematization of growth critiques in historical perspective. *Globalizations, 20*(3), 447–464.
Scott, A. J., Carter, C., Hardman, M., Grayson, N., & Slaney, T. (2018). Mainstreaming ecosystem science in spatial planning practice: Exploiting a hybrid opportunity space. *Land Use Policy, 70*, 232–246. https://doi.org/10.1016/j.landusepol.2017.10.002
Shmelev, S. E., & Shmeleva, I. A. (2018). Global urban sustainability assessment: A multidimensional approach. *Sustainable Development, 26*(6), 904–920. https://doi.org/10.1002/sd.1887
Singleton, A. D., Spielman, S., & Folch, D. (2017). *Urban analytics*. Sage.
South Downs National Park Authority (SDNPA). (2019). *South Downs Local Plan: Adopted 2 July 2019 (2014–33)*. SDNPA. https://www.southdowns.gov.uk/wp-content/uploads/2019/07/SD_LocalPlan_2019_17Wb.pdfS.

Spash, C. L. (2024). *Foundations of social ecological economics: The fight for revolutionary change in economic thought*. Manchester University Press.

Spash, C. L., & Smith, T. (2019). Of ecosystems and economies: Re-connecting economics with reality. *Real World Economics Review, 87*, 212–229.

Stibbe, A. (Ed.) (2009). *The handbook of sustainability literacy: Skills for a changing world*. Green Books.

Trisos, C. H., Merow, C., & Pigot, A. L. (2020). The projected timing of abrupt ecological disruption from climate change. *Nature, 580*, 496–501. https://doi.org/10.1038/s41586-020-2189-9

United Nations. (2015). *Transforming our world: The 2030 agenda for sustainable development. A/RES/70/1*. United Nations. https://sustainabledevelopment.un.org/content/documents/21252030%20Agenda%20for%20Sustainable%20Development%20web.pdf?ref=truth11.com

United Nations. (2023, February 6). *Humanity must act urgently to avert total global catastrophe*. Press release, GA/12489. https://press.un.org/en/2023/ga12489.doc.htm

United Nations Conference on Environment and Development (UNCED). (1992). *Agenda 21*. United Nations. https://sdgs.un.org/sites/default/files/publications/Agenda21.pdf

United Nations Environment Program (UNEP), and International Environmental Technology Centre (IETC). (2002). *Melbourne principles for sustainable cities*. Integrative Management Series No. 1. UNEP & IETC.

Voulvoulis, N., Giakoumis, T., Hunt, C., Kioupi, V., Petrou, N., Souliotis, I., Vaghela, C., & binti Wan Rosely, W. I. H. (2022). Systems thinking as a paradigm shift for sustainability transformation. *Global Environmental Change, 75*, 102544.

waynevisser. (2015, August 3). *UN sustainable development goals – Finalised text & diagrams*. https://www.waynevisser.com/report/sdgs-finalised-text

Williams, L., Sovacool, B. K., & Foxon, T. J. (2022). The energy use implications of 5G, Reviewing whole network operational energy, embodied energy, and indirect effects. *Renewable and Sustainable Energy Reviews, 157*, 112033. https://ssrn.com/abstract=4008530

World Commission on Environment and Development (WCED). (1987). *Our common future*. WCED. https://sustainabledevelopment.un.org/content/documents/5987ourcommon-future.pdf

World Economic Forum (WEF). (2021). *Net zero carbon cities: An integrated approach*. Insight Report. WEF.

Zhang, X., Bayulken, B., Skitmore, M., Lu, W., & Huisingh, D. (2018). Sustainable urban transformations towards smarter, healthier cities: Theories, agendas and pathways. *Journal of Cleaner Production, 173*, 1–10. https://doi.org/10.1016/j.jclepro.2017.10.345

Chapter 7

Placemaking, Conservation, and Heritage

Peter J. Larkham, Emma Love and Miguel Hincapié Triviño

Birmingham City University, UK

Abstract

Particularly in response to rapidly changing circumstances and environments, conservation involves identifying and retaining an element of heritage, stability, and familiarity in both existing areas and informing the design of new areas. Yet this is a complex and contested process. It involves processes of valuation and selection: so whose heritage is being selected, prioritized, promoted, and retained, and whose is marginalized, redeveloped, and vanishes? And individuals and communities do change over time, so the views and values of those communities are also likely to change. Incomers do not necessarily share the same values as long-term residents. On a wider scale, what is generally accepted as worthy of conservation also changes with, for example, postwar modernism, brutalism, and postmodernism becoming accepted but difficulties with problematic heritage – of war, destruction, slavery and exploitation, for example – being contentious and potentially splitting communities. What one generation values, particularly if it is (relatively) new, can be seen by others as disfiguring, and this is very evident in the contentious heritage identification and conservation of urban art and graffiti. We use a range of examples from the United Kingdom, Europe, and elsewhere to identify and critique the processes and products – the landscapes of heritage manipulation, the decision-making processes, the power of individuals and communities. All these are critical factors in the complex interrelationship between placemaking and conservation, new and old.

Keywords: Conservation; heritage; preservation; character; graffiti; England; Colombia; Ecuador

Introduction

Conservation – also known as "historic preservation" – is a process involving the identification, selection, and retention of landscape features of heritage significance, whether at the scale of a town, district, locale or tiny detail. All can play important roles in place identity: in defining the character or appearance of places which decision-makers might wish to preserve or enhance, to use the terms of UK legislation (1967 Civic Amenities Act, as amended). This chapter explores how conservation and heritage can be used as elements of placemaking but does so through the use of challenging examples rather than the usual comfortable heritage more familiar to many. The real world is full of complex and problematic heritage, difficult to conceptualize in terms of traditional conservation or to incorporate into conventional placemaking.

It is widely recognized that the urban landscape embodies the values and aspirations of its current occupiers and users but also those of their predecessors (Conzen, 1966). This allows people to take root in an area, acquiring an appreciation of its historical dimensions (although, of course, not everyone will value this in the same way). Historical elements of the urban landscape thus become assets to society both intellectually and as emotional experiences (Whitehand, 2021, p. 22). Retaining some such features can be significant not only for place identity but also in establishing the qualities of stability and familiarity: the environmental psychologist P. F. Smith said that "familiarity breeds contentment" (Smith, 1975) (Fig. 7.1A). A term associated with this is "topophilia" – love of, or identity with, a place (Tuan, 1974). Alternatively, too much change, carried out too quickly, can be unsettling and destructive to communities and place identity: both amateur and professional urban designers have argued

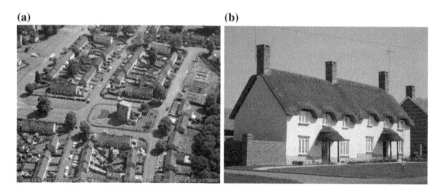

Fig. 7.1. (A) Johnstone Castle, Scotland: Remains of Fortified House Surrounded by Modern Housing. *Source:* CC-BU-SA/2.0 - © Thomas Nugent - geograph.org.uk/p/4874607 image cropped to focus on castle. (B) Recent Housing With Traditional Thatched Roofs, Tolpuddle, Dorset. *Source:* Peter J. Larkham (2015).

against this (HRH the Prince of Wales, 1989; Tibbalds, 1992). Too much change can destroy places – "topocide" (Porteous, 1988). There may also be questions of the "authenticity" of heritage or of heritage-related design (Fig. 7.1B).

Selection processes are a significant factor. Who makes decisions, on what basis, and with what input from experts, communities, or even individuals? At the very local scale, selection and management processes can often be divisive, as not everything can be conserved, and resources are often very limited. The views of national or specialist interest groups may conflict with those of local communities (Adams & Larkham, 2022; Larkham & Adams, 2016). As legal processes are often involved in identification and designation, an "authorised heritage discourse" (Smith, 1996) emerges. Whose heritage is being selected, prioritized, promoted, and retained – the authorized heritage – and whose is marginalized, redeveloped, and vanishes? There is often a very local, not formally designated, "unauthorized" heritage. Values and tastes can be very individual. Yet conservation should not be predicated solely on visual appeal, the "niceness" factor. It may be important to retain some features from past generations for historical or technical reasons, though this might not be popular with all. Much heritage decision-making is thus contested, and much heritage can be difficult or "dissonant" (Tunbridge & Ashworth, 1996). For example, difficulties with dissonant heritage – of war, destruction, slavery, and exploitation – are contentious and may potentially split communities, and dissonant heritage structures have been destroyed, vandalized, renamed, or removed. "Cancel culture" has become "cancel heritage" in recent years.

This raises the issue of time. Values and tastes change over time. Individuals and communities also change over time, both intrinsically and through movement: so the views and values of those communities are also likely to change. Incomers do not necessarily share the same values as long-term residents – which can result in conflict. New residents can seek the de-designation of authorised heritage identified by a previous generation of residents, as has happened in Leicester; and if de-designated, it becomes much more vulnerable to change. On a wider scale, what is generally accepted as worthy of conservation also changes with, for example, postwar modernism, brutalism, and postmodernism becoming accepted; it has become a familiar and accepted part of the urban landscape and experience for many and no longer provides the "shock of the new."

This complex and interrelated set of factors has a clear link with placemaking: whether in the creation of new places and the shaping of their character and identity or in the remaking of existing places, whether or not the community changes as part of that process. The UK fourth-generation New Town of Milton Keynes, for example, now has 27 designated conservation areas (Milton Keynes City Council, n.d.), although most relate to existing villages now assimilated by the New Town. Old items can be reused, from the detail scale of a prewar doorway incorporated into a new office block in Hamburg (Fig. 7.2A) to the retention of an early-medieval church in Exeter, "incongruously dished up on a platter of municipal planting in the middle of a paved square," a "pathetic and inappropriate centrepiece" (Cherry & Pevsner, 2004, pp. 394, 421) for the Guildhall shopping precinct of 1972–1976 (Fig. 7.2B). Although, particularly in

Fig. 7.2. (A) Old Doorway Incorporated Into New Office Block, Hamburg; (B) Medieval Church in Exeter Incorporated Into Guildhall Shopping Precinct. *Source:* Peter J. Larkham (2010, 2015).

the Exeter example, an important heritage item has been retained – it is perhaps the oldest Christian site in the city (The Parish of Central Exeter, n.d.); observation during numerous visits suggests that it is hardly the focus of place identity or community. This chapter uses a range of examples to explore the interplay between placemaking and heritage, and particularly the role of communities and other stakeholders and the definition of complex and problematic heritage.

Community Participation in Conservation for Placemaking

Participation of local communities and other stakeholders is a crucial aspect for the management and sustainable development of landscapes and places (Selman, 2004, pp. 365–392). International organizations emphasize that programs and projects should incorporate tools for the participation of diverse sectors of society as they contribute to identifying values, developing visions and goals, and collective agreement in actions (ICOMOS, 2003, 2013; UNESCO, 2011, 2017). Similarly, research shows the importance of community participation as civic engagement, local empowerment, or public–private partnership strategies, where renewed importance is given to citizens, not as passive receivers but as bringers of interests and promoters and executors of initiatives (Ellery & Ellery, 2019; Selman, 2004). However, the role of a community and the methods employed for engagement are usually framed by an array of circumstances, including who holds power in conservation decisions and who benefits from – or perhaps is disadvantaged by – them (Tunbridge, 1984). This can have a substantial influence in the ways in which places are being shaped, whose views and values are being manifested, and whose interests are represented in a place (Mason & Avrami, 2002).

Participation in the making of places and landscapes depends on the multiple types of relationships that communities develop with and within the areas, which motivate the implementation of practices and activities (Stephenson, 2008). Among those, identity and place attachment are fundamental types of relationships driving communities to participate (Claval, 2007; Manzo & Perkins, 2006). Buggey and Mitchell, for instance, state that "the meanings that people attach to the landscapes and their active involvement in the process, have become core elements in retaining the essential character while accommodating change..." (Buggey & Mitchell, 2003). For Aponte, this is a two-way process: places and landscapes influence the formation of individual and collective identities and character, which, once formed, shape and configure the specific compositions around us (Aponte, 2003). The multiple relationships over time take many shapes, including sociohistorical structures, social action, human activity, events, and group functions (Stephenson, 2008). Therefore, while some might assume that conservation of the character of places and landscapes happens "naturally," it is people – communities, and most usually local ones – through their cumulative actions (processes and practices) who contribute to the formation of both heritage and community and thus place (Aponte, 2003).

The research on community participation in conservation for placemaking is as broad as there are different interpretations and meanings derived from the relationship of human beings and place. Recent analysis has proposed two theoretical approaches to this complex interdisciplinary area of research: participation as the human interaction with natural forces and participation as the role of communities in democracy and decision-making, which can also lead to influence in social justice (Roe, 2012). In the first approach, place formation can happen more spontaneously, deriving from the multiple interactions of people in a place, productive, and nonproductive. In the second, there is usually a rational thinking and motivation, where local communities, as local actors attached to a place, discuss objectives, set strategies, and develop informed and arranged activities. This distinction can have implications in the conservation and decisions for placemaking. While spontaneous activities can be mapped out as pattern formation, in conscious forms of social action, community interests and values can be more easily identifiable.

Changing Communities and Heritage: Moseley Road Baths, Birmingham

These Edwardian public baths provide a useful example of changing communities and heritage; even their construction was an aspect of placemaking (Adams & Larkham, 2022). As Birmingham, newly promoted to city status, sought to expand in the late 1800s, civic leaders offered to construct a library and public baths in a target expansion area, in a grand baroque style, acting as a new focus

Fig. 7.3. (A) Moseley Road Baths and Library. *Source:* Oosoom at English Wikipedia, licensed under CC BY-SA 3.0 (B) Example of Campaigning and Events in the Derelict Baths: "100 Swimmers." *Source:* © Attilio Fiumarella/Some Cities (https://work.attiliofiumarella.com/).

for the area (Fig. 7.3A). The facilities were well used, as local histories demonstrate (Beauchampé, 2013, sections 4–7; Collins, 2020). While some traditional swimming baths were closed in the 1990s, Moseley Road remained open, and by 1994, the baths received statutory protection as Grade II Listed Buildings, reflecting their richness of décor and the rare survival of original features showing social segregation and shifting attitudes to personal hygiene.

However, the community was changing, with in-migrants from the Indian subcontinent, Southeast Asia, and the West Indies who were attracted to the city partly because of its booming post–Second World War economy (Chan, 2006). Users' accounts of the baths tend to convey particular tensions at the perceived discrimination associated with scheduling swimming activities around certain historically rooted ethnic and class divides, expected "bodily and cultural practices" (Collins, 2020, p. 11), and the different degrees of access afforded to men and women. Despite emerging tensions, the List grade was changed to II* in 2004, when there were only four other public baths in England with this level of heritage protection. Yet funding declined further, and the building began to suffer serious decay. In 2008, restoration was costed at £20-22 million (Elkes, 2008). In 2015, the City Council suggested closing the building, prompting it to become one of only two UK buildings to be included in the World Monuments Fund's Watch List. This threat mobilized local action: new users and pressure groups appeared, including a Moseley Road Baths Action Group and the Friends of Moseley Road Baths, bolstered in part by a committed, sometimes-voluble social media following and strong LinkedIn connections; and the original use, for community swimming, remained active. High-profile protests were organized (Fig. 7.3B). A threat to heritage, despite a lack of unanimity among users earlier, drew this disparate community closer together: it was a catalyst to creating identity and place. This seems to have succeeded: in 2021, the first phases of a £33 million conservation plan began (World Monuments Fund, n.d.), and a further stage began in October 2023.

Involving Local Communities in Building Conservation for Placemaking: Bogota (Colombia) and Cuenca (Ecuador)

The programs for façade conservation in the historic environments of Bogota (Colombia) and Cuenca (Ecuador) are relevant examples of the varied complexity of community involvement in placemaking and the use of heritage. In Bogota, the program "Candelaria is your Home" (*Candelaria es Tu Casa* in Spanish), led by the City's Institute of Heritage between 2013 and 2015, aimed to enhance façades and public spaces in the Historic Centre conservation area also known as *La Candelaria*. It included different forms of participation and engagement, from negotiation between public institutions and homeowners to the involvement of private sponsors for delivery. The first stage focused on strategic street corridors to demonstrate the effectiveness of image transformation and to catalyze further change. These were Streets 10th and 11th, Avenues second and third – active walkways for pedestrian movement. Further stages covered neighbor areas of residential use in the surroundings (Quiroga Galindo and Team Candelaria es Tu Casa, 2015).

Two elements played a crucial role in preparing and delivering this three-year program. First, local communities and stakeholders urged the Heritage Institute to improve and positively transform these environments. The Institute structured a team of technicians and conservation professionals to respond to this dynamic and build trust with local actors in institutional response. The enhancement of strategic areas later motivated other homeowners and residents to replicate activities, either by themselves or with the technical support of the Heritage Institute, particularly in deciding the color palette and the technical execution using traditional building methods. In addition to the trust built, a second key aspect was the impact of image quality enhancement in attracting visitors and strengthening local businesses and shops along the areas, supporting economic sustainability. The level of influence also pulled the investment of private companies, who saw the potential of this program and invested economically in materials and building costs.

The idea of "quick wins," broadly used in urban regeneration theories, suggests that short-term actions in an area can mobilize and promote even higher transformation and results (Boyle, 1993) (Fig. 7.4). Besides the residents–Heritage Institute partnership, Candelaria is Your Home motivated other private businesses to sponsor the intervention in listed buildings and further streets. The total impact of the program managed to enhance 1,014 façades between 2013 and 2015, and approximately 500 people directly benefited (Quiroga Galindo and Team Candelaria es Tu Casa, 2015). After the "quick wins," the Institute promoted other instruments of participation, such as a "Façade Community Club," consisting of a local network of neighbors that continued the improvement of façades beyond the years of the institutional program (Fig. 7.5).

Fig. 7.4. Before, During, and After Intervention of a Heritage Building in Bogota Historic Centre – La Candelaria. *Source:* Bogota Institute of Heritage (2015).

Fig. 7.5. Before and after Intervention of a Heritage Building in Bogota Historic Centre – Santafe Neighborhood. *Source:* Bogota Institute of Heritage (2015).

The case of Cuenca (Ecuador) exemplifies a similar process, although this time not led by a public institution but initiated and delivered by a local public university in conjunction with the residents of the historic center. The Program for Building Maintenance, executed between 2014 and 2018, represents how

Placemaking, Conservation, and Heritage 133

collective voluntary work for improving image quality in public space can promote higher levels of appropriation and place attachment (Achig-Balarezo & Tenze, 2019). The program was delivered in two stages, first in San Roque neighborhood in 2014 and, later, in Las Herrerías street in 2017–18. Both stages centered the attention in roof management, façades restoration, and public space cleaning and management.

A particular characteristic of this intervention was the form of action through a *Minga* – a pre-Columbian form of voluntary collective work that aims to benefit a community and their environments (Guevara, 1957). The University took the lead to design the program as an academic activity, identifying a few streets and neighborhoods, based on their aesthetic and architectural integrity and significance. The *Mingas* were scheduled as street parties, gathering many actors and inviting the residents to intervene and support. Activities of maintenance were mostly carried by the University, while locals either did some painting or prepared food and drinks for everyone. As per the communities' and academics' testimonies, placemaking through the celebration of a *Minga* highly valued the idea of "making together" for the common good and emphasized less on the physical change of the infrastructures (Achig-Balarezo & Tenze, 2019). This shift of focus from the management of physical objects to the collective party and its intangible relationships redefines its significance as a process of placemaking (Figs. 7.6 and 7.7).

The two cases of Latin America are relevant examples of multiple actors' engagement for the conservation of historic environments and placemaking. In the case of Bogota, residents of the historic center – *La Candelaria* – motivated and engaged with institutions for façades and public space enhancement, which

Fig. 7.6.   Neighbor in Las Herrerias Street, Supporting the *Minga*.
Source: Maria Cecilia Achig (2019).

Fig. 7.7. Before and After the Herrerías Maintenance Campaign. *Source:* Maria Cecilia Achig (2019).

resulted in quick changes in visual appearance, but also the configuration of community programs for sustainability. In Cuenca, the value of placemaking is visible through the *Mingas* as street parties for architectural enhancement. As communities and participants manifested, the *Minga* facilitated the gathering and interaction of local actors as something crucial to the conservation process, not necessarily with a focus on the product (number of buildings conserved) but in the celebration and the idea of making together. This can affect the way conservation is perceived and the value framework assessing social interaction and community work in placemaking.

"Difficult" and "Different" Heritages and the Impact on Placemaking

Bankside Gallery (Hull, UK)

The city of Hull in northern England has displayed a creative way to changing place and identity. The frequently controversial medium of graffiti has been utilized to identify and memorialize the heritage of a housing estate that is in the process of being demolished.

Like many other cities, Hull has districts that require redevelopment and an increasing demand for new homes or upgrades to the ageing and existing housing stock. One large area to the east of the city center, Preston Road, was problematic because of the historical hybrid approach to planning, architecture, and housing provision. This led to a mix of both traditional and nontraditional prefabricated construction, the latter including the concrete "Winglet" housing which was earmarked for redevelopment. Many of the nontraditional properties had known defects and improvement was considered unviable, so the City Council gave a commitment to build approximately 500 new homes and demolish 514 Winglet properties (Hull City Council, n.d.). However, the neighborhood was experiencing an increase in antisocial behavior, and it was considered to be a crime hotspot. The bleak landscape, with the remaining empty properties, became the playground of the disenchanted, providing opportunities and shelter for

Placemaking, Conservation, and Heritage 135

Fig. 7.8. Graffiti on Abandoned Housing, Preston Road, Hull.
Source: CC-BY-SA/2.0 - © Paul Harrop - geograph.org.uk/p/4874607.

criminality (Fig. 7.8). The original purpose of this housing estate, to provide homes for families and a sense of place for its community, was now changing: its fate became aligned with a new sense of purpose – an opportunity for antisocial behavior.

During its year as the UK City of Culture in 2017, Hull welcomed visitors and benefited from investments in city projects. During this time, and aligned in some way to the City of Culture label, a group of local graffiti writers decided to start to promote the positivity which graffiti can provide for local communities, and their attention was soon drawn to the derelict area of Preston Road. Bankside Gallery was formed to provide an opportunity for local people to understand and implement graffiti within their own communities (visithull.org, n.d.). The City Council supported the novel idea that 22 of the derelict properties in Preston Road could be used as an outside art gallery, and the area was visited by over 100 graffiti writers from across the United Kingdom, keen to help, even though the work would be a temporary addition to the landscape, by adding color and support to this initiative. This project by Bankside Gallery has now provided a host of other places where graffiti writers can visit to add color, legally with the local council's support, across Hull. Furthermore, the work of Bankside Gallery in establishing the relationship between difficult spaces and graffiti improved the antisocial behavior of Preston Road, with the local fire service reporting a 41% cut in call outs during the time the gallery was in situ (HullCCNews, 2019). Bankside Gallery continues to work with the local community, and their work, including the Preston Road gallery, is regularly featured as the topic of society and community improvement questions by local schools.

Doel, Antwerp, Belgium

Graffiti has also played a part in recognizing the changes in the 700-year-old Belgian town of Doel, not far from the city and port of Antwerp. A substantial nuclear power plant with two cooling towers is located there, along with a classic windmill. The visual contrast is substantially enhanced by the fact that the once-thriving community of about 2000 residents had declined in 2021 there were only some 19 people living there. No new tenants are allowed to move into the town, but observation shows that the majority of the unoccupied homes are still standing, and many are still completely furnished.

Rather than being abandoned artifacts, the ruins of Doel resemble the constructed environment left behind by abandoned lives. There are no more generations of the Doel community to follow, and an empty school, where the sounds of the town's children playing would have filled the air, serves as a somber mute reminder of this. A grand but now-defunct police station, deserted corner shops, a typical Flemish town hall, a children's play area with rusting swings, and abandoned bus stops remain. There are traces of prior habitation everywhere, creating an eerie backdrop to the truth that this community was once thriving and alive, picturesque, and healthy. However, with the 19 existing residents still tenaciously clinging to life and their houses, the community nevertheless has a sliver of its resolve. In addition to having heavy locks and bolts on the front doors and substantial shutters or bars on the windows, the surviving properties are well-kept, with potted plants outside and net curtains in the windows. Living in a largely deserted town has its drawbacks, such as the prevalence of night-time gang activity, with looters and stolen car racers being the most typical visitors. In the daytime, a small but constant stream of curious tourists can be seen gaping in shock at the postapocalyptic landscape. However, they and other advocates for the town are also acutely aware that a battle must be waged to prevent Doel from being permanently erased from Antwerp's history. The heritage of Doel remains in a physical sense with these buildings, but the change from a placemaking perspective is very apparent (Fig. 7.9).

The fabric of Doel as a town, although virtually empty of permanent occupants, undergoes constant change. Cresswell (2004) suggested that when determining the meaning of place, a consideration is the attachment that a community gives to the space. For Doel, this could be considered an external community, the wider graffiti nation, which has adopted the empty situation and spaces as an opportunity to create a new landscape.

Graffiti artists from all around the world have become interested in this difficult backdrop over the years. It provides a perfect and generally safe canvas for graffiti events, enthusiasts of urban art, and photographers of urban environments. Large-scale planned events have taken place, duly recorded on the walls of the properties themselves and on many social media platforms, by the

Placemaking, Conservation, and Heritage 137

Fig. 7.9. Graffiti in Doel. *Source:* Emma Love (2015).

local populations where the pilgrims came from, and have subsequently contributed to the history of graffiti as a placemaking tool itself. It is seen as an honor to have traveled there and painted in such a difficult environment, as well as a responsibility to convey the misery of the town and the effects that the timeline of events had on its residents to people all over the world. In 2020, a festival-related business seized the chance to carry out this exact action by holding a music event. Paradise City and Klub Dramatik, two organizations renowned for bringing people together in unexpected settings, teamed up to create the Doel Festival, and their aim is to continue to show that Doel remains a living and viable place; the festival has become an annual event, gaining the attention of many festival participants and high-level acts (paradisecity, n.d.).

Leake Street Tunnel, Waterloo, London

The Leake Street Tunnel, underneath London's Waterloo Station, has a long history that predates its current condition as a canvas for graffiti. Built in the 19th century as a railway tunnel, it was later used to store goods and cars. The tunnel eventually started to deteriorate and become disused, run-down, and with poor lighting. Banksy, a well-known street artist, created the "Cans Festival," a street art event that invited graffiti artists from all over the world to paint the tunnel's walls (Banksy explained, n.d.). As a result, in 2008, the tunnel changed from being an abandoned location to a dynamic canvas for creative expression.

The Leake Street Tunnel is an example of how graffiti within a city, generally viewed as a negative feature, can be revitalized into a positive characteristic. With the encouragement of the management company, the tunnel embraces and supports graffiti, and in doing so has established as a dynamic tool for placemaking that promotes a sense of collective identity and ownership within an urban setting.

138 Peter J. Larkham et al.

The tunnel's metamorphosis demonstrates how graffiti can facilitate this process. Because graffiti is participatory, both residents and outside artists can contribute to the tunnel's visual narrative, creating a sense of shared commitment and ownership. Schacter (2008, pp. 51–52) suggests that graffiti writers, by using existing and unused hidden spaces of cities for graffiti, can "modify and transform their environment to make it more personal" which in turn gives the public gaze the opportunity to determine their own construct of 'modern life'. Both locals and visitors have taken notice of the tunnel's transition from a depressing underpass to a vibrant art destination, which has improved foot traffic and the area's economic viability. Notably, one art festival attracted 1.5 million visitors over a four-day period in 2018 (Leake Street Arches, n.d.).

As further evidence, the tunnel received a prestigious Placemaking Award in the first London Infrastructure Awards in 2018 – a huge accolade for a dark, underused railway tunnel covered with ever-changing aerosol designs, created by unpaid collaborators (Fig. 7.10). However, this honor recognized Leake Street as

Fig. 7.10.   Graffiti in the Leake Street Tunnel. *Source:* Emma Love (2022).

the epitome of placemaking through the reframing of public realm projects, active participation in the local neighborhood's creative community, and by cultivating a reputation that encouraged others to participate with the city. Its close links to Southbank and Waterloo regeneration continue to build on this with Leake Street tied to this and, in turn, becoming recognized as a creative hub within London.

In 2017, a commercial developer and sustainable regeneration expert, London & Continental Railways (LCR), negotiated a 250-year lease from the land owners Network Rail and the Department for Transport to become the landlord and management company for the tunnel. An early decision was to improve the lighting not only as an investment in the public realm but to also encourage graffiti writers, street artists, and visitors to the tunnel. As part of LCR management's refocus and as part of their placemaking strategy, the tunnels received a new name, "Leake Street Arches," and promotion of the opportunities it could offer the local neighborhood, including a local community forum. With such an unusual and creative backdrop, the tenants they have attracted have also been creative independents, currently occupying 23,250 square feet within the arches which are housed in the tunnel. As key stakeholders in the development, the graffiti community, notably the local graffiti writers, have been consulted in the progress and placemaking plans of the tunnels (London & Continental Railways Limited, n.d.).

Graffiti as Placemaker

Although the connection between placemaking, heritage, and graffiti may not be immediately apparent, it is this focal point that demonstrates how placemaking is not always a linear process. Graffiti can be seen as a "radical and alternative form of creating heritage" (Bates, 2014), with the potential to have a substantial impact on a location, especially one that presents challenges to such established communities or, conversely, areas in need of redevelopment. Graffiti writers "are actively involved in place-making, like other private interests, and they exploit urban settings to meet their own particular wants, motivations, and aspirations" (Docuyanan, 2000, p. 105). In Preston Road, Doel and Leake Street, graffiti has had a positive influence, although in very different ways. Bankside Gallery has grown into a financially sound business that continues to bring attention to a marginalized area in a Northern town and raise funds to build on the work previously done. Doel is still in the same precarious situation, but thanks to an unlikely ally in the graffiti community, it is now a more outspoken player in continuing discussions about its future. Leake Street Tunnel continues to draw interest from the graffiti and wider community and provides the backdrop for a variety of now successful enterprises literally within its walls.

According to Christensen and Thor (2017), graffiti and street art provide "place-specific reciprocity (among urban people) and a translocally and globally connected feeling of space-molding." While Docuyanan, Christensen, and Thor see graffiti as a placemaking process, Preston Road and Doel seem instead to be examples where the opposite has really happened. The places enabled the graffiti process through the challenges they provided. Graffiti has contributed to the process of change by adding to each of their respective placemaking histories, although as a transient aspect, the graffiti has provided a permanent element to the history of place in each of them.

Conclusions: Challenging Heritage and Placemaking

The heritages examined in this chapter have been deliberately problematic and provocative, in order to better examine their potential input into processes of placemaking. Birmingham's example of colonial-era values, when the expanding city was itself colonizing its neighbors, and whose slipper-bath provision indicates a paternalistic provision for an impoverished population, can be seen as a good example of placemaking when first built. Its grandeur demonstrated the imposition of a new civic identity. While the values of paternalism and colonialism are currently widely criticized and structures embodying them have been vandalized or even torn down, these facilities themselves have in fact become popular to a wide and varied set of new users, including migrant communities. The building and its facilities have become appropriated by these communities, who wish the baths and library to be returned to full use and who appear unconcerned by the meanings embedded in the structure itself. Instead the contentious issue is over resource allocation, and prolonged campaigning has brought funding, including from external sources so that work could continue despite the current (2023) desperate financial position of the local authority itself. This one structure has thus been part of two phases of placemaking.

The examples from Cuenca (Ecuador) and Bogota (Colombia) demonstrate how community engagement in processes of regeneration can identify and work with structures of local significance, which many escape the attention of high-level actors such as international organizations and their expressed values (UNESCO and its Charters). The *Minga* community-level approach here saved and rehabilitated structures, so there was a heritage dimension but perhaps operating more as an unauthorized heritage discourse; and as these were existing places and communities, this was a process of reaffirming and reinforcing the position of "place" in these communities.

Graffiti poses a particular problem for both heritage and placemaking. Graffiti is usually a subversive, "outsider" activity, and in laying claim to territory through extensive physical markers, it can alienate existing communities. However, the examples presented here show how graffiti can be harnessed and new place identities shaped in places where communities have been moved away and locales left neglected or abandoned. The graffiti artists themselves form a new community, albeit transient not resident, and often communicating virtually. The identity of these places has been remade, although this too could be transient as replanning may demolish the structures and as the palimpsest layering of graffiti obscures its predecessors. Yet in some instances, graffiti communities have recognized the graffiti-culture-specific value of some graphic elements and have sought to protect them.

Thus, in considering how heritage and conservation can influence placemaking, these examples challenge us to think outside the norms of the authorized heritage discourse and established communities. They stress the processes of change: whether of communities through migration, of values and attitudes through the passage of time, and of different conceptions of heritage including the everyday, the temporary, and the counterculture. Placemaking is inherently a complex process, and, while these examples add to the complexity of placemaking considerations, they usefully push us to think outside the box of conventional, comfortable heritage.

References

Achig-Balarezo, M. C., & Tenze, A. (2019). The "Minga" community participation for the maintenance of vernacular heritage buildings in the historical center of Cuenca, Ecuador. In *ISPRS annals of the photogrammetry, remote sensing and spatial information sciences, IV-2/W6* (pp. 9–16). https://doi.org/10.5194/isprs-annals-IV-2-W6-9-2019

Adams, D., & Larkham, P. J. (2022). Contesting urban monuments: Future directions for the controversial monumental landscapes of civic grandeur. *International Journal of Heritage Studies, 28*(8), 891–906.

Aponte, G. (2003). Paisaje e identidad cultural [Landscape and cultural identity]. *Tabula Rasa, 1*(1), 153–164.

Banksy explained. (n.d.). *The Cans Festival, 2008.* https://banksyexplained.com/the-cans-festival-may-2008/

Bates, L. (2014). *Bombing, tagging, writing: An analysis of the significance of graffiti and street art* (Unpublished Masters Thesis). University of Pennsylvania.

Beauchampé, S. (2013). *Pool of memories: A history of Moseley Road baths.* Friends of Moseley Road Baths.

Boyle, R. (1993). Changing partners: The experience of urban economic policy in West Central Scotland, 1980–90. *Urban Studies, 30*(2), 309–323. https://doi.org/10.1080/00420989320080311

Buggey, S., & Mitchell, N. (2003). Cultural landscape management challenges and promising new directions in the United States and Canada. UNESCO World Heritage Paper 7. In *Cultural landscapes: The challenges of conservation* (pp. 92–100). UNESCO World Heritage Centre.

Chan, W. F. (2006). Planning Birmingham as a cosmopolitan city: Recovering the depths of its diversity? In J. Binnie, J. Holloway, S. Millington, & C. Young (Eds.), *Cosmopolitan urbanism* (pp. 216–231). Routledge.

Cherry, B., & Pevsner, N. (2004). *Devon.* Yale University Press.

Christensen, M., & Thor, T. (2017). The reciprocal city: Mediating space through street art and graffiti. *International Communication Gazette, 79*(6–7), 584–612.

Claval, P. (2007). Changing conceptions of heritage and landscape. In N. Moore & Y. Whelan (Eds.), *Heritage, memory and the politics of identity: New perspectives on the cultural landscape* (pp. 85–93). Ashgate.

Collins, H. (2020). Mermaids, knitted costumes and pink carbolic soap: Making meaning and translating social space in community-led pools. *Language and Intercultural Communication, 21*(1), 69–82.

Conzen, M. R. G. (1966). Historical townscapes in Britain: A problem in applied geography. In J. W. House (Ed.), *Northern geographical essays in honour of G. H. J. Daysh* (pp. 95–102). Oriel Press.

Cresswell, T. (2004). *Place: A short introduction*. Blackwell.

Docuyanan, F. (2000). Governing graffiti in contested urban spaces. *Political and Legal Anthropology Review, 23*(1), 103–121.

Elkes, N. (2008, February 28). *Moseley Road Baths thrown a £1 million lifeline – And changes are on the way*. Birmingham Mail.

Ellery, P. J., & Ellery, J. (2019). Strengthening community sense of place through placemaking. *Urban Planning, 4*(2), 12. https://doi.org/10.17645/up.v4i2.2004

Guevara, D. C. (1957). *Las Mingas en el Ecuador*. Editorial Universitaria. https://docplayer.es/74104025-Dario-guevara.html. Accessed on February 4, 2024.

HRH the Prince of Wales. (1989). *A vision of Britain*. Doubleday.

Hull City Council. (n.d.). *Preston Road regeneration*. https://www.hull.gov.uk/housing/housing-regeneration-and-development/preston-road-regeneration. Accessed on February 4, 2024.

HullCCNews. (2019, 11 April). *How graffiti led to a reduction in anti-social behaviour in Hull*. https://www.hullccnews.co.uk/11/04/2019/how-graffiti-led-to-a-reduction-in-anti-social-behaviour-in-hull/. Accessed on February 4, 2024.

ICOMOS. (2003). *ICOMOS Charter – Principles for the analysis, conservation and structural restoration of architectural heritage* [Conference Presentation]. ICOMOS 14th General Assembly, Victoria Falls, Zimbabwe.

ICOMOS. (2013). *The Burra Charter: The Australia ICOMOS Charter for Places of Cultural Significance*. Australia ICOMOS.

Larkham, P. J., & Adams, D. (2016). The un-necessary monument? The origins, impact and potential conservation of Birmingham Central Library. *Transactions of the Ancient Monuments Society, 60*, 94–127.

Leake Street Arches. (n.d.). *Leake Street arches*. www.leakestreetarches.co.uk. Accessed on February 4, 2024.

London and Continental Railways Limited. (n.d.). *Leake Street arches*. https://lcrproperty.co.uk/portfolio/leake-street-arches/. Accessed on February 4, 2024.

Manzo, L. C., & Perkins, D. D. (2006). Finding common ground: The importance of place attachment to community participation and planning. *Journal of Planning Literature, 20*(4), 335–450.

Mason, R., & Avrami, E. (2002). Heritage values and challenges of conservation planning. In J. M. Teutonico & G. Palumbo (Eds.), *Management planning for archaeological sites* (pp. 13–26). Getty Conservation Institute.

Milton Keynes City Council. (n.d.). *Conservation areas in Milton Keynes*. https://www.milton-keynes.gov.uk/planning-and-building/conservation-and-archaeology/conservation-areas-milton-keynes. Accessed on February 4, 2024.

paradisecity. (n.d.). https://paradisecity.be/paradise-city-and-klub-dramatik-present-doel-festival%EF%BF%BC/. Accessed on February 4, 2024.

Porteous, J. D. (1988). Topocide: The annihilation of place. In J. Eyles & D. Smith (Eds.), *Qualitative research methods in human geography* (pp. 75–93). Polity Press.

Quiroga Galindo, P., & Team Candelaria es Tu Casa. (2015). *Candelaria es Tu Casa: Recuperación cromática de las fachadas del centro tradicional – Parte I [Candelaria is your home: Chromatic restoration of the facades of the traditional centre - Part I]*. Instituto Distrital de Patrimonio Cultural de Bogotá [Cultural Heritage Institute of Bogota].

Roe, M. (2012). Landscape and participation. In P. Howard, I. Thompson, E. Waterton, & M. Atha (Eds.), *The Routledge companion to landscape studies* (pp. 335–354). Routledge.

Schacter, R. (2008). An ethnography of iconoclash: An investigation into the production, consumption and destruction of street-art in London. *Journal of Material Culture, 13*(1), 35–61.

Selman, P. (2004). Community participation in the planning and management of cultural landscapes. *Journal of Environmental Planning and Management, 47*(3), 365–392. https://doi.org/10.1080/0964056042000216519

Smith, P. F. (1975). Façadism used to be a dirty word. *Built Environment Quarterly, 1*(1), 77.

Smith, L. (1996). *Uses of heritage*. Routledge.

Stephenson, J. (2008). The cultural values model: An integrated approach to values in landscapes. *Landscape and Urban Planning, 84*(2), 127–139. https://doi.org/10.1016/j.landurbplan.2007.07.003

The Parish of Central Exeter. (n.d.). History & architecture of St Pancras Church. https://www.parishofcentralexeter.co.uk/history-architecture/st-pancras-church/. Accessed on February 4, 2024.

Tibbalds, F. (1992). *Making people-friendly towns*. Longman.

Tuan, Y.-F. (1974). *Topophilia*. Prentice-Hall.

Tunbridge, J. E. (1984). Whose heritage to conserve? Cross-cultural reflections on political dominance and urban heritage conservation. *Canadian Geographer/Le Géographe Canadien, 28*(2), 171–180. https://doi.org/10.1111/j.1541-0064.1984.tb00783.x

Tunbridge, J. E., & Ashworth, G. J. (1996). *Dissonant heritage: The management of the past as a resource in conflict*. Wiley.

UNESCO. (2011). *Recommendation on the historic urban landscape* [Conference Presentation]. UNESCO General Conference.

UNESCO. (2017). *Operational guidelines for the implementation of the World Heritage Convention*. UNESCO.

visithull.org. (n.d.). *The Bankside Gallery story*. https://www.visithull.org/discover/bankside-gallery-story/. Accessed on February 4, 2024.

Whitehand, J. W. R. (2021). Conzenian research in practice. In V. Oliveira (Ed.), *Morphological research in planning, urban design and architecture* (pp. 19–42). Springer.

World Monuments Fund. (n.d.). Moseley Road Baths. https://www.wmf.org/project/moseley-road-baths. Accessed on February 4, 2024.

Chapter 8

Handmade Spaces: Creative Placemaking in a Local Neighborhood

Silvia Gullino[a] and Heidi Seetzen[b]

[a]Birmingham City University, UK
[b]Kingston University, UK

Abstract

This chapter discusses the findings of a research project rooted in the unique context of a former Victorian square in South London squatted in the 1980s and 1990s. Over three decades, squatters (later homeowners and tenants) mended derelict houses, created two community gardens and green streets, and set up a vegetarian café locally. The square, an oasis in the middle of London, is now a fashionable neighborhood to live and visit because of its enduring artistic flair and alternative cultural "feel." Through ethnographic methods, our research focused on how residents transformed derelict buildings and neglected spaces and on the evolving dynamics of this neighborhood undergoing progressive gentrification, reflecting similar trends in many other neighborhoods in London. This chapter analyses these informal practices as examples of creative placemaking. Framed by the intricate interplay between the community's initiatives and the challenges posed by contemporary processes of regeneration and gentrification, we explore how such practices shaped both the material fabric of the place as well as its immaterial character: its sense of community and identity and the feelings and memories associated with its built environment. Informed by Lefebvre's theories on the social production of space and the right to the city, our analysis emphasizes the importance of informality, everyday practice, spontaneity, and self-management in shaping and sustaining a vibrant urban culture. By exploring how these elements intersect with forces of regeneration and gentrification, this chapter aims to contribute to a nuanced understanding of creative placemaking, the complex dynamics at play in the ongoing transformation of urban spaces, and the resilience of bottom-up, community-driven placemaking initiatives in the face of external pressures.

Placemaking, 145–162
Copyright © 2025 Silvia Gullino and Heidi Seetzen
Published under exclusive licence by Emerald Publishing Limited
doi:10.1108/978-1-83753-130-120241016

Keywords: Handmade placemaking; creative practices; gentrification; informal practices; Bonnington Square (London)

Introduction

In recent years, placemaking discourses have garnered considerable attention within social science and built environment disciplines, city authorities, and citizens (for example, Cresswell, 2014; Ellery et al., 2021; Gehl, 2010; 2011). While there is no singular, widely accepted definition of placemaking, it can be conceptualized as a process of remaking urban spaces to physically improve their attractiveness and distinctiveness and generate or enhance a sense of place (Akbar & Edelenbos, 2021; Cresswell, 2014). In brief, placemaking aims to reimagine and reinvent public places. Yet, as the multilayered analysis in this book makes apparent, such a definition can be problematic. Many questions remain open. How does placemaking take place, and for whom? Who are the actors involved, and what activities and outcomes does it entail? Moreover, how can more intangible concepts like "attractiveness," "distinctiveness," or "sense of place," subject to so much interpretation, be translated into practice?

Contemporary urban practices show no single way of approaching placemaking, and failing to recognize its complexities would lead to simplistic solutions (Jacobs, 1961; Madanipour, 2003; Zukin, 2009). Placemaking processes and practices are complex and operate in multiple ways. They include a variety of spatial scales (from large to small scale developments) and temporary scales (the pop-up city over the designed city), legal frameworks (from formally approved developments to informal ones, like guerrilla gardening/urbanism), and global/local approaches (top-down strategies and bottom-up tactics). Such a variety of options and configurations can lead to different placemaking outcomes (see, for example, Harvey, 1989; Jacobs, 1961; Lydon & Garcia, 2015; Madanipour, 1999; Montgomery, 1998).

This chapter recognizes the multifaceted nature of placemaking and the fact that it can be driven by various competing forces (physical, political, economic, social, and environmental), agendas, and actors (public, private or communities), aiming to regenerate urban spaces. It is within this broad framework that it explores a particular approach to placemaking where residents have actively been at the heart of reshaping their local environment through informal and creative practices over 30 years (Blokland, 2017; Healey, 2020). By doing so, it specifically explores the intangible and emotional aspects of creative placemaking. We argue that exploring the intertwinement of the material and immaterial aspects of placemaking is central to creating meaningful and socially sustainable communities that are not only physically and aesthetically attractive but that foster a sense of individual belonging, community, and identity (Cresswell, 2014; Tuan, 1977).

These less-tangible associations with place are fragile, contingent, and subject to ongoing negotiation among residents and users. Yet they are also a foundation for creating a sense of place that enables emotional connections. Moreover, they are often the motivating factor behind residents' involvement in reshaping and regenerating the places they call home (Pile, 2010; Relph, 1976; Tuan, 1977).

Our analysis draws upon an ethnographic research project which explored how placemaking in urban environments, rather than just being the "fixed" outcome of formal urban design, can be seen as the result of social, relational, and participative processes (Pink, 2015). The project ran in different phases between 2009 and 2014 when both authors were working at Kingston University, London. The project explored the value of everyday, ordinary (rather than formally designed) spaces by focusing on a small, formerly squatted neighborhood in South London (Rose et al., 2010). Located between Vauxhall Station and the Oval in the Borough of Lambeth, residents had significant involvement in regenerating and creatively adorning houses and public spaces. Over a period of 30 years, the area has undergone a community-led transformation process as residents have consolidated practices of collective action to transform their local environment, including the self-renovation of derelict buildings and the creation of new community gardens on sites bombed and damaged during the Second World War.

The aim was to explore residents' direct involvement in the making of place and their self-organized practices in renovating run-down buildings and neglected open spaces. This transformation occurred over three decades, as a result of creative and incremental practices, without a precise design process or consultations and without a planner/designer involved (Jacobs, 2006; Rose et al., 2010). Over time, the derelict square became a vibrant cultural community, renowned for its bohemian atmosphere, communal gardens, a friendly deli, and an old vegetarian café but also for its squatting history. Since the early 2000s, the urban context surrounding the square has undergone progressive urban transformation (from Vauxhall and Nine Elms down to Battersea). The square has been increasingly seen as a fashionable neighborhood by middle-class young urbanites and professionals who appreciate its old housing stock, its location (close to the center of London with good public transport links), and its enduring artistic flair and alternative cultural "feel" (Zukin, 2008). The fact that something of the square's "older" culture has endured over time is noteworthy and fed into our research interest.

In this chapter, we revisit the ethnographic and archival data that we gathered over an almost ten-year period in order to explore the slow creative placemaking processes initiated in the square in the early 1980s by squatters who settled in its derelict properties and their self-organized community practices (Berning, 2011; Blokland, 2017). Influenced by Lefebvrian critiques of urban development, discussions around the social production of space and the right to the city (Harvey, 2008; Lefebvre, 1968, 1991; Purcell, 2014), our analysis underscores the significance of informal and creative placemaking practices anchored in everyday use, spontaneity, and self-management in shaping vibrant urban cultures. It also explores the precarious nature of such placemaking practices and how wider-scale contemporary urban changes can jeopardize them. We argue that residents' creative practices and their material involvement in the production of place can be threatened by external urban transformations and different patterns of gentrification (Fisker et al., 2018; Hou, 2010).

The discussion is structured into six sections. This section and section two discuss the focus on informal creative placemaking practices and link our research to wider debates around the Lefebvrian notion of the right to the city, as well as critiques of urban gentrification and commodification. The third section traces the history of Bonnington Square, the ethnographic methodologies employed during the research project and the creative practices in the making of the place. The fourth presents the themes that emerged from our ethnographic research. It particularly focuses on the connection between the making (tangible) and the experience of the place (intangible). The fifth section analyses the square's multilayered patterns of gentrification, suggesting that gentrification threatened not just social fabric of the square but its established practices and associated sense of place. We conclude by suggesting that informal and creative practices are one expression of participatory placemaking. These can be undermined by contemporary processes of regeneration and gentrification. In this instance, it entailed the transformation of social, cultural, and creative practices and the loss of spontaneity and informality, which had long shaped residents' sense of place in Bonnington Square.

Placemaking and Our Right to the City: Informality, Creativity, and Our Sense of Place

Debates about creative placemaking are very wide-ranging. In recent years, ideas around informal and creative practices have gained currency in discussions around urban spaces and places and in social theory more generally. This is the case, for example, of contemporary discussions of Do-It-Yourself (DIY) urbanism (Simpson, 2014; Talen, 2015) or literature around the potential of creative placemaking practices to enable partnerships and participation (Markusen, 2014).

DIY urbanism, also paired with "tactical," "pop-up" and "guerrilla" urbanism, refers to any unconventional bottom-up transformation, often of an ad hoc nature, which individuals employ to address local issues often short term and/or at the margin of legality (Lydon & Garcia, 2015; Madanipour, 2017; Mould, 2014; Pagano, 2013). It tends to be resident-generated, low-budget, and often temporary (Ferreri, 2015; Talen, 2015). Markusen's (2014) definition of "creative," on the other hand, emphasizes intentionality, formalized relationships, and wide stakeholder involvement. Creative initiatives here animate places and spark economic development, but they do not include the spontaneous.

While we recognize the significance of the creative practices described at these two ends of the spectrum, the creative dimension we draw attention to in this chapter differs from either of these. The practices which we explore here sit in between the individualism, spontaneity, and informality of the former and the organized formality of the latter. We showcase forms of creative placemaking which combine a distinctive material and immaterial or emotional dimension (Fisker et al., 2018; Hou, 2010).

Here, Lefebvre's influential discussions of the "social production of space" and the "right to the city" provide a helpful lens through which to conceptualize the interconnectedness of these two dimensions (Lefebvre, 1968, 1991). By challenging the idea of urban spaces solely produced by institutionalized stakeholders, Lefebvre's work has long held that space is not a passive backdrop to our unfolding social life but is actively produced by social, economic, and cultural processes. It emphasizes the role of people's everyday practices in shaping local environments. It also provides a framework for understanding the relationship between space, society, and urban development. From this perspective, creative placemaking can be viewed as a process of production involving tangible elements (partly captured in what Lefebvre defines as "perceived spaces" or spatial practices including physical transformations) and intangible elements (described as "lived spaces," encompassing experiences, memories, identity, and social interactions) (Lefebvre, 1968, 1991; Shields, 1998).

Connected to the social production of space is Lefebvre's concept of "right to the city," which puts forward an idealized notion of the city. Urban spaces are imagined as a collective product shaped by inhabitants, who are enabled to become more actively and practically involved in transforming and managing urban life. At the heart of the idea is an emphasis on the use (or inhabitation) of space over the ownership of space. In his writings, Lefebvre critiques modern cities as increasingly shaped by capitalist surplus, practices of buying and selling, and investment and class relations over everyday spatial practices. Cities and spaces are conceived through the principle of property, ownership and monetary worth, often to the detriment of many residents.

Picking up on Lefebvre's right to the city, Harvey (2008) argues that urban life has essentially been commodified. However, against the background of urban gentrification and the commercialization of social or public spaces, he argues the right to the city formulates an alternative, less impoverished vision of the urban and our relationship to it. This vision puts "users of space" before "owners of space." Crucially, the right to the city not only posits that all users should have access to the resources of the city (although this is part of it), but that users and inhabitants need to be involved in shaping and creating the landscapes in which they live. It is this emphasis on bottom-up creative practices, ongoing involvement, and everyday shaping that resonates with our research and analysis here.

Purcell (2014) draws our attention to Lefebvre's distinctive use of the concept of "right." He suggests that the right to the city is not a right in the traditional socio-legal sense: to be fully included in the machinery of the state. It is not an end point at all but a point of departure, the beginning of a process of renewal. It is part of a new contract of citizenship, a contract that is not a static text but one which gives rise to a process of renegotiation, envisaged as a withering away of the state and increasing self-management. This interpretation coheres with Lefebvre's overall approach to society, space, and the city. By challenging the static representations of space that dominated the approach to space taken by many planners and architects, space is a production process created by the interplay of practices, representations, and the lived: the space that people experience. Similarly to the production of space, the right to the city is not fixed but procedural, enabling the continual creation of the city by its users.

This emphasis on process and fluidity also resonates with Lefebvre's concern with use and his argument that we need to de-alienate the city from contemporary economic practices (Lefebvre, 1968). Using always entails a process of shaping, creating, and meaningfully investing in the objects and spaces, whereas financially investing in it does not necessarily. In this sense, Purcell (2014) argues, Lefebvre's conception of the right to the city reorients urban environments away from "their role as an engine of capital accumulation and toward its role as a constitutive element in the web of cooperative social relations among urban inhabitants" (Purcell, 2014, p. 149). This web of cooperative social relations is what Lefebvre often refers to as "the urban," rather than "the city." Purcell describes it as "a space for encounter, connection, play, learning, difference, surprise, and novelty" (2014, p. 149). Thus, it is open-ended and emerges spontaneously from everyday informal and often creative practices. Reading it against the background of our research, we can see a sense of place emerging through the creative practices of inhabitants.

In the next two sections, this chapter introduces the square and the ethnographic research methods we employed. Drawing on these theoretical discussions, our analysis of Bonnington Square highlights the importance of informal creative practices, both tangible and intangible, and shows the way in which they can enable the development of a distinctive sense of place, emotional attachment to a place, as well as experiences of sociability and enduring social networks. Furthermore, we also raise concerns about the vulnerability of such creative practices and the risks posed by wider urban transformation processes, in particular, gentrification.

Exploring Bonnington Square: An Ethnographic Research Approach

Bonnington Square, a beautiful, Victorian, and green neighborhood situated in the heart of Vauxhall (Fig. 8.1), captured our attention due to its reputation as a residential neighborhood with a distinctive and alternative history. Tucked away from the buzz of the city, it was originally built for railway workers between 1870 and 1890 (London Gardens Trust, 2015) and was owned by the Inner London Education Authority (ILEA). The square sustained bomb damage during the Second World War, followed by a significant deterioration of its Victorian housing stock and open spaces during the postwar period. Most of the houses on the square were used as council housing until the 1980s when the ILEA designated the area as a future playing field for a nearby school (now itself transformed into a gated community). As the original tenants had moved out, the council gutted the houses, boarded the windows, and erected metal gates (Berning, 2011). In the late 1970s, the Greater London Council made a compulsory purchase order of the now run-down neighborhood to expand the premises of a local school. Before the houses could be torn down and the playing field built, the school closed, and the uninhabited buildings were left to decay.

The first squatters arrived in Bonnington Square in the early 1980s and managed to halt the demolition. During the 1980s and early 1990s, different waves of people arrived from everywhere to squat in the square. It was an eclectic community of artists, students, and political activists who lived in its old Victorian buildings or in vans parked on the street. Over at least two decades, they creatively transformed the area, renovating derelict houses, creating gardens on sites bombed and damaged during the Second World War, and adorning buildings and public spaces with murals, stained glass windows, artistic installations, and plants. Over time, the

Handmade Spaces 151

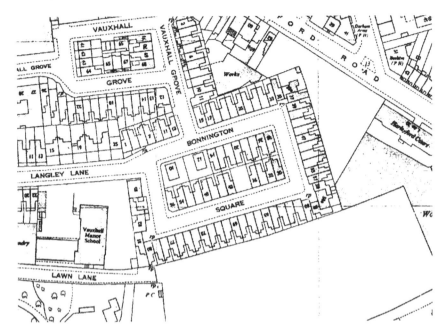

Fig. 8.1. Bonnington Square, London, in the 1970s. *Source:* © Crown Copyright and Landmark Information Group Limited (2024). All rights reserved.

derelict square became a vibrant cultural community. In 1998, the Borough of Lambeth enabled the residents to form themselves into co-operatives to buy the properties in which they were living.

Bonnington Square's community gardens and green streets, a locally run vegetarian café, and a local deli constitute an oasis in the city. The square is now a fashionable neighborhood to live and visit because of its enduring artistic flair and alternative cultural feel. The fact that one of the authors of this chapter lived in the square for seven years (2007–2014) intensified our interest in Bonnington Square and its distinctive sense of place (Rose, 1997). This personal connection to the square deepened our curiosity about how the placemaking of its urban spaces, rather than just being the "fixed" outcome of formal urban design, appeared as the result of informal, creative, and participative processes.

Using ethnographic methods (walking interviews and participant observations), the project explored the value of everyday, ordinary (rather than formally designed) spaces by focusing on the transformation of Bonnington Square over time (Evans & Jones, 2011; Jones et al., 2008; Pink, 2015). The project was run in different stages between 2009 and 2014. The core of our empirical work was based on walking interviews with 10 residents (during the first phase of the project, 2009–2010). The research participants, partly former squatters and partly new residents, were selected through a snowballing system. Each of them agreed to take us through the fascinating journey of their memories by walking with us around the square and guiding us to what they considered their meaningful places. The walking interviews – documented with photos, maps, and field notes – were entirely participant-led. Interviews were recorded, transcribed, and anonymized (Hennink et al., 2020).

In our walks, we explored how the square's handmade transformation took place over the years, as well as participants' meanings and attachment to specific spaces and how they were framed by changing urban contexts. We explored people's direct involvement in the making of place and their self-organized practices in renovating run-down buildings and neglected open spaces. Taking place over three decades, their creative and incremental practices were often without precise design processes or formal consultations. Although they all reflected a great sense of belonging, each walking interview was different as it revealed participants' unique attachment and connection to the square's past and present history. Some participants took us through the gardens showing us specific bushes and trees; some pointed out certain houses, corners, mosaics (Fig. 8.2), scribbles on particular walls, or in one instance, the location of an underground queer cabaret. Others chose to sit at the table outside of the local deli and share their memories.

Fig. 8.2. Example of a Mosaic Located in Harleyford Road Community Garden. *Source:* Silvia Gullino (2009).

As part of our research methodology, active participation in numerous local events was integral: from a street party to community festivals and volunteering in gardening activities. Moreover, attendance at crucial community meetings addressing pressing local issues, such as the contentious relationship with the local planning authority concerning the new development at Nine Elms, the selection of bicycle locks, the renovation of the community center building, and discussions on local gardens, was a key aspect. These meetings held significant value as they emphasized the lasting presence of engaged citizens, actively involved not only in square-related concerns but also in responding to the evolving socioeconomic dynamics of Vauxhall.

Making and Experiencing Handmade Places

Our walking interviews and direct observations revealed the unfolding of a nuanced narrative. Participants shared their accounts, intertwining tangible aspects such as the material transformation of the square – encompassing both buildings, gardens, and also small physical details – with an intangible and intricate tapestry of images, relationships, attachments, and memories (Degen & Rose, 2012). In the course of our research, the theme of handmade practices emerged strongly, highlighting how squatters shaped the space and remained involved in its ongoing maintenance (Tuan, 1977).

Initially, Bonnington Square's squatters were concerned with finding places to live and concentrated on making empty houses habitable. In the early 1980s, the square was seen as "bleak and desolate" (Vimeo, 2012). The houses were boarded up and in a neglected condition. At the start, life was difficult: "People lived here without any heating. It was very basic." People were dumping stuff on the street: "There were rats here. It was smelly and unsafe" (Interview 5, February 18, 2010). As some squatters recalled when reminiscing about the transformation of the properties and the placemaking of the gardens:

> [when we arrived] everything was stripped. The plumbing, the floorboard ... There were no pipes and the phone was off. That was all we had. So we ended up breaking into other houses ... a bath, a toilet ... we got bits and pieces from other houses. We all did ourselves (Interview 5, February 18, 2010).

After living on the square for a while, our participants began to focus on the square's appearance and culture. They created communal gardens on old bomb sites, decorated spaces with public artwork, and organized events and theater performances. They established a number of community spaces and forums which still exist today: a community center in which classes could be taught and meetings held, a communal kitchen which is now a collectively organized café, and two gardening groups which continue to maintain street planting and the square's communal gardens (Bonnington Square Pleasure Garden and Harleyford Road Community Garden) (Pearson, 2008).

The value of "handmaking" also emerged in relation to the placemaking of green spaces. In many of our interviews, participants emphasized the significance of maintaining street planting and gardens themselves, rather than allowing the council to take responsibility. In part, the concern was that the council would not be able to take the same care of the plants and trees as the original gardening groups had. When Bonnington garden was planted in 1990 by the Bonnington Square Garden Association, the group benefited from the fact that a few of its squatters had trained as professional gardeners. They transformed an old bomb site into the "Pleasure Garden," a covert reference to Vauxhall Pleasure Gardens, combining both indigenous and tropical plants (*The Guardian*, 2008; Pearson, 2008; Living London history, 2021) (Figs. 8.3 and 8.4).

However, it was not just the fact that residents did not trust the council to maintain the variety and individuality of planting. Many also felt that continuing their own involvement forged a special connection between themselves and the square:

> I think it is ok if we could get some gardeners that come and do the work. It would make our lives easy for us but it would change the

Fig. 8.3. The Pleasure Garden and, in the Background, an Old Mill Wheel Rescued From a Nearby Marble Factory. *Source:* Silvia Gullino (2009).

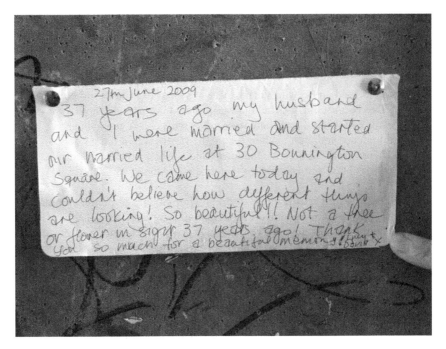

Fig. 8.4. A Written Note Left on the Community Board, Found During Our Fieldwork. *Source:* Silvia Gullino (2009).

ethos [of the garden] and I cannot say why and I haven't thought it through, but it is true ... It is not about ownership. It is responsibility (Interview 8, March 13, 2010).

Participants' narratives often shared a fond recollection of the enjoyment associated with being materially involved in the making and shaping of the square (both buildings and community spaces). In each interview, there was a sense of intertwinement of creative practices, emotional attachment, and place:

The gardening of the space is linked to that. You start to care more about that kind of thing when you have a sense of the future of the place and the feel a sense of place. And you think 'right I need to make it a bit nicer (Interview 8, March 13, 2010).

Of course, the fond recollections of past creative practices, doing up the houses, greening the square, creating gardens, or adding adornments constitute a nostalgic view of the past. Participants were themselves aware of this, describing "lots of tensions under the surface of communities" and the fact that, for example, the two gardens were managed by different groups of people "without much interactions." Some also said that while they missed the communal spirit, spontaneity, and creativity of the early years, they would not want to return to the chaos and instability of "that life." Life in the square was not always harmonious: there were inevitable tensions and the presence of frightening local characters:

> There used to be wild parties here ... there used to be different tribes because each household was a shared household. There were clans and it is not that there were not conflicts ... A guy living here threatened me with a knife one night. There was a dark side ... There were different factions and tribes, different ideas, personalities and leaderships (Interview 2, August 25, 2009).

The creativity and artistic ideals of Bonnington Square's squatter communities have left their mark over time. The communal gardens, the wealth of (often unusual) plants lining the square's relatively quiet streets and corners, and the flowerpots populating its pavements frame contemporary users' perception and sense of place. They also contrast with the much starker "urban-ness" characterizing much of the surrounding area.

Creative details are also still visible: a massive sculpture of a hand (an old theater prop) is displayed on the entrance to a garden, and an old mill wheel (an 1860s industrial artifact rescued from a nearby marble factory) (Fig. 8.2) has been erected against a wall where it acts as a giant trellis. Paths made from old tiles wind through another communal garden, murals made out of old pottery decorate walls, and stained-glass windows are dotted across the façades of buildings: "this peaceful garden ... my special place: this playing area. This path is made with reclaimed bricks ..." (Interview 1, July 1, 2009).

Such details are physical markers of the square's history and visible reminders of the physical efforts put in by squatters into the placemaking of the square. They also contribute to Bonnington Square's sense of place and emotional dimension or "feel" associated with this place. One of the most significant themes to emerge from our walking interviews was the emotions and feelings clustered around material features of the square (for example, a corner of a garden, a plant-pot mural, or a particular tree). As such, they were closely related to the residents' creative practices and their continued involvement in making and adding to the square's built environment, its buildings, and public spaces.

One interesting example here is a small "squiggle" painted just above a door that a long-term resident and former squatter, now part of a housing co-operative, pointed out to us in a walking interview when stopping in front of a house she used to live in:

> So this house here. I was in love with this crazy guy [laughter]. He and I lived on the top floor. And it was all a wreck outside anyway. So we just knocked the wall through. So all the top floor was open plan and you had a lovely view all around. It was so light and sunny in the summer. It was just like a dream house. [pause] And someone painted on there. They put 'Happy House, Happy

House'. And you would have thought that any builder worth their salt, they would have got rid of that, but they didn't. They let go of the words but – you know – that bit of paint? [interviewer: That squiggle?] I think they were too lazy to get rid of it altogether, but it actually had 'Happy House' on it (Interview 2, August 25, 2009).

Accounts like these show us the importance of residents' creative placemaking practices, both for the creation of a distinctive sense of place as well as for the development of emotional connections to places and to others. Lefebvre's discussion of the right to the city and urban culture advocated for urban spaces that allowed for "connection, play, difference, surprise and novelty" (Purcell, 2014). The creative practices that Bonnington Square's residents are trying to hold on to are reminiscent of this, embracing as they do the handmade, the informal, the socially based, the spontaneous, the eclectic reuse of material, and the at times conflictual negotiation of placemaking.

Threats to Creative Placemaking and "the Right to the City" in Bonnington Square

Over three decades, the sociocultural composition of the square has undergone substantial changes, influenced by both broad urban transformations and more localized shifts. During the empirical research for this project, a substantial portion of South London's formerly industrial Thames frontage (from Vauxhall to the Nine Elms district, including Battersea Power Station) underwent a vast regeneration program. In 2004, Vauxhall, Nine Elms, and Battersea (VNEB) were identified in the then London Mayor Ken Livingston's London Plan as an Opportunity Area (OA) with the potential for 18,500 new homes and 18,500 new jobs by 2041 (Mayor of London, 2004). Subsequently, in 2008, it was announced that the US embassy in London was to relocate to the area from Grosvenor Square, Mayfair (US Embassy & Consulates in the UK, 2008). At the time of writing, the redevelopment of the area, with the controversial emerging cluster of mostly luxury apartments and high-rise towers dubbed the Dubai-on-Thames (Bevan, 2014), is almost concluded, and Battersea Power Station development has recently opened as large residential, retail, and commercial space.

Locally, Bonnington Square underwent significant changes as well. Not only is the square no longer squatted, but over the previous two decades, it has also evolved into a desirable location for middle-class professionals. Property prices have risen considerably, and a local estate agent's advertisement at the end of 2023 described the square as "an iconic oasis brimming with nature in the heart of central London ... surrounded by trees, vines and tropical plants planted by members of the Bonnington Square Garden Association to bring inner city living and nature together in harmony" (Bonnington Square Agents, 2023) and attributed the responsibility not to squatters but instead to "a group of resourceful residents who transformed the houses and saved the square, through a process of diligent and determined self-build and restoration." Such descriptions are indicators of how much the square has changed. They also show how markers of the square's former alternative cultural identity have been repositioned within contemporary marketing strategies.

The cultural cycles of gentrification are familiar: artists and creative groups move into a run-down neighborhood where they create a particular kind of cultural capital, only to be progressively displaced by young professionals or middle-class urbanites (this process has been well documented in, for example, the work of Zukin, 1987, 2009, 2016; Zukin & Braslow, 2011). This resonates with what has happened in Bonnington Square, but gentrification has also been multilayered and complex. In particular, we can trace what we call internal and external processes of gentrification. With regard to its internal gentrification, one of the interesting aspects about Bonnington Square is that many of the original squatters themselves became "gentrified." They acquired proprietorial rights to the squatted houses (through housing cooperatives or privately) and left behind alternative lifestyles to embrace professional, business, or creative careers.

With regard to its external gentrification, our interviews identified two stages. From the 1990s to the early 2000s, there has been a slow gentrification by young professionals with a taste for the area's artsy image, who rented or purchased flats and houses in the square itself or in a smaller gated community nearby (originally a school). However, former squatters have not necessarily been pushed out nor is there a straightforward conflict between old and new ways of life, marginal or mainstream cultural practices. Old residents embraced the arrival of a delicatessen shop selling Italian coffee (often seen as a sign of gentrification). In our interviews, many agreed that change had not necessarily been bad, and they certainly did not want to go back to the squatting days (Interview 5, August 2, 2009).

While this first phase created some apprehension among all the squatters we interviewed, its threat to creative placemaking practices was not perceived as great as the concerns that accompanied the more recent second wave of regeneration and gentrification. This second phase was unleashed by a more concerted development push in the wider area from the early 2000s onward with the redevelopment of Nine Elms. Given the size and density of the Nine Elms development, its lengthy and disruptive construction process, the visual impact of the finished buildings, the anticipated increase in the area's residential population, and the added pressure on local services, it is not surprising that residents expressed concern in interviews and in community meetings we attended as observers, when the development was still in its infancy, about how it would affect their small neighborhood. Already worried about how the square's cultural landscape had been exploited in the marketing of the square and the effect that the erection of a smaller gated community already had on community life, the impact of the construction of 18,500 luxury flats in the square's immediate vicinity seemed difficult to imagine.

Notably, though, the concerns expressed by participants were less about being pushed out, a discourse frequently associated with gentrification (Hubbard & Lees, 2018). Instead, they were more about the threat posed by gentrification to the continuation of residents' creative spatial practices and their everyday involvement in the making of place. As discussed above, the ability to creatively and independently make and maintain the square was a crucial component of our participants' narratives. Indeed, here we might elaborate further. It was not just a focus on creative practices that defined the sense of place of former squatters and new residents but the fact that these practices were informal, spontaneous, and not restricted by external regulations. The interview extracts discussed earlier hint at the significance placed on the unplanned nature of creative practices and the fact that they spontaneously emerged out of material conditions. Against this background, gentrification suggested the death of creativity, spontaneity, informality, and independence. According to one participant:

> Putting a frigging tower down at the end there, which is going to be full of transient people doing their London thing ... There might be the odd exception, but in the main I think people aren't going to be thinking about flower pots and trees, and greening and space, and birdlife and bees, in the way people living here have come to, because of what's happened in their lives and settling here. Because we have a really interesting cross-section of people, in terms of how they relate to the space. Because it's all well and good if you have the kind of money that afford to come here. You're going to think you're in paradise, but whether you're actually going to get your trowel out and start attending workdays and put in is a different matter, and people who do love it and want the square to remain will do that (Interview 8, 13 March 2010).

During our walking interviews and the community events in which we participated, residents expressed anxieties not only about ongoing urban transformations in the surrounding Vauxhall, Nine Elms, and Battersea areas but also about the continuation of creative spatial practices and their everyday involvement in making place. The physical details which emerged in our walks – the flowerpots, the trees, the murals, and green spaces – had endured from the period of the squatters: they were visible reminders of the square's history and efforts put in by squatters to "regenerate and hand-make" the square. For some of the square's residents, these physical markers had become symbols of a different way of life. However, this way of life was now under threat. Participants in our research were afraid that rather than freely participating in the making and remaking of their neighborhood, their neighborhood would soon be no more than objects of cultural consumption. In other words, their right to "change themselves by changing the city" (Harvey, 2008) was endangered.

Conclusions

This chapter has covered some of the themes emerging from our research into a particular neighborhood. It is not an exhaustive account, but it presents a snapshot of the stories and experiences of the inhabitants of Bonnington Square over a particular time frame, at a point when residents felt that locally focused, participative creative practices, which had developed slowly and organically over time, were under threat by fast-paced and large-scale development.

Our analysis aimed to draw out the significance of participatory and creative practices in the making, experience, and negotiation of place and the extent to which such practices are vulnerable to different patterns of gentrification. With regard to the former, the walking interviews drew out the extent to which memories and emotions clustered strongly around physical features that participants or their friends and acquaintances had a role in building, making, repairing, or maintaining. They also illustrate how such material practices create a connection – sometimes described as a responsibility – between maker and made, urban dweller, and urban landscape.

Moreover, our participants' accounts also give expression to the fear that the freedom to engage in informal initiatives and to create new uses and forms of public space (our right to the city) is being threatened because spaces are no longer seen as living contexts. Marshalled into a wider process of economic accumulation and cultural consumption, they are no longer seen as places that their inhabitants can transform but rather as cultural commodities.

The narratives evoked by our participants resonate with the arguments made by Lefebvre (1968, 1991), Purcell (2014), and Harvey (2008) discussed above concerning our alienation from the potential vibrancy of urban life and the call for inhabitants' right to reshape the cities they inhabit. The fears expressed by our research participants reflect a sorrowful response to the potential loss of the informal, the open-ended, and the spontaneous – what Lefebvre describes as "the urban" – and a suspicion of the rise of the finite, the structured, and the commodified – what Lefebvre describes as "the city."

This lament focuses our attention on the importance of informal and creative practices in negotiating place and community and on the problems associated with the prestructured and commodified city, over which we have no purchase. It also posits creativity as a constitutive element in a melee of (not always harmonious) social relations and practices, which are increasingly being threatened by different patterns of gentrification.

References

Akbar, P. N. G., & Edelenbos, J. (2021). Positioning place-making as a social process: A systematic literature review. *Cogent Social Sciences*, 7(1), 1905920.

Berning, D. (2011, September 11). Life in a Victorian terrace. *The Guardian*. https://www.theguardian.com/artanddesign/2011/sep/11/victorian-terrace-home-architecture

Bevan, R. (2014, April 1). Dubai-on-Thames: The rise of London's tall buildings. *London Evening Standard*. https://www.standard.co.uk/culture/exhibitions/dubaionthames-the-rise-of-londons-tall-buildings-9227566.html

Blokland, T. (2017). *Community as urban practice*. Polity Press.

Bonnington Square Estate Agents. (2023). Welcome to Bonnington Square, a new kind of estate agency. Bonnington Square. https://www.bonningtonsquare.com/

Cresswell, T. (2014). *Place: An introduction*. Wiley.

Degen, M. M., & Rose, G. (2012). The sensory experiencing of urban design: The role of walking and perceptual memory. *Urban Studies*, 49(15), 3271–3287.

Ellery, P. J., Ellery, J., & Borkowsky, M. (2021). Toward a theoretical understanding of placemaking. *International Journal of Community Well-Being*, *4*(1), 55–76.
Evans, J., & Jones, P. (2011). The walking interview: Methodology, mobility and place. *Applied Geography*, *31*(2), 849–858.
Ferreri, M. (2015). The seductions of temporary urbanism. *Ephemera*, *15*(1), 181–191.
Fisker, J. K., Chiappini, L., Pugalis, L., & Bruzzese, A. (Eds.). (2018). *The production of alternative urban spaces: An international dialogue*. Routledge.
Gehl, J. (2010). *Cities for people*. Island Press.
Gehl, J. (2011). *Life between buildings: Using public space*. Island Press.
Harvey, D. (1989). *The condition of postmodernity*. Blackwell.
Harvey, D. (2008). The right to the city. *New Left Review*, *53*, 23–40.
Healey, P. (2020). *Collaborative planning: Shaping places in fragmented societies*. Bloomsbury.
Hennink, M., Hutter, I., & Bailey, A. (2020). *Qualitative research methods*. Sage.
Hou, J. (Ed.) (2010), *Insurgent public space: Guerrilla urbanism and the remaking of contemporary cities*. Routledge.
Hubbard, P., & Lees, L. (2018). The right to community? Legal geographies of resistance on London's gentrification frontiers. *City*, *22*(1), 8–25.
Jacobs, J. (1961). *The death and life of great American cities*. Random House.
Jacobs, J. M. (2006). A geography of big things. *Cultural Geographies*, *13*(1), 1–27.
Jones, P., Bunce, G., Evans, J., Gibbs, H., & Hein, J. R. (2008). Exploring space and place with walking interviews. *Journal of Research Practice*, *4*(2), D2.
Lefebvre, H. (1968). *Le droit à la ville*. Anthropos. Translated as The right to the city. In E. Kofman & E. Lebas (Eds.), *Writings on cities* (pp. 63–181). Blackwell.
Lefebvre, H. (1991). *The production of space*. Wiley Blackwell.
Living London History. (2021, September 6). *The fascinating story of Vauxhall's secret jungle neighbourhood*. Living London History. https://livinglondonhistory.com/the-fascinating-story-of-vauxhalls-secret-jungle-neighbourhood/
London Gardens Trust. (2015, August 28). *London Parks & Gardens – Inventory site record*. London Parks & Gardens. https://londongardenstrust.org/conservation/inventory/site-record/?ID=LAM006
Lydon, M., & Garcia, A. (2015). A tactical urbanism how-to. In M. Lydon & A. Garcia (Eds.), *Tactical urbanism* (pp. 171–208). Island Press.
Madanipour, A. (1999). Why are the design and development of public spaces significant for cities? *Environment and Planning B: Planning and Design*, *26*(6), 879–891.
Madanipour, A. (2003). *Public and private spaces of the city*. Routledge.
Madanipour, A. (2017). *Cities in time: Temporary urbanism and the future of the city*. Bloomsbury.
Markusen, A. (2014). Creative cities: A 10-year research agenda. *Journal of Urban Affairs*, *36*(Suppl. 2), 567–589.
Mayor of London. (2004). *The London Plan: The Spatial Development Plan for Greater London*. Greater London Authority.
Montgomery, J. (1998). Making a city: Urbanity, vitality and urban design. *Journal of Urban Design*, *3*(1), 93–116.
Mould, O. (2014). Tactical urbanism: The new vernacular of the creative city. *Geography Compass*, *8*(8), 529–539.

Pagano, C. (2013). DIY urbanism: Property and process in grassroots city building. *Marquette Law Review, 97,* 335–469.
Pearson, D. (2008, June 8). Pleasure garden. *The Guardian.* https://www.theguardian.com/lifeandstyle/2008/jun/08/shopping.gardens
Pile, S. (2010). Emotions and affect in recent human geography. *Transactions of the Institute of British Geographers, 35*(1), 5–20.
Pink, S. (2015). *Doing sensory ethnography.* Sage.
Purcell, M. (2014). Possible worlds: Henri Lefebvre and the right to the city. *Journal of Urban Affairs, 36*(1), 141–154.
Relph, E. (1976). *Place and placelessness.* Pion.
Rose, G. (1997). Situating knowledges: Positionality, reflexivities and other tactics. *Progress in Human Geography, 21*(3), 305–320.
Rose, G., Degen, M., & Basdas, B. (2010). More on 'big things': Building events and feelings. *Transactions of the Institute of British Geographers, 35*(3), 334–349.
Shields, R. (1998). *Lefebvre, love and struggle: Spatial dialectics.* Routledge.
Simpson, B. (2014). Insurgent public space: Guerrilla urbanism and the remaking of contemporary cities. *International Planning Studies, 19*(1), 105–108.
Talen, E. (2015). Do-it-yourself urbanism: A history. *Journal of Planning History, 14*(2), 135–148.
The Guardian. (2008, August 23). From squat to hot. *The Guardian.* https://www.theguardian.com/lifeandstyle/2008/aug/23/homes1
Tuan, Y. F. (1977). *Space and place: The perspective of experience.* University of Minnesota Press.
US Embassy and Consulates in the United Kingdom. (2008, October 2). *New U.S. Embassy in Nine Elms, London.* https://uk.usembassy.gov/our-relationship/policy-history/new-embassy/new-london-embassy-in-nine-elms/
Vimeo. (2012, February 11). *Bonnington Square.* Video. Vimeo. https://vimeo.com/36595608?signup=true
Zukin, S. (1987). Gentrification: Culture and capital in the urban core. *Annual Review of Sociology, 13*(1), 129–147.
Zukin, S. (2008). Whose culture? Whose city? In T. S. Oakes & P. L. Price (Eds.), *The cultural geography reader* (pp. 443–450). Routledge.
Zukin, S. (2009). *Naked city: The death and life of authentic urban places.* Oxford University Press.
Zukin, S. (2016). Gentrification in three paradoxes. *City & Community, 15*(3), 202–207.
Zukin, S., & Braslow, L. (2011). The life cycle of New York's creative districts: Reflections on the unanticipated consequences of unplanned cultural zones. *City, Culture and Society, 2*(3), 131–140.

Chapter 9

The Political Dimension of Making a Place: Framing the Right to the City in Placemaking

Débora Picorelli Zukeran, Claudia E. Carter and Miguel Hincapié Triviño

Birmingham City University, UK

Abstract

This chapter focuses on the political dimension of placemaking. While placemaking has the potential to foment political change, recent discussion about placemaking seems to revolve around its methods and outcomes. Departing from the perspective of placemaking as outcome, this chapter positions placemaking as a dynamic process, shifting attention to the actors involved and their motivations. This political dimension is explored by adopting a framework of the right to the city, enabling a critical examination of existing power structures and circumstances in the transformation of the urban landscape. Drawing on a few cases of placemaking to illustrate the questions about who has the right to make places, this chapter emphasizes the need for structural change in the transformation of urban spaces for public use. As the current approach for placemaking is criticized for fueling social inequalities, asymmetrical political processes, and spatial issues, such as gentrification and displacement, a new framework is required to reorientate placemaking toward a people-led approach. This chapter shows how, by employing the right to the city framework, placemaking can be interpreted beyond its physical outcomes as a unique set of conditions and circumstances that facilitate or hinder people's ability to make a place. Moreover, the right to the city provides a lens to examine the processes involved in the transformation of the urban landscape and acknowledges the potential of placemaking to challenge these processes.

Placemaking, 163–177
Copyright © 2025 Débora Picorelli Zukeran, Claudia E Carter and Miguel Hincapié Triviño
Published under exclusive licence by Emerald Publishing Limited
doi:10.1108/978-1-83753-130-120241018

Keywords: Placemaking; right to the city; sense of place; people-led; privatization of space; gentrification

Introduction

This chapter proposes the concept of "the right to the city" (Harvey, 2012; Lefebvre, 1968; Mitchell, 2003; Purcell, 2002) to reimagine placemaking focusing on its political dimension. Exploring its political dimension allows placemaking to be understood as a process, rather than an outcome. In doing so, the circumstances of that space transformation move into focus: who is/was involved and the motivations behind it. The act of making a place becomes intentional, and the people involved in the process (rather than investors or experts) become the agents of their environment. Taking a right to the city perspective therefore facilitates a critical lens to scrutinize current structures of power and influencers in the transformation of spaces. It acknowledges that those who inhabit the space should decide, or at least influence, how it is transformed, instead of unquestioningly adopting or accepting a market-driven approach.

This lens is pertinent to recent discussion on the effects of placemaking (critiques on gentrification, privatization, austerity, and spatial segregation) and the need for a people-led approach. Much has been discussed about the outcomes and methods of placemaking, but there is a lot of room to theorize about its process. In the current context of how urban spaces are created and controlled, a new interpretation of placemaking as a political act supports calls for a people-led approach on decision-making. A right to the city framework structures this new interpretation around the potential of challenging the current structures of power that hinder people's ability to claim their agency over the urban space.

This chapter begins with explaining common interpretations of placemaking as a concept and its critiques; it then highlights the importance of process alongside outcomes in placemaking projects and planning endeavors. These aspects lay the foundation to understand the importance of placemaking as a political act and how the right to the city provides a meaningful framework to help democratize urban change and neighborhood-level planning.

Understanding Placemaking: Concept and Critiques

Placemaking has no set definition, rendering all discussions about the impact of placemaking in urban development subject to how people understand the concept (Ellery et al., 2021). In any case, finding a universal and rigid definition of placemaking might be counterproductive to the idea of "making a place" because place is a multidimensional concept dependent on cultural, social, and geographical assumptions people have (Mateo-Babiano & Lee, 2020).The discussion of how placemaking is employed, either as a market-driven urban renewal tool (Bedoya, 2013; Stabrowski, 2014; Toolis, 2017) or as a community-driven tool for public participation (Project for Public Spaces, 2007), depends on the notion of place itself. This means that specific understandings of the concept of place affect how we understand and develop urban design, policies, and everyday life in society (Douglas, 2023).

Just as it is inevitable to discuss the notion of place without considering the element of space, either in contrast, parallel, or complementary (Massey, 2005; Relph, 1976; Tuan, 1977), it is the same for people, as place is inherently about people. While place and space are defined according to human experiences and interactions, the relationship to people is what differentiates place from space (Douglas, 2023). While space is associated with locality and physicality, places come into being through people inhabiting spaces, giving social meanings and values and forming attachments (Relph, 1976; Tuan, 1977). However, as much as places do not exist without people, people ultimately do not always have a protagonist role in making places. Just as people shape spaces, spaces shape people too, turning placemaking into a continuous process by creating meaningful experiences in, of, and for people (Hes et al., 2020; Wyckoff, 2014). Through this process of imprinting their values, perceptions, and cultural traditions onto a geographical space, people develop what is known as "sense of place" (Lew, 2017). A good analogy for this is when a house is turned into a home, a place people are familiar with and care about, just as when a space is turned into a place (Moore, 2020; Wyckoff, 2014).

Sense of place, as the bonds people develop to a particular space and the distinctiveness of that space (Foote & Azaryahu, 2009), reveals the political and social elements of the process of making places. When people imprint their values and meaning on spaces, they build their vision for the urban environment. Lefebvre (1991) highlighted that space is produced and reproduced through people's experiences and aspirations for their lives. The process of making a place is, therefore, a way to claim everyday urban life.

However, the process of making a place is not confined to the physical boundaries of a space but influenced, shaped, and transformed with reference to its wider context. Because the meanings and attachments formed within a space are plural and subjective to the life experiences of each individual or group, the process of making a place reflects social norms and structures. This means that the process of placemaking is influenced, shaped, and diverted by social relations in play. The social circumstances of an individual, such as their race, gender, or class, are likely to influence sense of place, feelings of belonging and entitlement, and how much power they exercise over their environments (Hayden, 1994; Manzo, 2005). If there is a great deal of inequality in society, this will appear in how people relate with this environment and, therefore, how space is shaped, transformed, and kept.

The discussions over the implications of placemaking in the urban environment reflect this understanding well. Over the past decade, as placemaking became more present in the vocabulary of practitioners, academics, and policy makers, a more critical perspective voiced concern over the exclusionary impact of placemaking (Bedoya, 2013; Douglas, 2023; Lees & Melhuish, 2013; Moran & Berbary, 2021; Toolis, 2017). The idea that placemaking could transform spaces into desired and attractive places to live in (Wyckoff, 2014) led placemaking to be linked to urban projects aiming to renew and revitalize existing areas (Moran & Berbary, 2021). However, as Moran and Berbary (2021) discuss, "renewal" and "revitalization" carry a meaning suggesting that what was before was not good enough or nothing at all, that those spaces are a shell ready to be made meaningful. Even though this reflection relates to the authors' specific context of settler colonial cities in North America, the issues of perpetuating the displacement of local inhabitants through these urban renewal projects are not exclusive to the Indigenous peoples in Canada. Douglas (2023) joins this discussion on how the narrative of placemaking is used to sanitize the urban landscape, using the case of homeless people in California and how placemaking projects do not account for or include them. The exclusionary concern around placemaking is also directed to the lack of an ecological approach, ignoring the needs and realities of nonhuman elements and disregarding them as users of the urban space (Boros & Mahmoud, 2021; Hes et al., 2020).

Many projects reduce placemaking to beautifying neighborhoods, making them attractive to investment and projecting an image of safety, order, and creativity, while disregarding the entrenched problems of racial and social inequality (Bedoya, 2013; Douglas, 2023; Mitchell, 2003). These projects follow a similar aesthetic and guidelines, as invoked in our minds when Moran and Berbary (2021, p. 644) describe them as "A colourful mural, flowers in bloom, and strings of warm-hued lighting" or when Douglas (2023, p. 39) says of pedestrian-oriented streets, "think brightly coloured temporary seating, maybe ping pong tables."

The focus on these aesthetics raises the question whether such placemaking is something aiming to create spaces to exhibit at the expense of those who inhabit them (Fincher et al., 2016). Bringing these recognizable and trendy elements to a neighborhood transforms its image to attract investment but also contributes to an immaterial dimension of displacement. This means not only the physical displacement of the local population but of their cultural identity and the loss of sense of place that they had developed (Bedoya, 2013; Fincher et al., 2016). Placemaking becomes a brand for urban renewal built on a positivity discourse of inclusion and diversity that disregards the power dynamics involved in the making of a place (Fincher et al., 2016; Moran & Berbary, 2021). By focusing on commonality, a generic and standard vision, placemaking forgets the differences that make up the plural society we have and produces spaces that reinforce social relations of power and generates urban capital to those who already have wealth (Douglas, 2023; Fincher et al., 2016; Sharp et al., 2005). An example of this is the gentrification of the neighborhood of Notting Hill, in West London. Curiously enough, the neighborhood was even the case study for the sociologist Ruth Glass (1964) when she coined the term "gentrification" itself. In the middle of the 20th century, Windrush immigrants arrived in London and experienced difficulties to find accommodation, having to move into areas of the city that were heavily bombed in the Blitz and where many of the buildings were still in disrepair. Many of the houses that were once inhabited by one family were now bought by landlords and housed several families. The area was overcrowded with families from the Caribbean in precarious situations. Soon, racist graffiti started to appear in the neighborhood, and the Caribbean immigrants were harassed and attacked on the streets. There was a clear sentiment that they were not welcome and did not belong there. Several community organizations emerged in order to provide help with housing and a sense of community. Soon after, the now-famous Notting Hill Carnival, a celebration of Caribbean culture, started. Notting Hill became a Caribbean place; it was home to a community that was persecuted and taken advantage of. After many tenants were able to buy their houses due to local community saving schemes, many of the houses reverted to single-family occupancy and attracted the attention of investors and middle-class families with the resources to renovate the derelict houses. In the late 1980s, the character of the neighborhood started to change, with many Black-owned businesses replaced by other businesses that catered to the needs of the new residents (Loffhagen, 2023; Martin, 2005). The immigrant residents were priced out of the place where they were first not welcome but nevertheless still had built a community.

The gentrification of inner-city neighborhoods, like Notting Hill, shows not only a reconfiguration of the physical space, who inhabits and accesses the space, but also the spatial identity itself. A neighborhood that was known for its overcrowded working-class buildings, and for having been the stage for the race riots in 1958 (Martin, 2005), is now one of the most affluent neighborhoods of London.

These critiques on placemaking around the loss of identity, the application of a standard aesthetic, privatization of public spaces, sanitation of the landscape, the displacement of the local population, or the little attention to the environment are fair and valid. A common underlying issue is who is included and who is excluded in the processes of creating and transforming urban spaces. If placemaking is to be used for its "potential to foster a sense of belonging, community, even power – especially perhaps for subaltern, underprivileged, excluded, or displaced people" (Douglas, 2023, p. 5), there is a pressing need to reimagine a redistribution of power over the urban space (Moran & Berbary, 2021), enabling placemaking to become a way for people to reclaim agency in how urban space is transformed. By focusing on the "how," the conversation is led to understand placemaking as a process, rather than an outcome.

Placemaking: Process or Outcome?

There is a clear difference between understanding placemaking as a process or as an outcome. When viewing placemaking only as the outcome, as a product, of what was achieved and built, then the relationship with what was before is much based on comparisons of "before and after" but from a perspective of the "now" and current values. It becomes a discourse where history is written by the winners, and which is focused on how this new space affects people now, and limiting or ignoring knowledge and interests pertaining to the prior situation. On the other hand, when seeing placemaking as a process, there is an inevitable focus on the "during." This is not to say that the result is not of importance or interest, but it is not the main or sole focus, and there is a general understanding that things may not come out as once planned. This is mainly because, when seeing something as a process, things evolve and may change: there may be errors, unforeseeable factors, and contextual circumstances. Moreover, it places attention to not only considering the particularities of each situation but to appreciate that making a place is a process of many different steps, not a single action. Doing so humanizes placemaking – a concept that is very much dependent on human interactions. And even if the results in two different places are very similar in terms of aesthetics, morphology, and function, there will be an understanding that the steps to get there were not, that they were derived from the specific context, ideas, and needs of the people living and/or working there and using and shaping that place.

The attention given to placemaking as an outcome is not limited to its practice but also its theories. Much of the discussion around placemaking revolves around its methods and outcomes (Toolis, 2017), as types of placemaking are identified (Wyckoff, 2014) and many toolkits, policies, and best practice reports are created. There is plenty of evidence of the application of placemaking as a practice of spatial transformation, but the theoretical dimension relating to its process remains vague and scarce (Fincher et al., 2016; Toolis, 2017). Perhaps it is this characteristic of being vague and elusive that allows placemaking to be adapted and used in a diversity of situations. Perhaps being open to interpretation is what allows multiple realities to develop and a plurality of sense of place in the same space. At the same time, however, this vagueness allows for some interpretations being more prominent than others.

What is certain is that placemaking is influenced and shaped by current trends of thought. When we observe the impact of placemaking as either the gentrification of inner-city districts or the participatory design of public spaces, we are looking at choices. For example, the privatization of public spaces happens because there is a deliberate choice of treating urban spaces as commodities – it is a choice to orientate urban development toward profit. It is a choice to understand and produce urban spaces in a certain way, according to certain ideals. The vague definition of placemaking is replaced by a subjective practice: the choices for placemaking have reasons behind them, theories and underlying values or principles that sustain and direct them toward a vision. Perhaps the vague definition(s) of placemaking remain that way because its practice is subjective to all different sorts of situations. However, subjectivity does not equate with vagueness. Therefore, it is important to theorize the process of placemaking, question assumptions, deliberate visions and goals, and open up placemaking to the plurality of residents and users.

Exploring the Political Dimension of Placemaking

Understanding the choices around placemaking means acknowledging that there were other possibilities that were never chosen. They are other possibilities of place suppressed or defeated in a contest over whose vision, resources and agency dominates (Arefi, 2014). The acknowledgment of other possibilities of place opens up a discussion of what has been and what could have been. How and why was this particular choice taken? Who was left behind? What were the other possibilities? Who influenced and made this choice? Examining the process of placemaking allows these questions to be addressed and answered. Redirecting the focus to the process, instead of the outcomes, sheds light on the political dimension of placemaking. This lens to placemaking recognizes that spaces are being produced, instead of merely spatially transformed. The difference lies in placemaking being concerned with how spaces come to be, who was involved (people and/or organizations), how resources were managed and deployed, and whether those spaces reinforce or challenge the status quo.

What this chapter proposes, by focusing on the process, is a new perspective of placemaking not as consequence but as intention. Reflecting on the distinction between place and space discussed above and how sense of place is developed, it is possible to form the notion that the making of places is intentional, even if not explicit. When people develop a sense of place, they give meaning and imprint their own perceptions and values on a space (Lew, 2017): they are choosing a possibility of place. It is in this notion of intention that placemaking is regarded as production of spaces: it is a combination of social, economic, and political relations, representing people's experiences of space in everyday life (Irandoost et al., 2019; Purcell, 2002). Therefore, placemaking is a conscious act.

It is through this consciousness that the act of making a place carries the potential of challenging how things are done. It reveals that the idea of making a place itself is not exclusive and restricted – even if the practice is – but something possible to anyone and everyone. By creating spaces that reflect people's identity, aspirations, and needs, they are enabled to reclaim agency over their environment. It ultimately challenges current structures of power by redirecting the decision-making process to those who inhabit or use the space. As the making of a place is a political process, it is formed by the way in which people understand the world. It is, in essence, an epistemological process supported by theoretical assumptions about life and the world. Therefore, a solid theoretical framework is essential to guide and support this interpretation of placemaking as a political and intentional process that ignites change.

A New Interpretation of Placemaking: A Framework of the Right to the City

This interpretation of placemaking is triggered by the question of who is included and excluded in the process of making places. It acknowledges, through the review of literature, that the act of making places is not universal, nor evenly accessible to everyone. But it also highlights the fact that people can be agents of their own environment; they can be makers of their own places, that spaces can reflect the culture and aspirations of those who inhabit and use them. These are the ideas that should frame an interpretation focused on the political dimension of placemaking. A framework around the political dimension of placemaking enables this potential of change to be explored, theorized, and applied to practice. And this is explored now in more detail through the theory of the right to the city.

By redirecting the decision-making process over the transformation of urban spaces to those who inhabit them, the making of places is no longer restricted or exclusive. It is interpreted as something that can be practiced by everyone, as a right, rather than a privilege or a concession. The right to the city is used not only to frame placemaking as a political process but also to reveal and explain dynamics of power and highlight what circumstances and factors enable or deter people on exercising the right of making a place.

Just as placemaking is a contested concept (Fincher et al., 2016), so is the right to the city. The right to the city is a concept first coined by Lefebvre in his 1968 book *Le droit à la ville* (*The right to the city*). In his conceptualization, the urban space should not be entirely controlled by market-driven forces but by the people who inhabit it. He drives an extensive analysis of the influence of capitalism over the urban space, including the commodification of urban life, the decrease of social interaction and urban governance being a privilege. The core of his idea was that decision-making processes would be diverted from the state to the production of spaces, meaning to those who inhabit the space. Many social movements have recently reclaimed the right to the city, and the concept has become a common topic in academic and policy discussions about growing inequality, undemocratic urban policies, the power of capital, and how these issues affect austerity, authoritarianism, and the denial of human rights (Purcell, 2002). The right to the city emerges from a context of exclusion, and among its many perceptions and definitions, it is a concept that, as a right, is not enjoyed by all. The right to the city proposes a radical structuring of social, economic, and political relations, as it calls for a decision-making process involving those who produce spaces, rather than those who exploit them (Harvey, 2008; Lefebvre, 1996; Purcell, 2002). The right to the city challenges structures of power in place to prevent people from feeling entitled to engage and construct the urban space. As Harvey (2008, p. 23) stated, "The right to the city ... is the right to change yourselves by changing the city."

The right to the city theorizes placemaking around its political dimension, but this dimension is not always evident. However, it does become clearer through observing the different ways of making places. They are not only different because they are made by different people but also because of different visions, claims, and disputes over urban spaces. The different ways in which people make places reveal differences in resources, motivations, and awareness. The right to the city explores this political dimension of placemaking as products of the combination of circumstances that render each situation unique. Considering the uniqueness of each process enables us to regard placemaking as a political act in its specific context.

The Digbeth Community Garden in Birmingham (UK) and the Political Dimension of Placemaking

The political dimension of a place can be the reason for its existence and strongly shape its identity. This is well illustrated in a community garden located in Birmingham: Digbeth Community Garden (see Fig. 9.1). The political dimension permeates every aspect of its process of placemaking: from the space to the activities there performed. The garden is situated in the center of Digbeth, an area

Fig. 9.1. Digbeth Community Garden. *Source:* Débora Picorelli Zukeran (2023).

in central Birmingham subject to intensive regeneration. The garden is the result of the gardeners' motivation to prevent extensive real estate development in an underutilized site and became the way to resist expensive regeneration and gentrification. The garden started from the convictions, perceptions and worldview of this group of people, and from their contempt of how the surrounding urban space was being transformed. For them, it is a matter of taking ownership of their environment. At the same time, they imprint their values and aspirations for a city in this space. There is a level of conviction that they are doing the right thing, almost as a duty of being inhabitants in the city. This conviction materializes in the way that they do not fear intimidation from the city council or any investors or developers and firmly believe that they own the space, since they have occupied it for several years. The space is very different from the surroundings, a well built-up area next to a railway line. It is a very green space with elements that are not usual for the area, such as flower beds, vegetable patches, and a frog pond. However, how the space is used is also rooted in their political motivation. This space not only re-signifies an empty space in central Birmingham but also the image of a community garden. The group works in an all-welcome, fee-free basis, instead of the more common allotment style of putting your name on a list and, as availability arises, renting a plot and signing up to certain do's and don'ts.

Digbeth Community Garden also does not restrict users' activities to gardening: it holds musical events, community feasts with the vegetables harvested from the garden, classes, and artistic performances. Creating this space, transforming it from a neglected and unused site, brings the idea of an alternative possibility of what a space in this part of Birmingham could be. Moreover, it puts into focus with and for whom it is being made.

The political dimension of placemaking, however, is not necessarily formed consciously. In the case of Digbeth Community Garden, it is clear how the gardeners' intention of claiming their agency over the urban space is what drives the placemaking to happen. But sometimes a place is made from struggle, as a last resort for marginalized groups to belong and to address their needs. These places are an indication of a deep segregation in urban enfranchisement which the next example illustrates. Their political dimension is not immediate; it is worked through the social relations produced within space.

Placemaking Under the Bridge With Garrido Boxe, São Paulo (Brazil)

The meanings given to space through people's lived experiences and interactions are what make the shaping of a place a political act. This is evident in the case of Garrido Boxe, a boxing gym under a flyover in São Paulo. The gym (see Fig. 9.2)

Fig. 9.2. Garrido Boxe gym in São Paulo. *Source:* Débora Picorelli Zukeran, 2018.

is the creation of a local man, Nilson Garrido, locally known as Garrido Boxe, who wished to address an issue – of drug abuse in street children and homeless people under the flyover and other left-over spaces – as he did not see a solution coming from the municipal authorities. The feeling of neglect was ever present, but it was the feeling of hopelessness that triggered him to act by himself. Those left-over spaces, just like him and his peers, were abandoned by the authorities, marginalized by the idea of a city that does not relate to them. The space under the bridge was what was available at the time and would make do: in the early days, much of the equipment was improvised, with boxers throwing punches on old tires and refrigerators. Boxing, though, was something Nilson Garrido knew, as he was a former boxer himself. The improvisation and makeshift situation not only show a scarcity of resources but also an ability to re-signify meaning of material elements. That space under a flyover was no longer only where people used drugs but also where sport is practiced. The unexpected activity slowly became natural for those in the area, changing the perception that the space under the flyover was dangerous, unpleasant, and bare. Through the use of the space and the social relations created, these people form the understanding that they can transform their environment. This is clearly noticed when surrounding residents began forming groups to manage other open spaces under the flyover and demanding more sport facilities from the local government. Perhaps it was this increasing awareness of their potential to challenge power that then triggered persecution tactics by the state: evictions, police raids, closure of services like water and electricity. Despite these measures of intimidation, the gym kept returning because it was not just the physical space that was transformed but its meaning to those people. They no longer saw it as a left-over space but as a space of recreation for public use.

Contextualizing Placemaking as Challenges to Structures of Power

Both cases show actions of people who are or feel excluded from the decision-making processes over nearby urban space. The right to the city frames their presence in space as a challenge to the structures of power that do not include or consider them. It is a reminder that making places is a product of social relations produced within space. Placemaking, for these two cases, becomes a way to claim their space in the city, their space as part of society, and pursuing their vision for the urban space. However, it is important to point out their differences in the processes of making a place. As mentioned before, understanding placemaking processes as unique draws attention to the circumstances in which a place has been shaped and used and investigates the reasons why they exist. It also justifies the need for spaces to be transformed reflecting the local context, and not replicating the same space all over the city. In the examples discussed above, we see differences in motivation, resources, awareness, and sense of entitlement. In the community garden, there is an awareness of how the system works and their right of having their voices heard. They do not fear eviction because they know how to use the tools to fight it. They navigate opportunities to raise resources, such as council grants and charity funds, to bring their vision to life. Furthermore, right from the start, they have a clear picture of what they are contesting and what counts as meaningful placemaking in their locality. On the other hand, Garrido's motivation emerged from a feeling of last resort: he only feels it possible to occupy a space that is as marginalized as he has been, and his sense of entitlement to that space and awareness of his rights as an inhabitant are only formed through the living experiences within space by himself and others. There is never a sense of complete stability because there are formal mechanisms that can claim that space, and he has no power or say over this. The gym under the flyover does not set out to confront the structures of power, as does the community garden. This confrontation, for those involved with Garrido's gym, comes through the realization of their ability to (temporarily) transform their environment and the awareness of their rights being overlooked. This is not to say, however, that Digbeth Community Garden's placemaking process is easier or less impactful than Garrido's. Both face obstacles in their own specific circumstances, and they would not necessarily be able to overcome each other's problems. Placemaking as a process looks at both community action examples as political acts and how they claim their right to the city in different ways.

In this interpretation of placemaking, the right to the city explores the political dimension of placemaking as a unique combination of factors and circumstances that facilitate or hinder people's ability to make places. In this framework, placemaking is intentional; it reflects the motivations, social relations, aspirations, and the vision people have for their environment. This consciousness reveals the potential of placemaking to challenge current structures of power. In parallel, the right to the city brings a lens to scrutinize the processes of transforming spaces and to acknowledge the potential of the placemaking act to challenge these processes, as it advocates for a redirection of the decision-making process to those who inhabit the space. Therefore, this framework brings the possibility for placemaking to be truly place-based and demonstrates the ability of people transforming their own environment.

Conclusion

The political dimension of placemaking allows us to explore its potential for change and extending its significance beyond physical transformations. Placemaking is fundamentally a process linked to social relations and contextual circumstances rather than a fixed outcome. This perspective provides insight into who shapes these spaces, the dynamics of inclusion and exclusion, and the underlying motivations driving the making of a place. In this understanding, placemaking is an intentional production of spaces: it is a combination of social, economic, and political relations, representing people's experiences of space in everyday life (Irandoost et al., 2019; Purcell, 2002).

It is through this consciousness that the act of making a place carries the potential of challenging how things are done. It ultimately challenges current structures of power by redirecting the decision-making process to those who inhabit the space. By doing so, it enables multiple realities to be reflected within the city: it creates spaces that reflect people's identity, aspirations, and needs, enabling people to reclaim agency over their environment.

The exploration of the political dimension of placemaking, particularly focused on the potential of structural change, is guided by a theoretical framework of the right to the city. By framing the making of place as a right, rather than a privilege or random occurrence, it addresses the bottom line of the critiques of placemaking: of who is included and who is excluded in the process of making places. It highlights what circumstances and factors facilitate or hinder people in exercising this right and the motivations behind them. It structures this interpretation of placemaking around the notion of the potential of placemaking to challenge structures of power. It is based on the belief that those who inhabit the space should have the opportunity of being heard and actively being involved in local decision-making processes. But, most importantly, this framework allows us to acknowledge the fact that people are capable of creating the space they want and need. Both cases discussed in this chapter illustrate the act of making a place as a way to claim one's space in the city; they depict actions by individuals who were excluded, in some form, from decision-making processes.

This chapter proposes an interpretation of placemaking that transcends the physical outcomes and explores its political potential. By doing so, it leads the discussion about city-making to not only reflect the multiple social realities – the diverse needs and aspirations of their inhabitants – but also provides channels to challenge and reshape existing power dynamics in the urban environment.

References

Arefi, M. (2014). *Deconstructing placemaking: Needs, opportunities, and assets*. Routledge. https://doi.org/10.4324/9781315777924

Bedoya, R. (2013). *Placemaking and the politics of belonging and dis-belonging*. Grantmakers in the Arts. https://www.giarts.org/article/placemaking-and-politics-belonging-and-dis-belonging

Boros, J., & Mahmoud, I. (2021). Urban design and the role of placemaking in mainstreaming nature-based solutions. Learning from the Biblioteca Degli Alberi case study in Milan. *Frontiers in Sustainable Cities*, *3*, 635610. https://www.frontiersin.org/articles/10.3389/frsc.2021.635610

Douglas, G. C. C. (2023). Reclaiming placemaking for an alternative politics of legitimacy and community in homelessness. *International Journal of Politics, Culture, and Society*, *36*(1), 35–56. https://doi.org/10.1007/s10767-022-09426-x

Ellery, P. J., Ellery, J., & Borkowsky, M. (2021). Toward a theoretical understanding of placemaking. *International Journal of Community Well-Being*, *4*(1), 55–76. https://doi.org/10.1007/s42413-020-00078-3

Fincher, R., Pardy, M., & Shaw, K. (2016). Place-making or place-masking? The everyday political economy of "making place". *Planning Theory & Practice*, *17*(4), 516–536. https://doi.org/10.1080/14649357.2016.1217344

Foote, K. E., & Azaryahu, M. (2009). Sense of place. In R. Kitchin & N. Thrift (Eds.), *International encyclopedia of human geography* (pp. 96–100). Elsevier. https://doi.org/10.1016/B978-008044910-4.00998-6

Glass, R. (1964). Aspects of change. In Centre for Urban Studies. (Ed.), *London: Aspects of change* (pp. xiii–xlii). Macgibbon & Kee.

Harvey, D. (2008). The right to the city. *New Left Review, 53*, 23–40.

Harvey, D. (2012). *Rebel cities: From the right to the city to the urban revolution*. Verso.

Hayden, D. (1994). The power of place: Claiming urban landscapes as people's history. *Journal of Urban History, 20*(4), 466–485. https://doi.org/10.1177/009614429402000402

Hes, D., Mateo-Babiano, I., & Lee, G. (2020). Placemaking fundamentals for the built environment: An introduction. In D. Hes & C. Hernandez-Santin (Eds.), *Placemaking fundamentals for the built environment* (pp. 1–13). Palgrave Macmillan.

Irandoost, K., Doostvandi, M., Litman, T., & Azami, M. (2019). Placemaking and the right to the city of urban poor: A case study in Sanandaj, Iran. *Journal of Place Management and Development, 12*(4), 508–528. https://doi.org/10.1108/JPMD-03-2018-0027

Lees, L., & Melhuish, C. (2013). Arts-led regeneration in the UK: The rhetoric and the evidence on urban social inclusion. *European Urban and Regional Studies, 22*(3), 242–260. https://doi.org/10.1177/0969776412467474

Lefebvre, H. (1968). *Le droit a la ville*. Anthropos.

Lefebvre, H. (1991). *The production of space*. Blackwell.

Lefebvre, H. (1996). *Writings on cities* (E. Kofman & E. Lebas, Eds.). Blackwell.

Lew, A. A. (2017). Tourism planning and place making: Place-making or placemaking? *Tourism Geographies, 19*(3), 448–466. https://doi.org/10.1080/14616688.2017.1282007

Loffhagen, E. (2023, August 25). The forgotten racial history of Notting Hill Carnival. *The Standard*. https://www.standard.co.uk/going-out/attractions/notting-hill-carnival-2022-forgotten-racial-history-police-b1021012.html

Manzo, L. C. (2005). For better or worse: Exploring multiple dimensions of place meaning. *Journal of Environmental Psychology, 25*(1), 67–86.

Martin, G. P. (2005). Narratives great and small: Neighbourhood change, place and identity in Notting Hill. *International Journal of Urban and Regional Research, 29*(1), 67–88.

Massey, D. B. (2005). *For space*. Sage. http://www.sagepub.co.uk/booksProdDesc.nav?prodId=Book227109

Mateo-Babiano, I., & Lee, G. (2020). People in place: Placemaking fundamentals. In D. Hes & C. Hernandez-Santin (Eds.), *Placemaking fundamentals for the built environment* (pp. 15–38). Springer. https://doi.org/10.1007/978-981-32-9624-4_2

Mitchell, D. (2003). *The right to the city: Social justice and the fight for public space*. Guilford Press.

Moore, Z. E. (2020). What is placemaking? Definition & examples. *Spaces to Places*. https://spacestoplaces.co.uk/blog/what-is-placemaking-definition-examples/

Moran, R., & Berbary, L. A. (2021). Placemaking as unmaking: Settler colonialism, gentrification, and the myth of "revitalized" urban spaces. *Leisure Sciences, 43*(6), 644–660. https://doi.org/10.1080/01490400.2020.1870592

Project for Public Spaces. (2007). *What is placemaking?* https://www.pps.org/article/what-is-placemaking

Purcell, M. (2002). Excavating Lefebvre: The right to the city and its urban politics of the inhabitant. *Geojournal, 58*, 99–108.

Relph, E. C. (1976). *Place and placelessness.* Pion. https://bac-lac.on.worldcat.org/oclc/300946176

Sharp, J., Pollock, V., & Paddison, R. (2005). Just art for a just city: Public art and social inclusion in urban regeneration. *Urban Studies, 42*(5/6), 1001–1023. https://doi.org/10.1080/00420980500106963

Stabrowski, F. (2014). New-build gentrification and the everyday displacement of Polish immigrant tenants in Greenpoint, Brooklyn. *Antipode, 46*(3), 794–815. https://doi.org/10.1111/anti.12074

Toolis, E. E. (2017). Theorizing critical placemaking as a tool for reclaiming public space. *American Journal of Community Psychology, 59*(1–2), 184–199. https://doi.org/10.1002/ajcp.12118

Tuan, Y.-F. (1977). *Space and place.* University of Minnesota Press.

Wyckoff, M. (2014). Definitions of placemaking: Four different types. *Planning & Zoning News, 32*(3), 1–10.

Chapter 10

Placemaking on a Wider Scale: Seeing the Bigger Picture

Kathryn Moore, Alex Albans and Peter J. Larkham

Birmingham City University, UK

Abstract

This chapter outlines a selection of significant ideas emerging from research investigating the implications of the redefinition of theories of perception presented in the book *Overlooking the visual* (Moore, 2010). This is based on a sequence of case studies beyond the academy, establishing a strategic landscape-led approach to placemaking at a regional scale that culminates in the West Midlands National Park, officially launched in 2018 at Birmingham City University. We argue that this is the perfect time to take stock, see the bigger picture, and take a new look at regional planning – not as it has been traditionally conceived, but from a landscape perspective. This is "landscape regional design." This is essential if we want to create better, more resilient places.

Keywords: Landscape; scale; regional planning; spatial planning; rethinking; landscape vision; West Midlands National Park

Introduction

Throughout the development of the work discussed in this chapter, exploring a new approach to regional design, there has been a continuing dialogue oscillating between the view that "this is planning" countered by "no it's not, it is landscape architecture." Further, as architects begin to appreciate the value of landscape, there is the misguided assumption that what we are discussing is actually "architecture." The lack of clarity in professional roles is not necessarily a problem. The main point is that any places we create need to be designed with considerable and appropriate expertise, contribute positively to quality of life and quality of the environment, while addressing global challenges. But, evidently, this is not happening. And where is the sense of urgency?

What is problematic is the absence of holistic, strategic spatial thinking (Moore, 2015). Moore argues that the inability to see the bigger picture is deep-seated, a consequence of the siloed thinking and reductive values embedded in almost every aspect of our lives as we are inexorably swept along in what Schama (1995, p. 14) describes as a "mindless race towards a machine driven universe, where measurement, not memory is the absolute arbiter of value."

Moore argues that it should be self-evident that expertise is required to design well and that it is a critical, investigative skill, applicable at any scale and in any context. Yet a long-standing overemphasis on teaching planning and design as technical disciplines, largely a matter of referring to technical guides and specifications, makes it almost inevitable that detail is substituted for spatial design and technology for ideas. Policy, often made by well-intentioned people who have little or no design expertise, is handed down to those who do, who then become responsible for ameliorating the consequences of such policy. In this way, strategies for landscape become merely technical appendices rather than setting out a clear strategic vision of its spatial structure. The wide range of checklists, procedures, and design codes now at our disposal simply reinforce this attitude, helping to evaluate and monitor the more easily quantifiable parts of the process. Yet this should not be mistaken for an indicator of quality. Good design does not necessarily equate with the details of sustainable technology, the number of miles of urban swales, the extent of green or brown roofs, or whether we need to plan for 35 or 40 dwellings per hectare. The design and specification of the details is, of course, hugely important – in fact increasingly so with the demands of sustainable development – but it really does require a well-designed conceptual and spatial framework, something that cannot be provided by land use planning alone (Moore, 2010, pp. 208–209).

Crossing professional and disciplinary boundaries between planning and landscape architecture, using artistic, landscape, and geographical expertise to re-evaluate the assumptions underlying practice-based research inquiry and the relationship between landscape and philosophy, represents a significant shifting of methodology away from the dominant scientific/social science paradigm and toward an approach that is deliberately more ambiguous and interpretative (see Moore, 2018a). Using this radical pragmatic perspective, the method requires an understanding of perception as intelligence and defines landscape as the relationship which a community has with its territory. The resulting research thus seeks to address whether ideas can transform a region and, if so, how? It has led to a significant number of high-profile outcomes spanning academic and public arenas including peer-reviewed papers, numerous exhibitions, developmental publications, and policy. Using extracts from these outputs as well as unpublished reports, papers, and presentations to national and international, professional, and academic audiences, this chapter draws on the experience of a sequence of case studies published in the online research catalogue (Moore, 2024), including the 2011 UNESCO proposal for an international landscape convention (discussed in Moore, 2012); High Speed 2 Landscape Vision (2011, exhibited in 2015); the Tame Valley Landscape Vision in North Warwickshire (2016); *Big Skies, Big Thinking*, for Thurrock Borough Council (2017); the Saturn Project Consortium, funded by EI Climate KIC with partners from Sweden, Italy, and the United Kingdom (Birmingham) (2019–2022); and the radical West Midlands National Park (WMNP). This last example, launched in 2018, is being delivered using the WWNP approach, supported by the WMNP Foundation, the WMNP Awards, and the WMNP Lab, and is a strategic project of BCU (Moore, 2018b).

Policy and Placemaking

Support for the design of good quality places has taken a beating over the last 15 years or so in the United Kingdom, as planning and urban design, accused of being bureaucratic and antidevelopment by the then Secretary of State during debates on major planning reforms (e.g., House of Commons, 2011), are forced to take a back seat; regional spatial strategies have been abolished, and the Commission for Architecture and the Built Environment (CABE) has been dissolved.

By 2017, the Organisation for Economic Co-operation and Development (OECD) reported that "The United Kingdom does not have an explicit national urban policy, but since 2011, it has been actively engaged in decentralising urban policy through its City Deals for English cities and for some cities in the devolved administrations" (OECD, 2017). This approach has not met with much success. By 2020, a housing audit for England stated that "whilst some limited progress has been made in some regions, overwhelmingly the message is that the design of new housing environments in England are 'mediocre' or 'poor'." The report adds "Collectively, we need to significantly raise our game if we are to create the sorts of places that future generations will feel proud to call home" (Carmona et al., 2020). At the report's launch conference, a housebuilders' representative refuted this criticism, demanding "If the proposals were so bad, how did they get through the planning system?" and, by association, brought into question the efficacy of professional education.

These troubles are not unique to the United Kingdom. At the 2022 World Urban Forum, a global conference on sustainable urbanization, all built environment professions were taken to task by a representative from the World Health Organization angrily proclaiming that "all of you professionals have let us down ... all over the world, every day people are dying because of poor spatial planning." Closer to home, in 2017, a recent Leader of Birmingham City Council was reported as saying that, despite 20 years of effort and considerable investment, there had been no impact whatsoever on multiple deprivation in the city.

Current practices seem to be failing. Questions are being raised about whether this is the right way to create better places. Current planning perspectives, situating placemaking at the scale of an urban quarter or entire settlements, have prompted the production of numerous technical guidelines, checklists, and toolkits to advise and support the development of master plans and detailed design layouts. But do these work? Are generic guides the best we can do? A perplexed conference attendee, contemplating an important town center regeneration project that had used various design guides and toolkits to the letter, asked the speaker whether the images shown were good or bad examples. Few could tell.

At last, things seem to be changing. The establishment of the Office for Place in 2023, created in response to the Building Better, Building Beautiful Commission

(BBBBC) and its report *Living with beauty* (BBBBC, 2020), is welcome. This is an important step forward. Do we need more measurable standards without asking whether we are measuring and valuing the right things? Will it support the creation of better places by helping to see the bigger picture, address global challenges and refocus professional education? And is it enough?

Seeing the Bigger Picture

Moore (2023) argues that "We need to refute the idea that we can rely on transformational technical fixes to sort out all our problems – the 'band aid solution ... starting with what we have today and trying to and make it less bad' – in effect 'shoe-horning new technology into old systems'. Technology is just one part of the picture, just as biodiversity is one part of landscape. Agriculture, forestry, cities and industries, water, soil and air are other interconnected parts. "It is foolhardy to think of these as being separate and discrete systems – to think that is just a habit that we have slipped into, that partly explains the apparently irresistible urge to focus on details and an overwhelming concern with measuring, quantifying and recording. Or equating landscape with environment. Or with grass and water. It is time to put these habits and preconceptions to one side." What we urgently need to be asking at this point is, what is the bigger picture? Where do we want to get to? What are we trying to achieve? What is the overall spatial vision for the landscape (all of it) for England?

A landscape-led, land use spatial strategy is desperately needed for the whole of England. Nothing like this exists currently – at least within the public domain. With no vision, and no strategy, spatial decisions are seemingly carried out in the dark without any overall knowledge of what we have already, what is needed, or where things might go to achieve an overall ambition, given the resources, aspirations, and environmental pressures. Instead, we focus on technical fixes rather than big ideas.

Fiona Reynolds, writing for the Bennett Institute of Public Policy, concurs, observing:

> As a small, densely populated country with huge pressures on land, it's astonishing that England has no mechanism for resolving the many and complex demands made on this key resource. We need land to produce food, to build on (whether houses, jobs, shops and public services, or for transport, energy and water infrastructure), to provide space for nature, trees and water, and to combat climate change and achieve net zero. While some of these uses clash, many could be entirely compatible, but they will not happen in the right way and the right place by chance (Reynolds, 2024).

With recent talk of building several New Towns and major infrastructure projects (see, for example, Willetts, 2023), and the United Kingdom in the midst of a second agricultural revolution and plummeting biodiversity, this is becoming very concerning, and the cost of continuing to neglect the bigger picture is becoming more evident day by day. The Land Use Framework study being promoted by the Geospatial Commission of the Department for Science, Innovation, and Technology (Geospatial Commission, 2023) is to be welcomed, especially if it is shaping the bigger picture, recognizing the significance of the landscape as the physical, cultural, and economic resource to help us address global challenges and is not just drowning in details and data.

Landscape as Infrastructure

A step change is needed to deal with global threats, to overcome the inbuilt inertia in systems and institutions – old habits really do die hard. We need to challenge the pervasive belief that to continue with business as usual is a feasible option. As a society, it is time for us to be braver: more ambitious, more determined to deal with the global challenges we face and, perhaps, less comfortable.

The holistic and strategic approach epitomized by the WMNP sees the world from the other end of the telescope. As an economic, social, and environmental project, it of course includes nature and biodiversity, but is so much more.

Moore (2010, p. 235) concludes that:

> ...the deeply flawed conception at the heart of epistemology and theories of perception has consistently deflected us from developing effective strategies to teach the arts, having serious discussions about quality and ultimately from achieving the measure of design expertise needed to match society's aspirations to create well imagined and properly sustainable environments.

The development of the WMNP, based on a systematic reappraisal of practice, using practice-based research, tests the implications of the redefinition of theories of perception presented in Moore (2010). It is part of a long-term strategy to bring a radical shift to placemaking, planning, and landscape architecture, ensuring that it is not just a sticking plaster solution, palliative rather than preventative, but has real impact.

A New Kind of Regional Planning

The new look at landscape presented by Moore (2010, 2015) recognizes landscape as the bedrock of society, the infrastructure upon which we depend, for everything. Moving debate away from business as usual, this is about using the enormous restorative and resuscitative capacity of the land to deal more effectively with every one of the global challenges faced by society. Underpinning this approach is the recognition that landscape shapes our culture and identity and that the powerful relationship between communities and their territory, largely ignored in planning policy in the United Kingdom, gives us agency to address the global challenges we face, informs the creation of places, shaping the experience people have of where they live, work, and visit at whatever scale – not through toolkits and guidelines but by changing attitudes and perceptions of place.

The role of landscape is, then, vital: not just to make a fast buck but critical in tackling the accelerating climate emergency, pollution, urbanization, food and water security, and loss of biodiversity. But it continues to be a blind spot in regional economic strategies (Nefs, 2016), in fact in any kind of spatial strategies. The *Roadmap for a just and regenerative recovery*, adopted by both UN Habitat and the World Urban Forum in 2022, embeds a new perspective on the contribution of landscape to social, environmental, and spatial justice across all 17 Sustainable Development Goals (SDGs) (UN Habitat, 2022). Embracing culture, place, and identity, it argues how important it is to understand the complex interrelationships of the critical global challenges and the extent to which this renewed understanding of landscape can help us deal with them, at scale.

Current and New Designations

The damaging consequence of traditional landscape designations focusing solely on the basis of preserving existing natural beauty and conservation value is made evident in the initial proposal for an international landscape convention (ILC).

> Certain remarkable, valuable, historical and beautiful landscapes are given sanctuary, but at present, the everyday landscape, the social, economic and physical context of our lives, has no champion. Fragmented into various components that are green, grey or blue, agricultural, historical or ecological, landscapes are often undervalued and neglected, seemingly belonging to everyone, but actually to no one. Each week, across the world, communities are experiencing benefits, but also feeling the impacts of industrialisation, urbanisation, and the search for energy. Lives are endangered or affected by poor or badly planned development. Problems are caused by demographic shifts and changing patterns of work and habitation, as well as climate change, the depletion of natural resources, de/reforestation, difficulties relating to food production, biodiversity, heritage, and a host of other issues relating to aspects of land use change and development. The quality of the landscapes of daily life is constantly being eroded. A more strategic and holistic approach is desperately needed to provide support to communities in dealing with these global threats and challenges (Moore et al., 2011).

A more strategic and holistic approach is precisely what is being delivered through the West Midlands National Park (Moore, 2018b). Including all of the towns and cities and all land uses of the West Midlands, the WMNP is striving to deliver more for the region, nature, climate, and people, not just by conserving or restoring current/past landscapes but by cocreating a long-term vision and policies for its future transformation and resuscitation. Based on an analysis of current pressures, constraints, and opportunities and in the context of the global challenges, it is utilizing the overwhelming desire of communities (particularly younger generations) to play a part in addressing these issues.

This is not a traditional national park. Through advocacy, challenging and inspiring better practices, rewarded through its annual WMNP Awards, the WMNP is putting quality of life and quality of the environment at the top of the agenda. This is helping to shift attitudes and institutional behaviors toward the land. Driven by the need to reduce deprivation across the region and across multiple indices, it is by bringing the values of the national parks to urban populations, that we can create a better sense of place, identity, belonging, and hope for the future.

The idea of a new West Midlands National Park is strongly supported by The UK Government's Landscapes Review. Referring to the WMNP and the London National Park City, the report states that "these are not asking for new laws, or powers, but exist as a way of getting people to act and think differently. We applaud them" (Defra 2019, p. 20).

Design Expertise, Drawing, and Mapping

Drawing and Mapping

The role of research, drawing, and mapping in the development of the WMNP cannot be overestimated. The process of drawing and mapping enables us to see a place differently, give voice to its infrastructure, explore the power of the physical, cultural, everyday landscape, and express new ideas and proposals for the region. It is not simply a question of collecting more and more data. Examining, overlaying, and inferring relationships between multiple factors and disciplines including geography, hydrology, economics, transport, and communications, the biosphere, identity, culture, employment, nature, health and well-being, the expert analysis and interpretation this information is used to build up an overarching physical, cultural, and economic landscape led context for transformation. Words and images and images and words explain each other. From these, we learn something new, and this is what changes perceptions.

This is why the maps have such great political and policy impact. A member of the UK Government's *Landscapes Review* panel agrees, noting that "the review's report, quite remarkably, endorsed the application of National Park principles to cities. That we did so was due directly to Professor Moore's vision and maps. This shows how, by reframing the way we think about National Parks, urban populations could benefit," adding that the maps are "a way of getting people to act and think differently" (pers. comm. to K. Moore).

Mapping digital data is not without its problems. A recent report for Natural England examines how data availability affects the creation of regional landscape strategies concluding that:

> ...the starting point in compiling geographically accurate, integrated maps for a holistic landscape perspective in the UK is to obtain

information that can be compared, overlayed and interrogated in once place and at scale. Extensive mapped information is available online. Nevertheless, a great deal of information is in formats that preclude comparative interrogation (behind paywalls, as embedded/ interactive maps etc.) It is therefore difficult to build up the bigger picture, infer relationships, or identify opportunities and constraints. Further issues relating to the type, format and availability of information are compounded by problems originating in the way data is aggregated into output areas or tiles. Embedded within websites, web portals or apps, the benefits of interactive maps are clear. Mapped data is easily accessible on phones and screens, and so is convenient and portable. A whole range of physical, economic and cultural information is available in incredible detail, however, it is not possible to scale from the screen or overlay information to infer unexpected or known spatial relationships. Details are lost when zooming out and the vitally important bigger picture of contextual relationships, constraints and opportunities disappears. It is almost impossible to compile maps to understand the social and environmental impacts of spatial decision making, and we are only just beginning to understand the impact of geography and planning on the quality of life, quality of the environment, economic success and self-confidence. Based on a reductive approach, some of these problems have existed for many decades. But interactive maps exacerbate the problems, contributing to the apparent lack of awareness of the need for any kind of vision, encouraging instead a focus simply on detail, a tweaking or adjusting what is already known, a filling in of available "blank" space and an increasing detachment of place from geography and the quality of experience (Moore et al., 2023).

Reimagining Landscape Through Radical Mapping

The WMNP exploratory maps are rhetorical tools, there to provoke debate and to present alternative futures. The research philosophy and methodology are explored in *Overlooking the visual* (Moore, 2010) and *Seeing the bigger picture* (Moore, 2024). The section below is an extract from the mapping section of the online research catalogue.

The large-scale spatial structure of landscape rarely figures in our consciousness – not as we move around places in everyday life or even in our imagination. The structure and detail is lost on a screen and is virtually impossible to read on maps, particularly of urban areas, buried by the graphic emphasis on buildings and roads. Often left off altogether, as characterless, blank, flat, voids, landscape has become invisible, forgotten. It is presumed to be of little or no consequence.

Arguing that drawing is an analytical skill and that "rather than mediating between the conceptual and the visual, drawing can be seen simply as a way of working out an idea" (Moore, 2003), the research uses radical mapping in a number of ways, including as a tool to understand and rediscover the physical materiality of regions, history and culture, hydrology, scale, and monumentality. The drawings, artistic representations expressing form and ideas in combination with the images used in presentations and accompanying spoken narratives create, as a whole, an incredibly effective way to engage and inspire stakeholders, to persuade and change perceptions.

Feddes (2017) observes that the process is about "discovering 'landscape where you thought it couldn't be'... right under your nose....." He adds that it is significant because "once you presume the cohesion of a river valley, instead of the later fragmentation, the area can get a new identity and revitalise. This change of perception is the turning point" (Feddes, 2017).

The method of overlaying of a range of regional maps with different kinds of scientific data in the anticipation that the objective answer will emerge once enough data have been amassed has a long history in landscape planning (see Walker & Simo, 1994), and in many quarters, although this, colloquially known as McHarg's layer cake method, may not be utilized, the planning process in general is presumed to be capable of being objective, neutral, and based on facts alone. The philosophical starting point of this research is fundamentally different, subverting the idea that it is ever possible to be objectively neutral. Every image is stuffed full of analysis from the beginning. The maps aim to show places in a way that cannot be experienced by wandering around but that is absorbing and new, that gains attention and is memorable and so become part of our identity and culture. They create powerful connections to our territory. Inverting the usual way of representing the world, prioritizing topography, rivers, and streams over roads and buildings can be mind-blowing.

Their purpose is to express ideas at an ambitious, visionary, and strategic level to focus on the bigger picture, without devolving to details and lists (such as where is the cycle track and where are the benches?). As in a caricature, these are based on detailed knowledge and express ideas with a carefully constructed imprecision, smudginess, and layering that is not confrontational, threatening, or slick (Fig. 10.1). At exhibitions, people can touch the drawings and engage with the feeling and texture of the paper. As illustrations, these are dramatically different and, it appears, a welcome respite from the usual well-honed, pixel-precise digital creations that are so beguiling. These are unexpected, artistic, rhetorical tools to initiate debate, to provoke the imagination, and to intrigue.

The collision of the analogue with the digital, with precise georeferencing that wraps the drawings over LIDAR imaging, serves to ground the diagrams in the physical world and emphasize that these ideas are not hypothetical but could have a reality. These ideas could be interpreted to fit the region like a glove.

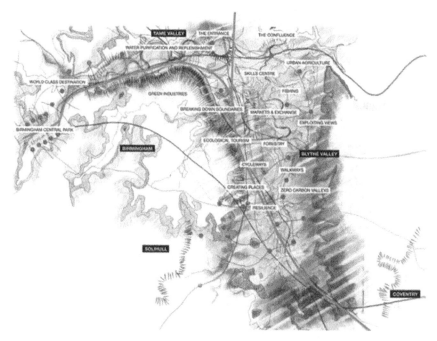

Fig. 10.1. A Refinement of the Proposal for the Tame Valley Landscape Vision: An "Unthreatening Drawing." *Source:* Kathryn Moore (2012).

Mapping and the Tame Valley Landscape Vision

Unexpectedly, through mapping, it was found that the rivers and streams of the headwaters of the Tame connect the divided communities across the West Midlands. Making a map can take minutes or years to think about or execute and a couple of hours or many weeks to build up the courage to begin. Mapping is about deciding and selecting what to draw, how to draw it, what paper to use (weight, color, thickness, texture), what size, what ideas to express and how to express them, what colors to use, what materials, the thickness of lines, the scale and how and where to make the first mark and where to finish. A blank piece of paper is just as daunting when drawing as it is when writing.

The research is predicated on the presumption that is only possible to be objective if we are informed, if we make judgments from a position of knowledge, aware of our prejudices, preconceptions, and desires. The hard part is to recognize what these are and then to have the courage to put them to one side if necessary. The knowledge required to map a region depends not on metaphysics, the genius loci, subconscious, or universal laws (the kind of things that pervade landscape architectural discourse and design process methodologies research) but on knowledge learned and gathered over time, applied, and interpreted to an understanding of a place (at whatever scale), its history, problems, ambitions, and potential, and its social, economic, and natural contours. Driven by curiosity, this is what gives us the intuition to know where to search, who to speak to, which books to select, or which websites to browse to amplify our understanding. It also drives the interpretation and method of the representation of the information gathered.

To undertake this work, maps at the same scale in a printed format are traced and overlain. The contours are vital. Redrawing the contours is not just a technical task but a critical, analytical investigation that requires knowledge to make sense of what it is you are looking at. It requires geographic, landscape, and artistic sensibility to understand what you are seeing as the world emerges, contour by contour, stream by stream, place name by place name as connections are made across the territory, as maps are redrawn, overlaid, and redrawn again (Fig. 10.2). Generating considerable knowledge, it can open up an unknown world, like reading a new book. Tracing a contour, for example, the 100m contour of the Tame Valley, exposes its topography, making unexpected connections between different parts of the region – all at the same height! A three-dimensional, sculptural form emerges, folded, eroded, and fractured, intersected and disguised by a dramatic infrastructure of rivers and streams, canals, railways, and roads.

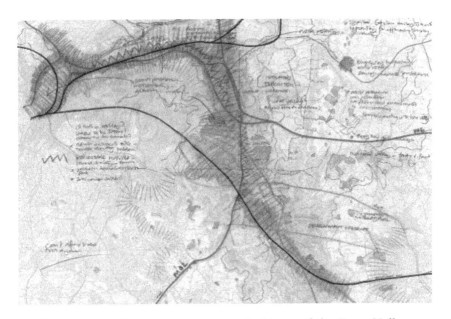

Fig. 10.2. A Contour-Based Analytical Map of the Tame Valley.
Source: Kathryn Moore (2012).

It takes courage, passion, and knowledge to undertake the challenges of this kind of untamed, exploratory practice that is by no means well behaved in a traditional disciplinary sense. Described as guerrilla landscape architecture by Feddes (2017) and in many ways it aligns to the self-initiated design activism of Mathur and Da Cunha (2016).

Likewise, a drawing (Fig. 10.3) set the foundations for the West Midlands National Park (WMNP) (Moore, 2018b), now embedded in the psyche and policies of the West Midlands's institutions, organizations, and communities, evident in policy, bids, discussions, and ambitions for the future development of the region. The map shows the immense rolling topography, the junction of two of largest river systems in the United Kingdom, the vast scale of the basin that is the upper headwaters of the Tame and the crucible of the industrial revolution, nestled in the uplifted plateau that contains the West Midlands. At public exhibitions, we are frequently asked if it is Mordor (Moore, 2024).

Public Participation

Quite rightly, the placemaking agenda focuses on public participation. However, Moore (2010) warns against the knee-jerk reaction that passes all responsibility for decision-making to local communities, advising that "It doesn't matter if it's a technical or scientific report, criticism of a scheme, or the creation of a project for implementation, conservation or management. It makes no difference if we are concerned with the city center, school playground, national parks, the urban

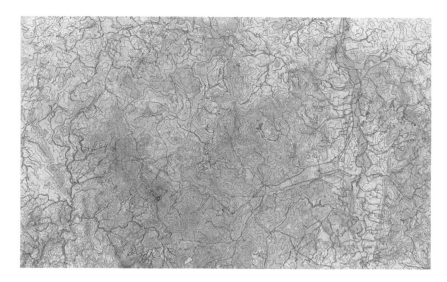

Fig. 10.3. A Contour and Waterway Analytical Map of the Blythe and Tame River Catchment. *Source:* Kathryn Moore (2017).

realm, or the seaside. Or what stage of the development process the project has reached, whether it is the feasibility, planning, strategic review, the detailed design, or its long-term management. Each of these development stages requires different kinds of knowledge and skill, but essentially, they all involve design. It is a question of research and decision-making."

Designing is about making propositions and presenting a vision for the future. Central to the discipline is the forward thinking, the anticipatory and predictive nature of its practice. On this basis, anyone who has a responsibility for the landscape, whether they deal with words rather than drawings, a computer rather than a pencil, they are effecting, predicting, or managing spatial change. It all has a visual dimension. Focusing on content rather than process and acknowledging the importance of expertise calls into question the current vogue for the public to be involved at every level of decision-making and thinking. In the swing from authoritarianism to public consultation, we can become so obsessed with the process, we ignore content, blithely adopting the attitude that the process will deliver whatever the process delivers.

There is a genuine risk here that we are washing our hands of professional responsibility and we should know better. The outcomes of community planning and design in the 1970s were "rarely exceptional" (Relph, 1987, p. 234), and the same is true today. There are too many images of community-designed spaces that are just too dismal to show. If nothing else, they prove that no matter how many people are consulted, no matter how many views are collected, someone has to synthesize the information and work out the spatial implications of it all, and that takes specialist knowledge – expertise. Whatever form the consultation takes, it should not be seen as an alternative to the making of often difficult design decisions because these decisions are the nuts and bolts of the process, an artistic rationale if you like. But, like it or not, the lesson would appear to be that designing (on whatever scale) is not a democratic activity, any more than mending a broken arm, making a legal judgment, or fixing the plumbing; one way or another, they all require expertise. If you want your boiler fixed, don't send for a chartered accountant. Flagging up the extent to which professional responsibility seems to have been abandoned in the name of public participation is not to signal a return to an old-style autocracy, with high-handed 'experts' telling the populace what is good for them. This is to confuse arrogance with an attempt to define an appropriate process.

Public participation should be a good investigative collaboration, a discussion about how best to develop a comprehensive brief. The pragmatic argument makes it easier to understand where to draw the line in that process (Moore, 2010).

In developing the WMNP, advocacy and engagement are absolutely vital, but it is a different kind of advocacy, achieved through WMNP maps and presentations. The success of this new research, exploring the art of design at a regional scale, is a testimony to the pragmatic argument developed in *Overlooking the visual* that the "breath-taking nature of the aesthetic experience is dependent on and limited by what we know" (Moore, 2010, p. 69). It is so significant because, as Shepheard adds, "it rescues design philosophy and aesthetics from the ivory tower and reintroduces them to everyday practice" (quoted in Moore, 2010 p. ix). This is precisely what brings materiality back into the picture.

The Impact of This Approach

Evidence of the impact of connecting philosophy and theory to practice comes from a range of sources. Moore's design-led research and exploratory drawings for the Black Country Consortium resulted in a vision for the region's landscape that included geology, topography, and culture called "above, beyond, below" (2004/5). A landscape-scale vision framing the whole Black Country as an Urban Park, it contributed significantly to the shared statutory development plan, the Black Country Core Strategy, and Black Country as Garden City project. Highlighting the international significance of the region's unappreciated and forgotten industrial heritage and geology, this work emboldened the local authorities of Dudley, Sandwell, Walsall, and Wolverhampton to apply for UNESCO geopark status, an inscription confirmed in 2020.

Conclusion

We have ignored landscape for too long. BCU's WMNP Lab recognizes landscape as the bedrock of society, the infrastructure upon which we depend – for everything. Through research, drawing, and mapping, we are discovering and seeing a place differently, giving voice to this infrastructure, showing the power of the physical, cultural, everyday landscape. This ensures that landscape is no longer a "blind spot" (Nefs, 2016) but a vitally important resource to be looked after, resuscitated, celebrated, the very fabric of our identity, self-confidence, and worth.

Utilizing this power is the only real way to address the challenges we face, including the climate emergency, spatial and environmental justice, and multiple deprivation. Already adopted by the West Midlands Combined Authority, Birmingham City Council, and others, our approach is of interest to a number of UK Government agencies, including the Department for Business and Trade, the Department for Leveling Up, Housing and Communities and the Department for Environment, Food and Rural Affairs (Defra). The WMNP Lab and the International Federation of Landscape Architects are in discussion with UN Habitat and a range of other UN agencies and NGOs to discuss the development of an international landscape convention.

The final missing link in achieving real impact across England (and the United Kingdom more widely) is the translation of this into trans-departmental government policies that lead and drive investment into the right places and in the right way. We need to change the way in which money flows.

This chapter has considered placemaking at the widest spatial scale and with a focus on landscape: both are novel departures from the bulk of the existing literature and professional practices, which tend to be smaller scale and settlement based; although, of course, it is perfectly possible to consider an urban landscape-based approach. It has also charted a novel mapping approach to design-based research. The value of these new perspectives is demonstrated in large-scale plans for the West Midlands region, and the way in which these have been developed with major stakeholders and with a wide range of community involvement. That involvement, through a wide range of exhibitions, meetings, media reports, and so on, was both a mechanism for residents and users providing information and responding to initial suggestions and for communicating strategies and proposals.

This is placemaking at a grand scale. The drawing and dissemination processes sensitized stakeholders, residents, and other users to the character, appearance, values, and potential of a large, much-changed, and underappreciated region. In deliberately using the term "National Park" to equate this landscape with the highest valued seminatural landscapes of the United Kingdom's existing National Park designations, from the Lake District to the South Downs, this has challenged preconceptions, existing values, and indeed an entire political/bureaucratic process of identification, designation, and management.

The value of this to placemaking is clear. No matter how well a small-scale place is made, usually urban-related and at the quarter or settlement scale, it is always part of the wider landscape. If that wider landscape is better appreciated, and this appreciation developed through a design and communication process such as this, then that place takes on a wider value and significance as part of a wider – regional – place-made identity. This approach has been developed within the English quasi-judicial planning system but has generated a great deal of international interest and is capable of being adapted to any city system or region in any country that possesses the prerequisites of sufficient appropriate and accurate data, from topographic survey onward, and encourages a bottom-up approach to public engagement and involvement in plan development and implementation.

Acknowledgments

This chapter is the formal publication of ideas and examples that have been previously available only as a range of exhibitions, maps, policy proposals, and related documents. Some of the text is taken from Moore's research catalogue content (https://www.researchcatalogue.net/view/1173624/1175605).

References

Building Better, Building Beautiful Commission (BBBBC). (2020). *Living with beauty*. BBBBC. https://www.gov.uk/government/publications/living-with-beauty-report-of-the-building-better-building-beautiful-commission

Carmona, M., Alwarea, A., Giordano, V., Gusseinova, A., & Olaleye, F. (2020). *A housing design audit for England*. Place Alliance & CPRE. https://www.cpre.org.uk/wp-content/uploads/2020/03/Place-Alliance-A-Housing-Design-Audit-for-England_2020.pdf

Department for Environment, Food and Rural Affairs (Defra). (2019). *Landscapes review: National Parks and AONBs*. Final Report. Defra. https://assets.publishing.

service.gov.uk/media/5d8a19a3e5274a083d3b78bd/landscapes-review-final-report.pdf

Feddes, F. (2017). Discovering landscape where you thought it couldn't be. In *Report of the international symposium 'Confrontations in the metropolitan landscape'* (pp. 3–4). Deltametropolis Association. https://deltametropool.nl/app/uploads/2018/09/171204_verslag-internationaal-symposium_MN.pdf

Geospatial Commission. (2023, May 23). *Finding common ground: Integrating data, science and innovation for better use of land*. Geospatial Commission. https://www.gov.uk/government/publications/finding-common-ground-integrating-data-science-and-innovation-for-better-use-of-land

House of Commons. (2011). *Abolition of Regional Spatial Strategies: A planning vacuum*. Second Report of Session 2010–11. https://publications.parliament.uk/pa/cm201011/cmselect/cmcomloc/517/517.pdf

Mathur, A., & Da Cunha, D. (2016). Aqueous Terrain. *Journal of Architectural Education, 70*(1), 35–37.

Moore, K. (2003). Overlooking the visual. *Journal of Architecture, 8*(1), 25–40.

Moore, K. (2010). *Overlooking the visual: Demystifying the art of design*. Routledge.

Moore, K. (2012). *Towards an international landscape convention* [Conference presentation]. UN Food and Agriculture Organisation meeting on Globally Important Agricultural Heritage Systems, Rome. https://laliniciativablog.files.wordpress.com/2013/05/prof-kathryn-moore-towards-an-international-landscape-convention.pdf

Moore, K. (2015). *A new look at landscape*. Birmingham City University. https://core.ac.uk/reader/145241200

Moore, K. (2017). *The Tame Valley landscape vision development*. Tame Valley Wetland Partnership. http://www.tamevalleywetlands.co.uk/wp-content/uploads/2017/01/TVWW_Report_Final_WEB.pdf

Moore, K. (2018a). Towards new research methodologies in design. In E. Braae & H. Steiner (Eds.), *Routledge research companion to landscape architecture* (pp. 312–323). Routledge.

Moore, K. (2018b). *Creating a new National Park for the West Midlands: A new 21st century idea*. Birmingham City University. https://bcuassets.blob.core.windows.net/docs/National%20Park.pdf

Moore, K. (2023). *Contribution to rethink climate*. BBC Radio.

Moore, K. (2024). The art of design. Research catalogue. https://www.researchcatalogue.net/view/1173624/1175605

Moore, K., Albans, A., Daniels, R., & Nikologianni, A. (2023). *Re-imagining resilient landscapes - an integrated, holistic approach. A case study of the West Midlands National Park*. Unpublished report for Natural England.

Moore, K., Mitchell, N., & Rossler, M. (2011). *Proposal for an international landscape convention*. Presented to the UNESCO Board.

Nefs, M. (2016). *Blind spot*. Deltametropolis.

Organisation for Economic Co-operation and Development (OECD). (2017). *The state of national urban policy in United Kingdom*. https://www.oecd.org/regional/regional-policy/national-urban-policy-United-Kingdom.pdf

Relph, E. (1987). *The modern urban landscape*. Croom Helm.

Reynolds, F. (2024, 17 January). Why England needs a land use framework and why it is needed now. Bennett Institute for Public Policy blog. https://www.bennettinstitute.cam.ac.uk/blog/why-land-use-framework-now/

Schama, S. (1995). *Landscape and memory*. Harpercollins.
UN Habitat. (2022). *The HPF 2022 roadmap to recovery*. https://unhabitat.org/sites/default/files/2022/04/final_hpf_roadmap_220426.pdf
Walker, P., & Simo, M. (1994). *Invisible gardens*. MIT Press.
Willetts, D. (2023, 6 June). Sunak urged to build more new towns to tackle collapse in home ownership. *The Guardian*. https://www.theguardian.com/uk-news/2023/jun/06/sunak-urged-to-build-more-new-towns-to-tackle-collapse-in-home-ownership

Chapter 11

Conclusion: The Future of Placemaking

Peter J. Larkham[a] *and David Higgins*[b]
[a]Birmingham City University, UK
[b]Higgins Research, UK

Abstract

This chapter reinforces the overall premise of the book: placemaking is here to stay, has become an integral part of decision-making for the built environment, has much of value to offer, and should encompass all layers of our diverse urban communities. Nevertheless, even dominant paradigms need critical attention, and this chapter reinforces the contributions of the individual chapters and the overall message that placemaking needs to be more holistic, to demonstrate more "joined-up thinking", in a fast-changing world in which our growing urban areas need to prepare for climate change and other uncertainties.

Keywords: Placemaking; smart real estate; sustainability and the environment; placekeeping; urban communities; reshaping places

Introduction

Placemaking, a once obscure term, has gained unprecedented popularity over the last few decades and now forms the platform for conversations around the future of real estate. Recognizing its transformative power, the breadth of ideas that have come to shelter under the heading of "placemaking" is extensive. From being a derided neologism, the concept has become mainstream in academic, professional, and even political thinking about how places could be shaped, how they change over time, and how users interact across communities. It is so pervasive that it has become familiar to a wider lay public: the residents and users of urban areas. Its relationship with older terms such as "town planning" and "urban design" remains rather uncertain – and indeed it is interesting to compare placemaking with the acceptance journey of urban design, from a new term in the 1950s to general acceptance in the 1990s. Even then, we were still concerned about different definitions and usages (Rowley, 1994) or ambiguities (Madanipour, 1997). But how far are these rather abstract concerns actually helpful?

If "geography is what geographers do," as was claimed in the early 1930s even as it struggled for acceptance as an academic discipline (Johnston, 1980, citing Parkins, 1934, and others), then perhaps placemaking is whatever its users wish it to be, and we should be less concerned about spellings (with or without hyphen, one word or two) and precise definitions, fascinating though these philosophical discussions might be. In some cases, of course, it might help if users define *their* intended usage. Placemaking is about places and is applied through deliberate mechanisms including urban planning and design and in unintentional ways through juxtaposition and construction. The key point is that placemaking is here to stay – as it provides a holistic approach to transforming spaces as to make them more functional and attractive to meet community member needs and aspirations.

Placemaking has become a dominant paradigm. It is the fate of all dominant paradigms that they are eventually discredited and replaced: the histories of science and social science are full of such transitions, and a problem is that an outgoing dominant paradigm is rejected and replaced for reasons of intellectual fashion even while it has useful contributions to make. Therefore, we argue that it is useful to review a concept even as it is dominant. We should learn from the critiques, identify and full gaps, and extend the concept to deal with other fields and changing circumstances. For example, many city centers are being transformed by ultra-high-rise residential towers, which bring people back to the city but radically change an area's character and appearance. The architect Ian Simpson, producing a vision for a future Manchester, said "This is a unique opportunity to bring life into the city centre. We can't afford to miss it ... There can never be too many towers ... Some people think that what I do is the work of the devil. They think we should be building these towers on streets. But we live in a rough tough city and the towers are a king of refuge. We are designing them in real places. They are not gated communities" (quoted in Sudjic, 2024). How can placemaking respond to the challenges of the impact on the wider city, the localized impacts around the buildings themselves, and should we also consider the internal structure, design, and function of the towers themselves – which have as many dwellings as some older housing estates! And increasing urban greenery has become an integral part of placemaking, and indeed after COVID, there are studies correlating access to, or even sight of, greenery with increased health and well-being. But, as Fitzgerald's sharp and provocative critique points out, this is often a wishful thinking greenwash: more greenery will not solve a housing crisis, or the problem of redundant historic high streets, or many other issues (Fitzgerald, 2024). Thus, what has become an orthodoxy of the dominant placemaking paradigm needs review.

It is therefore timely that the placemaking literature should encompass fields such as the legal system, real estate and property asset management, and digitalization. In addition, as concerns about climate change grow, many aspects of placemaking do align with recognized global sustainability goals. Placemaking needs to consider inanimate actors such as ecosystems and those rarely recognized as placemakers such as those temporarily occupying places. These are explored with new perspectives through free-standing chapters and contributions incorporated to support other aspects of placemaking chapters in this book.

Chapter 1 shows placemaking as a process which needs to broaden to incorporate different users, whether actual placemakers (communities, local governments, property developers, etc.) and/or beneficiaries of placemaking activities, such as underprivileged residents of smaller communities in developing economies or multinational organizations with extensive exposure to standalone trophy buildings and the surrounding environment. Likewise, important aspects of heritage need to be expanded, for example, incorporating less-traditional heritage details, which may still play a part in reshaping places, their perceptions and uses, and hence contribute to sustainable placemaking. Placemaking needs to be extended to all scales of activity including the widest, regional and perhaps even national, scales: reconsidering the image and perception of a region can be transformative, and examining the placemaking impact of major infrastructure projects and similar is too often ignored, to the potential disbenefit of the project and those affected by it. In short, placemaking needs to be a holistic activity, inherent in how we think about, design, and manage the places in which we live and work.

Chapter 2 reminds us that placemaking and related activities only exist within a legal framework. Placemaking is examined within the context of the English planning law and policy framework, which provides a basis for decision-taking while upholding the capacity of communities and decision-makers to create the places which they require and desire. This chapter also considers the limitations of the existing system, particularly given the contribution of planning in achieving the creation of beautiful, sustainable places and the need for change to facilitate this process.

This approach is, of course, applicable in any administrative system with a clearly developed judicial and land-use/spatial planning system. We should recognize, though, that some forms of placemaking might exist outside these conditions, for example, in informal housing (*barrios, favellas,* and similar) or more temporary situations (refugee camps, postcatastrophe housing: see Scipión et al., 2019) or as other facets of bottom-up or guerrilla urbanism. Indeed, exploring such informal placemaking could be a powerful research agenda.

Chapter 3 examines a fundamental issue rarely given explicit consideration in placemaking – although it could be said that those investing in real estate are well aware of it – the relationship between place, space, and value. If owners or investors see no added value, placemaking will not happen. Owners could, of course, be national or local governments, and land for large projects can be expropriated: but institutional investors (especially pension funds in the last half-century and more) are the main owners of investment grade real estate in many developed economies. In today's socioeconomic situation, in the United Kingdom at least, creating value in real estate is changing with additional determinants affecting location, use, and performance. Foremost are extreme risk events which, with climate change, will occur more often and with increased severity. Political instability is also a growing problem, whether at a global scale (seen recently with the effects of Russia's invasion of Ukraine) or locally (the instability of the United Kingdom during rapid changes of Prime Minister in 2022).

In addition, with structural change, new products and processes are entering the marketplace, particularly with new digital technology that is changing the ways in which we work, live, and socialize. New ways to work and live are offering additional real estate revenue streams for building owners, although there is a trade-off between potential improved returns and increased operational risk. Decision-making models are adapting to the changing marketplace. In detailing the changing marketplace, valuing techniques need to change in order to better account for fluctuation in demand, rental structures, diverse revenue streams, and additional operation costs. This can lead to increased emphasis on real-time granular property data – again, an issue of digitalization for large-scale data acquisition and analysis – and management skills.

Chapter 4 builds an interesting picture as to supporting evidence of technological progress, as in recent years new digital technology has often been promoted, and often by politicians, as a "good thing" – driving practice on the ground rather than through evaluated evidence of what works. The contemporary world cannot escape the rush to become digital, but there remains a need to have a collective vision for what kind of places we want and then harness smart thinking and digital technology to deliver it. In saying this, we should be aware that there remain locations that are digitally impoverished: how can these secure the benefits of digital-driven placemaking?

There appear to be two key risks inherent in technology-driven placemaking thinking and activity. First, there is a risk of disjointed incrementalism (Lindblom, 1959, once widely warned about in town planning courses) through technological developments making changes to places that are, in themselves, "improvements" but which defeat wider efforts. The political or financial short-termism of such activity, often based on smaller-scale projects, relates well to what Lindblom also referred to as "muddling through." Secondly, there is the risk of continuing not to include the externalities (nature, design quality, noise reductions, etc.) as valued items in technology-driven placemaking, either because they are not easy to monitor/measure and so are not integrated (missing opportunities for creative solutions), difficult to assign responsibility for them (they fall through the regulatory cracks), or they are negotiated away in successive "unbalanced decisions." This is, of course, hardly new: the "new" spatial planning approach was intended to promote a large-scale and "joined-up" way of thinking (cf Tewdwr-Jones et al., 2010), though whether it has succeeded is debatable (Abis & Garau, 2016; Grădinaru et al., 2017). A third risk could be mentioned, that there is a potential return to unchallenged belief in the efficacy of "blueprint" planning, this time digitally driven with a false security in data and systems.

A further problem is that place governance and relevant decision-makers seem often to be ignorant of how to use the rapidly developing technology in ways that are more than simply relating to more efficient "service" delivery – because there are questions about how that efficiency is measured, and who obtains the benefits of that efficiency or, indeed, of the service delivery. Further, it appears that the layers of governance are increasingly separated (community, parish, local

Conclusion: The Future of Placemaking 201

authority, region, and national) as a result of differences in understanding of the technology or access to knowledge/data.

Nevertheless, Chapter 4 suggests that there are silver linings if we choose to use them – access to green space within 15 minutes, multifunctional use of land as a norm, harnessing public demands for green and biodiversity to influence placemaking more effectively, and so on. The technology disrupts outdated governance processes and forces more integrated, inclusive approaches, which can bring wide and multiple benefits. It potentially places more power into the hands of citizens as the technology enables more knowledge sharing and hence bottom-up contributions.

Chapter 5 further examines the topic of digital- and technology-informed placemaking but as part of a wider approach, a new way of thinking about placemaking: Holistic Smart Placemaking. The chapter underscores the significance of taking a holistic approach to placemaking in cities by incorporating smart strategies. It emphasizes that placemaking is a vital element for enhancing urban quality of life, and to achieve this, a comprehensive view that integrates smart approaches is essential. There is a significant research gap relating to how systems thinking and systems integration can be integrated into the practice of smart placemaking within cities. Applying these concepts can contribute to making placemaking more resilient, connected, and smart.

In addition, Chapter 5 introduces the concept of viewing a city as a system of interconnected and integrated smart places, which includes attractions, communication hubs, public spaces, and infrastructures. It emphasizes that smart placemaking leads to various positive outcomes such as economic prosperity, environmental sustainability, health and well-being, safety and security, cultural preservation, innovation, and resilience.

Chapter 6 explores links between placemaking and sustainability. Business as usual is no longer an option if we are serious about sustainability and the type of placemaking that has characteristics of social, ecological, and economic resilience. And, as Chapter 2 implies, widespread ongoing changes are likely to mean that resilience is needed more than ever in our growing urban communities. Currently, however, we are experiencing a double-bind with many suggested "sustainability" policies falling into the "weak sustainability" camp: this is likely to store up more social and economic unknowns and be unable to halt or reverse ecological decline and global warming (and all the negative impacts associated with rapid climate change). A significant shift in mindset/worldview is urgently needed, overcoming the Cartesian split of human-nature, science-art/humanities, and associated modes of dualistic thinking (which has become the post-Enlightenment Western mainstream culture) and instead reconnecting within more holistic thinking, deciding, and doing.

Chapter 7 deals with the placemaking interplay between history, heritage, and conservation. It is well known that these factors are often used in reshaping place identity and place promotion, and that heritage selection processes are important. But for every heritage that is included within an authorized heritage discourse, there is excluded heritage, often dissonant heritage, and excluded or marginalized communities. The included heritage is usually sanitized, edited, and even faked or trivialized by incorporation into modern pastiche designs. Hence, this chapter emphasizes the importance of identifying a wider range of stakeholders in these processes. These may be minority, disadvantaged, or migrant communities; their conceptions of heritage may be different, or their aspirations for the places in which they now live might be challenging to existing or former users. This is particularly the case when new users revalue the heritage inherited from very different previous communities.

For many, place is shaped not just by the "special," things traditionally identified as heritage, but by the ordinary and everyday. Some seek to put their stamp on their place by unconventional means – graffiti, street art, temporary structures and "meanwhile" uses, and so on. All these have meaning and, if they persist, may become considered as valuable, as heritage, and hence could have an important role in placemaking. This chapter pushes us to think outside the usual comfortable links between heritage and placemaking: to accept and understand variety, and that, like heritage itself, placemaking is an extremely diverse activity.

Chapter 8 provides a detailed exploration of placemaking in a single, small locale: one later-19th century square in south London. It builds on Lefebvre's concept of the "right to the city" and focuses on the informal placemaking activities of the square's residents. What is particularly interesting about this example is that, since the end of the Second World War, the residents have changed significantly, as has the local authority's attitude to them and the square itself. It became semi-forgotten, neglected and boarded-up, and thus subject to squatting. Yet the squatters engaged in a form of placemaking at the smallest scales but still with meaning for them. Over time, the square changed, and some of the squatters remained, becoming legal occupiers. Using an ethnographic, walking interview process, this chapter charts how residents, some of long standing, attach meaning to place elements and reshape their place. Yet nearby large-scale commercial redevelopment, promoted by its stakeholders as a form of placemaking and interpreted by others as a form of gentrification, is seen by these research participants as a threat to their place, their activities, and values. This chapter highlights the value of the unplanned, small-scale, spontaneous activities of residents and place users: this could and should also be seen as a valid form of placemaking.

Chapter 9, like Chapter 8, builds on a particular philosophical approach to urbanism and placemaking. Placemaking is seen as a political act: a process more than an outcome. It is framed as a right, rather than a privilege or a random happening. The examples considered here represent a bottom-up approach to reshaping place, which could be considered as challenging dominant structures of power and control in the city. The placemakers are not municipal officials, elected representatives, or even property owners: nevertheless, they have seized opportunities to shape the places they want and need, providing opportunities for wider communities. A key message is that we should consider placemaking at multiple levels and as an act that should reflect multiple social realities of a diverse urban population. In this way, this chapter aligns with critiques that there is more to placemaking than producing good-looking places that increase property prices for owners and investors.

Chapter 10 considers placemaking at the widest spatial scale and with a focus on landscape: both are novel departures from the bulk of the existing literature and professional practices, which tend to be smaller-scale and settlement based. It has also charted a novel mapping approach to design-based research. The value of these new perspectives is demonstrated in large-scale plans for the West Midlands region and the way in which these have been developed with major stakeholders and with a wide range of community involvement. That involvement was both a mechanism for residents and users providing information and responding to initial suggestions and for communicating strategies and proposals.

This is placemaking at the widest possible scale. The drawing and dissemination processes sensitized stakeholders, residents, and other users to the character, appearance, values, and potential of a large, much-changed, and underappreciated region. In deliberately using the term "National Park" to equate this landscape with the highest-valued semi-natural landscapes of the United Kingdom's existing National Park designations, from the Lake District to the South Downs, this has challenged preconceptions, existing values, and indeed, an entire political/bureaucratic process of identification, designation, and management. The value of this to placemaking is clear. No matter how well a small-scale place is made, usually urban-related and at the quarter or settlement scale, it must sit in a wider landscape. If that wider landscape is better appreciated, and this appreciation developed through a design and communication process such as this, then that place takes on a wider value and significance as part of a wider – regional – place-made identity.

The message of this book is unequivocal. Placemaking is extremely relevant to us all: it is not a fad or fashionable jargon but a fundamental activity, that could achieve much by appropriate use of technology, changing ways of thinking, incorporating new elements, and the full range of aspects already considered. But we should not be uncritical of the currently dominant paradigm: some rethinking is timely. Placemaking needs to be smarter, to use appropriate technology in more sophisticated ways, and to engage more closely with the full range of stakeholders. That range includes those who are not property owners, wealthy or influential: placemaking needs to include and generate benefits for, every layer of urban society. The potential benefits to the places we make and remake, and hence to the physical and mental health and well-being of residents and users, are widespread. The potential disbenefits of not doing so, at a time of climate crisis, political instability, and growing populations, will result in worsening quality of life, rising inequality, and eventual catastrophe.

Looking to the future, placemaking needs a companion concept: *placekeeping*. Once we have shaped appropriate high-quality places, we must pay attention to keeping them high quality. That means appropriate management and maintenance. This is a long-term issue: as places age and materials decay, as landscaping matures, as society's needs and tastes change, and as the physical world changes through climate change and other factors, we need to continually consider what makes places high quality. If we do not do so, the investment of one generation is likely to be lost, and this is wasteful. Short-termism should no longer be acceptable – we should certainly be designing, building, and placemaking for the long-term future.

References

Abis, E., & Garau, C. (2016). An assessment of the effectiveness of strategic spatial planning: A study of Sardinian municipalities. *European Planning Studies*, *24*(1), 139–162.

Fitzgerald, D. (2024). *The city of today is a dying thing: In search of the cities of tomorrow*. Faber.

Grădinaru, S. R., Iojă, C. I., Pătru-Stupariu, I., & Hersperger, A. M. (2017). Are spatial planning objectives reflected in the evolution of urban landscape patterns? A framework for the evaluation of spatial planning outcomes. *Sustainability*, *9*(8), 1279.

Johnston, R. (1980). Geography is what geographers do ... and did. *Progress in Human Geography*, *4*, 277–283.

Lindblom, C. E. (1959). The science of 'muddling through'. *Public Administration Review*, *9*(2), 79–88.

Madanipour, A. (1997). Ambiguities of urban design. *Town Planning Review*, *68*(3), 363–383.

Rowley, A. (1994). Definition of urban design: The nature and concerns of urban design. *Planning Practice and Research*, *9*, 179–197.

Scipión, D., Silva, Y., Kapetas, L., Grace, M., Lim, W. Z., Wall, R., & Proverbs, D. (2019). *Building resilience in flood disaster management in Northern Peru*. Newton Fund Project Report. Birmingham City University. https://www.open-access.bcu.ac.uk/8911/

Sudjic, D. (2024, January 6–7). Manchester, inside out. *Financial Times* House & Home, 6.

Tewdwr-Jones, M., Gallent, N., & Morphet, J. (2010). An anatomy of spatial planning: Coming to terms with the spatial element in UK planning. *European Planning Studies*, *18*(2), 239–257.

Printed and bound by CPI Group (UK) Ltd, Croydon, CR0 4YY
03/12/2024

14604564-0001